Short Answers to the Tough Questions

Expanded Edition

How to answer the questions
libertarians are often asked

Dr. Mary J. Ruwart

THE ADVOCATES FOR SELF-GOVERNMENT

Cartersville, Georgia

Published in the United States
by the Advocates for Self-Government
269 Market Place Blvd. #106, Cartersville, GA 30121-2235
800-932-1776, info@TheAdvocates.org, www.TheAdvocates.org

FIRST EDITION
Published August 2012

Ruwart, Mary J.
Short Answers to the Tough Questions, Expanded Edition
By Dr. Mary J. Ruwart

ISBN 13: 978-0-9754326-6-2

1. Politics   2. Political issues   3. Libertarianism
4. Libertarian Q&A   5. Libertarian FAQ
I. Title   II. Ruwart, Mary J.

Cover design and typography by JPL Design Solutions
Manufactured in the United States of America

*This book is dedicated to libertarians worldwide
who are called upon to answer the tough questions
and want to give it their best shot!*

ALSO BY THE AUTHOR

Healing Our World: The Other Piece of the Puzzle (1992, 1993)
Healing Our World in an Age of Aggression (2003)
Short Answers to the Tough Questions
Healing Our World: The Compassion of Libertarianism (2013)

ALSO FROM THE PUBLISHER

Libertarianism in One Lesson: Ninth Edition
by David Bergland

Liberty A to Z: 872 Libertarian Soundbites You Can Use Right Now!
by Harry Browne

Secrets of Libertarian Persuasion
by Michael Cloud

Unlocking More Secrets of Libertarian Persuasion
by Michael Cloud

Minimum Wage, Maximum Damage
by Jim Cox

The Haiku Economist
by Jim Cox

Discovering Self-Government: A Bible-Based Study Guide
by Virgil L. Swearingen

Table of Contents

Preface

For most of us, learning about the libertarian ideal was a life-changing event. Our entire perspective on politics and, at a deeper level, on life itself shifted. We recognized that war and poverty result from a misunderstanding of how human nature works. The realization that these age-old plagues can be largely eliminated by adopting the non-aggression principle results in an incredible enthusiasm to share the good news with others.

When we try to do so, however, we discover that societal indoctrination is so strong that our friends and relatives often dismiss libertarian ideas as impractical, idealistic, or just plain wrong. Very few of them are willing to give us much time to dissuade them, either.

Yet without a more widespread understanding of how liberty works in the real world, our society cannot reap the benefits that freedom can bestow. Our mission, should we choose to accept it, is to entice our listeners with brief explanations that pique their interest and encourage them to ask us for more information.

Short Answers to the Tough Questions provides examples to stimulate the curiosity of your listeners. These questions and answers have been compiled from my own experience as a guest lecturer in schools and universities, as a Libertarian Party candidate, and in writing the "Ask Dr. Ruwart" column for the *Liberator Online,* the free newsletter published by the Advocates.

These "short answers" are compelling because they challenge the way the questioner views the world. Most people believe that government is the solution, instead of the problem.

Although short answers can pique their interest, showing them a different way is likely to require references to how liberty works in the real world. My book, *Healing Our World,* cites hundreds of studies that you can use to show your listeners the practicality of libertarian solutions. A complimentary download of the 1993 edition is available at my website, www.ruwart.com; the 2003 edition is available there and at the Advocates for Self-Government's website (www.theadvocates.org). Throughout *Short Answers*, I'll be citing some chapters in *Healing Our World* that provide detail beyond the short answers.

Some of the "tough questions" have been combined, paraphrased, or edited for ease of reading, but the essence and tone have been preserved. I have included some duplication where alternative phraseology might be useful. I've also included some questions that are openly hostile so that you can get a feel for how to handle them. You'll also find some gems from my readers who have come up with great short answers of their own.

My answers to the tough questions are far from perfect; however, most have been "field tested" and work well for me. Ultimately, you will find your own style and develop your own unique answers if you are in front of audiences with any frequency. Your unique background and experience will give you insights and perspectives that are different than mine; these are likely to work better with the people that are part of your intimate circle.

Readers have asked for more elaboration, so some answers are longer than others. Feel free to use these answers or reprint them (citing the Advocates and me).

Finally, please let me know what you think of *Short Answers!* You can reach me on Facebook or through my website www.ruwart. com. Visit the Advocates' website (www.theadvocates.org) for more communication tips as well.

Whether you use this book to improve your communication of libertarian ideas or simply to enhance your understanding of how liberty works, I hope you'll find it inspiring and enlightening.

Mary J. Ruwart, Ph.D.
Burnet, Texas

Publisher's Introduction

The Advocates for Self-Government is proud to present this new and greatly expanded edition of Dr. Mary Ruwart's libertarian communication classic, *Short Answers to the Tough Questions*.

Libertarians are constantly asked questions on a wide variety of issues. To answer them effectively, libertarians need short, accurate, convincing and memorable answers – preferably learned and practiced in advance.

Many years ago Mary Ruwart realized that. She began preparing such answers for her own use. The results were so dramatic that she began sharing her short answers with other libertarians, in speeches at libertarian events.

One of the key missions of the Advocates for Self-Government is to empower libertarians to become successful and persuasive advocates for our ideas. So in 1997 we asked Mary to write a regular column for our free email newsletter the *Liberator Online.* Readers were invited to send us questions they had difficulty answering, and Mary would craft short answers.

"Ask Dr. Ruwart" has since become one of the libertarian movement's greatest resources. Mary's column has been read by tens of thousands of libertarians around the world and has been widely reprinted.

Over the years, the audience for "Ask Dr. Ruwart" has grown – and changed. As the circulation of the *Libertarian Online* increased, questions began coming in not just from libertarians, but from non-libertarians curious about libertarianism. Mary's column now serves a double purpose: educating the public about libertarianism and helping libertarians answer those tough questions every libertarian faces.

Over the years Mary has answered hundreds of questions, on virtually every topic imaginable. This book collects the best and most useful answers, some rewritten and updated. From abortion to the War on Drugs, from flag burning to the post office – if it's something libertarians are commonly asked about, you'll find it here.

Libertarians will find this book an incredibly useful tool. You will benefit best if you read her answers, put them in your own words, and learn them by heart. By having a selection of persuasive soundbites for common questions on hand, rather than relying on last-minute inspiration, you will quickly become an appreciated and quotable spokesperson for liberty.

As a bonus, you can find even more answers from Dr. Ruwart, sorted by subject matter and searchable by keywords, at our website www.LibertarianAnswers.com.

Would you do us a favor? Please share with us your experience of using the book so we can then share with other libertarians – and future libertarians! Thank you.

As this book shows, liberty brings with it abundance, peace, tolerance and happiness. Because you are interested in libertarianism and in sharing these vital ideas with others, you are helping make our world a better place – thank you!

Sharon Harris
Advocates President
Cartersville, GA

PS: If you have a question that's not included here, be sure to write it up and send it in to Mary at ruwart@TheAdvocates.org. The answer to your question could show up in "Ask Dr. Ruwart" or even in a future book!

What Is a Libertarian?

L ibertarianism is based on a single ideal, the non-aggression principle, so libertarian rhetoric tends to be remarkably consistent.

Q *What is the libertarian non-aggression principle?*

A Libertarians oppose the initiation of force to achieve social or political goals. They reject "first-strike" force, fraud or theft against others; they only use force in self-defense. Those who violate this "non-aggression principle" are expected to make their victims whole as much as possible.

This "Good Neighbor Policy" is what most of us were taught as children. We were told not to lie, cheat, steal, or strike our playmates, except if they hit us first. If we broke a friend's toy, we were expected to replace it.

Most of us still practice what we learned as children with other individuals, but we have grown accustomed to letting government aggress against others when we think we benefit. Consequently, our world is full of poverty and strife, instead of the harmony and abundance that freedom (i.e., freedom from aggression) brings.

Simply put, libertarians take the non-aggression principle that most people implicitly follow in their interactions with other individuals, and apply it to group actions, including government actions, as well.

You might have heard the Libertarian Party (LP) referred to as the "Party of Principle." This is because the LP bases its programs and policy positions on the non-aggression principle.

Q *Do all libertarians belong to the Libertarian Party?*

A A libertarian is anyone who agrees with the non-aggression principle, and tries to live it in his or her daily life. Membership in a particular party or organization is not required!

Many libertarians view the Libertarian Party as the best vehicle for injecting their ideas into the political debate, and for electing libertarians to public office. Others work to try to steer the Republican and Democrat parties in a more libertarian direction. Still others prefer to devote their energy to libertarian organizations that are strictly educational and non-political in nature.

Some libertarians eschew political activism altogether. They simply live their lives by the non-aggression principle and try to be a good example.

Q *What is the difference between the fundamental beliefs of libertarianism and the two major parties?*

A One popular libertarian response is, "The Democrats want to control you in the boardroom; the Republicans want to control you in the bedroom. Libertarians want you to be in control of yourself."

Other parties, including the minor ones, feel that they know best how to spend your hard-earned money. Democrats like to spend your money on social programs and restrictions of your economic freedoms; Republicans like to spend your money on excessive military build-up and restrictions of your personal freedoms.

Libertarians want you to spend your own money and restrict none of your freedoms. That's why Libertarians want to do away with taxation. Taxation, even with representation, is still tyranny.

Q *I've heard people say that Libertarians have no moral values.*

A Libertarianism is based on the moral premise of non-aggression or the Good Neighbor Policy. Consequently, libertarians believe that no one is entitled to spend your money or tell you how to live your life. It's your life and your choice.

The Democrats and Republicans, on the other hand, believe that they are entitled to tell you what to do and how to spend your money. If you don't agree, they are willing to take your money or bend you to their will – at gunpoint, if necessary.

Which position do you think is the moral one?

Q *Are we ever entitled to use the coercive mechanism of the state in an unprincipled manner? Does the state not have the duty to justify its actions reasonably? How is state coercion by way of "policy" any different from being attacked by a gang?*

A Any policy that uses aggression (first-strike force, fraud, or theft) is unprincipled. We are never "entitled" to use the coercive mechanism of the state in an unprincipled, first-strike manner. It cannot be justified, because the ends invariably reflect the means used to obtain them. State coercion does not truly differ from a gang attack.

Q *While engaged in a friendly debate among friends, I tried to explain the moral foundation of libertarian ideals. I used the example of illegal prostitution and they agreed that they as individuals have no right to use force to prevent someone from enlisting the services of a prostitute. But they thought it is OK for the police to do so, because they are enforcing laws that the majority of Americans believe in, and that without those types of laws, our country would be submerged into anarchy, etc.... How to respond?*

A Libertarians believe that no one should be permitted to use first-strike force or fraud against others. On the other hand, by today's standards, it's OK to strike first as long as the majority agrees to do so. In which society do you have more chaos and violence? Is it OK to enslave blacks if the majority agrees? Is it OK to beat your wife if most men think it's fine? Such questions make it obvious that a libertarian society is based more on "law and order" than our current one!

Black economist Walter Williams said it best: "Slavery was legal; apartheid was legal; Stalinist, Nazi, and Maoist purges were legal. Clearly, the fact of legality does not justify these crimes. Legality, alone, cannot be the talisman of moral people."

Q *My friends think that if the majority of people find something acceptable, everyone else must abide or suffer the consequences of breaking the law. How should I respond?*

A Ask your friends if it's ok to enslave blacks if the majority agrees. Is it ok to beat your wife if most men think it is fine? Is it ok to shoot homosexuals if the majority approves? Such questions should help them see that wrong doesn't become right just because 51% of the people agree.

Q *I have been told that libertarianism is a combination of liberal and conservative ideas. Is that correct?*

A One can indeed look at libertarianism as the best of liberal and conservative views.

Conservatives tend to prefer individual choice over government control in many economic issues much (but not all) of the time. Liberals tend to prefer individual choice over government control in many (but not all) personal issues.

Libertarians, in sharp contrast, believe in individual choice in all areas. Libertarians believe that individuals should be free to make their own choices, as long as they don't assault others, steal from them, defraud them, or harm their property.

Libertarians want you to be free to choose; conservatives and liberals want to control you in some areas and give you limited freedom in others.

Libertarians honor their neighbors' choices; conservatives and liberals want to use the government to take some of those choices away.

Q *What the [epithet deleted] is a libertarian? Is a libertarian someone who constantly takes liberties?*

A Libertarians believe that stealing from, defrauding, or assaulting your neighbor is a crime, even when it's done by government for your benefit.

A libertarian is someone who wants to make their own choices – and honor yours – rather than having government force the will of majority or special interests on all of us. Libertarians recognize that liberty is something that we cannot have for ourselves without giving it to others. You might say, therefore, that libertarians are people who *give* liberties rather than take them.

Q *I have become very interested in libertarianism during the last few months. I want to study it deeper. If you had to pick one book to read to get started, which would it be? Then maybe books number 2 and 3? Can you steer me in the most effective way so I can catch up?*

A Naturally, I'm partial to my own book, *Healing Our World*, which you can order from the Advocates (2003 edition) or obtain as a free download (1993 edition) at my web site, www.ruwart. com. When you combine *Healing* with one of Harry Browne's books (*The Great Libertarian Offer* or *Why Government Doesn't Work*), you'll have a good balance. *Libertarianism in One Lesson* by David Bergland is a concise treatise on rights that will round out your "education." All of these are available from the Advocates by phone, mail, or online at www.theadvocates.org.

Q *How can I find out if I'm a libertarian?*

A One good way is to take The World's Smallest Political Quiz at www.theadvocates.org. The Quiz shows you where you believe in freedom of choice and where you are not so sure. The Quiz helps you place yourself as a libertarian, conservative, liberal, centrist or authoritarian.

Enjoy the Quiz and have fun sharing it with your friends. It turns small talk into big ideas!

Q *I think I'm a Constitutionalist rather than a Libertarian. I want the government to follow the precepts of the Constitution, nothing more or less.*

A Most libertarians would be delighted to see the government turn from its present course and follow the Constitution. Unfortunately, the history-making U.S. Constitution failed to recognize the aggression inherent in excise taxes, tariffs, etc. These fatal flaws would bring us back to where we are today, even if we could somehow turn back the clock and start over.

Libertarians attempt to correct this fatal flaw. They recognize that "freedom" means freedom from aggression, especially aggression through government. Freedom means self-government, not government by representation.

Aggression through government, in the form of taxes and regulation, takes away our freedom, even if a majority of the House and Senate vote for it. The U.S. Constitution was a giant step for humankind, but libertarians recognize that another step is yet to be taken. Check out libertarian ideas further, and see if you agree!

Q *In Article I, Section 8 of the U. S. Constitution, the powers of Congress, and for that matter the U. S. federal government, are outlined. Which of these powers could be defined as "non-libertarian?"*

A Article I, Section 8 gives Congress the power to lay and collect taxes, duties, imposts, and excises. A libertarian government could only charge user fees for services voluntarily contracted for. A libertarian government could not regulate commerce, establish post offices and roads, or relieve debtors of their obligations through bankruptcy.

A libertarian government could conceivably undertake the other activities listed in Section 8. Some libertarians, myself included, believe that even these functions could be left to the private sector.

Q *I know there are countries in Europe where taxes are extremely high and socialism dominates. Are there any people in, maybe France, that are upset by this? Are there libertarians in Europe?*

A Yes, the libertarian movement is worldwide! The International Society for Individual Liberty (www.isil.org) networks with libertarians throughout the world and has facilitated the publication of freedom literature in dozens of different languages. The Atlas Network is also engaged in international activities (www.atlasnetwork.org).

Q *The "free rider" dilemma has long been a problem in society. How do libertarians approach this problem? This is quite similar to "the prisoner's dilemma." I have yet to see any literature that has dealt with this issue.*

A The Prisoner's Dilemma has been dealt with extensively in reiterative computer games. The strategy that promotes individual and collective growth is called TIT-for-TAT, which is cooperative in its initial interaction between participants. In subsequent interactions, TIT-for-TAT reflects back the reaction it got from the other, "teaching" the other that cooperation is win-win.

As described in my book *Healing Our World*, TIT-for-TAT is similar to the libertarian philosophy: first, do no harm; if another harms you, reflect their own actions back through self-defense and/ or a demand for restitution.

Q *At its core, the libertarian philosophy seems to base all of it theories on one hypothesis: that people left to their own devices will always do the right thing. Doing the right thing, such as contributing to charities in the absence of government programs, requires that people, as a whole, rise up to a higher level.*

It simply is not their natural tendency. People are greedy, stingy organisms. They tend not to part with their time and money for charitable causes. Businesses tend not to really care about the environment or worker safety in the absence of government regulation. Examples to the contrary are few and very far between.

How do you address this foundational flaw in libertarian philosophy? Or am I all wet?

A Actually, libertarianism assumes that people will look after their own selfish interests. Because interaction is voluntary in a libertarian society, people can only cater to their own selfish interests by paying attention to what others want.

For example, if you want to make millions selling widgets, you have to make your widget better or less expensive than the competition. In a libertarian society, you can't put your competitors out of business through regulations and licensing laws, so you have to serve the customer best.

Businesses in a libertarian society also have to compete to attract and retain good workers, and providing a safe working environment is one way to do that.

Similarly, if you want someone to pay you a high price for your property, you have to take care of it. If you don't want to be sued by people who own the downstream fishing rights for a river, you don't dump your toxic waste upstream.

People will take care of the environment best when they own a piece of it and profit from it. Private forests, even those primarily grown for paper, are better tended than our national forests overseen by bureaucrats. (See the chapter on the environment for more discussion of this subject.)

As for charitable giving, Alexis de Tocqueville commented on the high level of generosity he observed during his travels in the early days of the United States. People who are free and prosperous are more likely to share with those who have less.

Q *This question was raised while I was discussing libertarian ideas with a member of the Green Party. Would a libertarian government in the United States permit socialist zones within the country?*

A If a group of individuals in a community all agreed to abide by socialistic principles, they could certainly contract among themselves to do so. They could not forcibly require those who hadn't agreed in writing to abide by their rules, however.

Q *I recently read about popular sovereignty and decentralism, the idea that state or local governments should make most of the decisions concerning the surrounding community, with a much-reduced role for the federal government. Would someone who subscribes to this idea be considered a libertarian? If so, would this make a good approach to selling libertarianism?*

A Libertarians are the ultimate decentralists: libertarians want to take government from the nation, state, and community down to the level of the individual. The closer to this ideal that we come, the more libertarian our society should be.

Switzerland, for example, has a part-time national government and strong canton (state) governments. The Swiss have one of the highest per capita incomes in the world, in spite of some very socialist canton governments. Since wealth creation increases as liberty does, devolution of power may be an effective strategy for moving a country towards libertarianism.

Q *Zen politics takes the best of all possible worlds and runs with it. If ten million people were about to starve to death and I could release the grain to feed them because of my position in government, and* *it would get them to their next harvest, would I do that or just say "Let 'em eat cake, I'm a Libertarian!"*

A A practitioner of Zen once said to me, "Libertarianism is the most spiritual of all political philosophies." His reasoning was that the moral and the practical are inseparable. Moral actions produce "good" in the real world.

For example, libertarians don't tell starving people to "eat cake;" they prevent starvation by creating an abundance of "cake." Virtually all poverty in the world today is a result of governments aggressing against their people. Free countries, on the other hand, end poverty by removing the laws that foster it. They create an abundance of wealth because the poor aren't legally ostracized from supporting themselves.[1]

Q *Libertarianism seems to me to be an impractical philosophy. Worse, it seems that many libertarians must be waiting hopefully for a lawless society of gun-toting vigilantes where the only rule is the survival of the fittest (most powerful, most aggressive, most arrogant, most greedy). That's about as bad as any bad government. So how could libertarianism promote good and responsible government?*

A A libertarian society is, by definition, one where nobody is the first to harm (strike, defraud, steal from) another. If someone fails to obey this one-and-only law, then he or she must make things right again with the one who is harmed.

I'm not sure where you get the idea that such a society would be lawless, where only the fit would survive. That's actually what we have now. Special interests that control government really have an edge over the rest of us. Sovereign immunity protects government officials, even when they kill innocent women and children (e.g., Waco, drug raids, etc.). We're forced to deal with big corporations because taxes and regulations drive out their smaller competitors.

In a libertarian society, we'd have more law and order because the government wouldn't be exempt from following the non-aggression principle. The wealthy and connected couldn't use government against the weak and disadvantaged as they do today.

Q *The dream of libertarianism seems to be a non-violent society. Force is seen as the only enemy. Do you think this is possible? I disagree with the idea that force should be done away with.*

A Libertarians don't want to do away with force, just "first-strike" force. If neither of us strikes first, no fight is possible. If you are behaving peacefully, and I assault, defraud, or steal from you, then defensive force is permissible in a libertarian society.

Q *I saw a reference in one of Michael Cloud's Liberator Online "Persuasion Power Point" columns to "natural or God-given" rights. The column also mentioned Christianity and the Bible. As an atheist, I was surprised at this. Is belief in God a necessary part of libertarianism?*

A Libertarianism is for everyone – even people with widely diverging beliefs on religious matters, like atheists and Christians.

The libertarian philosophy is embraced by Christians, Jews, Muslims, atheists, agnostics, pagans, etc. The common denominator that brings people from all these diverse belief systems to libertarianism is simply a desire for peace and plenty (as opposed to war and poverty) and the shared belief that the way to achieve this is to build a society based on the non-aggression principle or the Good Neighbor Policy.

The non-aggression principle is the core concept of libertarianism: the idea that people should be free to live their lives in any peaceful way they choose, as long as they don't harm others or their property. You can come to believe in the non-aggression principle from many approaches. Your intellect will take you there. The Ten Commandments can take you there, too. The pathways are many, but they all lead to the same destination.

Isn't it remarkable that groups with such divergent beliefs can agree on liberty?

Q *What is the difference between Ayn Rand's Objectivism and libertarianism?*

A In my opinion, the differences are more cultural than real, in political matters. Both Objectivism and libertarianism are based on the non-aggression principle of honoring our neighbors' choice (not initiating physical force, fraud or theft) and making things right with our victims if we don't.

Objectivism is a comprehensive philosophy of life that includes not just political beliefs but strong and unified beliefs on virtually every aspect of human existence, including religion, art, romance, and so on. Libertarianism, in contrast, is a strictly political philosophy.

Rand believed that government's proper role was protection of rights and that government should have a monopoly on defensive force to fulfill this role. Many libertarians agree with her. Others believe that governments are poor protectors of rights and that competition in this realm is right and proper.

Q *If taxation is theft – which I believe it is – we are the thieves, to the extent that we vote for political figures who tax (steal) in our name. The Bible preaches against theft. If one is a Christian, being a thief doesn't seem to be a good thing to be. Do you agree?*

A You're exactly right: when we vote for taxes, we are voting to steal from our neighbors. Stealing is contrary to Christian principles. Hence, all true Christians should be against taxation – and for libertarianism!

Q *What is the difference between anarchists and libertarians?*

A Some libertarians believe that government should handle the courts, police, and national defense; others of the anarchist persuasion believe that all the functions of government can be provided by the private sector.

What Does a Libertarian Government Look Like?

A libertarian government would be very different than what we have today since it would not be funded through taxation.

Q *What, succinctly, is the job of government?*

A Government, if it has a role, is to protect its citizens from aggressors, both foreign and domestic.

A libertarian-style government would therefore limit itself to a police, court, prison system and military. These institutions would deter crime more effectively than today's system by assuring that criminals paid restitution to their victims, as well as the costs of government enforcement.

Q *Do libertarians want any government at all? If so, where do they propose to get the revenue to finance it?*

A Some libertarians believe that all functions of government can best be provided by competitors within the private sector. Other libertarians believe that the government should have a monopoly on the courts, police, and military. Both groups would fund these activities through user fees or their equivalent.

For example, convicted criminals would be expected to compensate their victims and pay for costs of apprehension and prosecution.[2]

Military funding would probably come from a variety of sources. If some Americans wanted to help a nation under siege, they could raise funding as a charitable effort. Volunteer militias might be popular for local defense. Historical evidence suggests that such activities can be adequately funded without resorting to the aggression of taxation (see the chapter entitled "National Defense" for more detail).

Q *Wasn't the failure of a libertarian-like society the reason that government was created in the first place? Is it possible that a result of such a society would be true anarchy, in which the strong banded together against the weak?*

A Just the opposite is true. Government is, in essence, the privileged class dominating the disadvantaged. The Big Lie is that government is the friend of the poor and the foe of the well-to-do.

Government is force; force is expensive. The poor pay little in taxes and campaign contributions. Do you think our elected officials serve those who fund them and put them in office, or do you think they turn against their benefactors to help the disadvantaged once they are elected?

Q *My questions to you: (1) If you are in favor of abandoning all taxation, how do you distinguish your proposal from the anarchist proposal? (2) Do you think that your proposal for the elimination of all taxation represents the mainstream libertarian point of view?*

A Libertarians generally view taxation as theft and are against it accordingly. The taxation plank of the Libertarian Party platform states that members "oppose all personal and corporate income taxation, including capital gains taxes" and "support the eventual repeal of all taxation."

Some libertarians, however, cannot envision a government that operates without taxes. To them, "no taxes" mean "no government." However, a government limited to providing defense against aggressors, both domestic and foreign, could indeed operate without taxation (see the chapters entitled "Restitution" and "National Defense" for more details).

Q *I read an article in which libertarians attacked supposedly wasteful "pork-barrel spending" in the U.S. budget. Why are you guys so full of yourselves? Some of these projects are very useful – like those that have to do with finding new sources of energy, with perfecting our culture, with job training, and with animal research. Sure, some useless stuff shouldn't be funded, but those projects intended to upgrade our way of life deserve support.*

A Libertarians find many of your favorite projects "useful" and would like to see them carried out by the private sector. However, libertarians are against tax funding for any project, because taxation is, in essence, theft.

For example, let's say you want to encourage animal research. You might invest in a company that performs such research or donate to a non-profit organization for that purpose. Your neighbors may think that animal research is unethical and won't invest in or donate to such work. Instead, they might invest in alternative fuel. Everybody contributes to what they feel is important and boycotts what they feel is offensive.

If such research is tax-funded, however, your neighbors will be forced – at gunpoint, if necessary – to support something that they don't want. (If you don't think that it happens at gunpoint, imagine what would happen if you didn't pay your taxes!) Your neighbors, in turn, will force you to pay for projects they favor, but you don't. Everyone loses, because the government bureaucracy takes a hefty "overhead" to collect your taxes and decide where they should go.

Libertarians believe that stealing from our neighbors is wrong whether we do it as individuals, as majorities, or as governments. Wrong means used to achieve good ends backfire every time.

For example, two-thirds of our welfare tax dollars go to the middle-class social workers who administer the programs. Private charities, on the other hand, deliver two-thirds of each dollar to those in need.[3] We help the poor best through private charities, not tax-supported welfare. When we let government administer projects that we find useful, we get less "good" for our dollar.

In summary, libertarians don't judge a project's utility at all. Libertarians simply want to stop the theft of your money through taxes so that you can decide which programs your funds should support. You'll never have to worry about funding pork-barrel spending again!

Q *I think that when you take someone's tax money by force, you need to listen to how that person wants their money to be spent. Why not let individuals decide how their individual tax dollars are spent, instead of coercing them into supporting a libertarian system they may disagree with?*

A Libertarians do let individuals decide how their tax dollars are spent by not collecting them in the first place. That way, people have their money in their pocket to spend as they please.

Q *I am coming around to libertarian ideas, but so many libertarian policies, while moving in the right direction, seem to go way too far. For instance, the idea of no taxation, only user fees, seems great. But it seems that some taxation would be necessary to pay government workers, maintain ambassadors and embassies to other nations, host state visits from other nations, and (a necessary evil) pay lawyers to defend the government against lawsuits, as well as a host of other little things that there couldn't be a user fee for. Can zero taxation really stand up to reason?*

A Yes! Government workers would be paid by those individuals or groups that made their employment necessary. Lawyers defending the government in lawsuits, for example, would be paid for by the guilty party. Since government officials would not enjoy sovereign immunity in a libertarian society, they could be liable for attorney fees and damages for any wrongdoing (see the chapter entitled "Restitution" for more detail).

Since a libertarian government would not be restricting trade between nations, establishing embargoes, setting tariffs, handing out taxpayer guaranteed loans, etc., our top officials would not be wining and dining dignitaries from other countries as they do today. Naturally, heads of state from other countries could visit the U.S. at their own expense. Without the ability to pick the U.S. taxpayer's pocket, however, few would bother.

If embassies were maintained in foreign nations, they would be supported by fees from travelers or others who might use their services.

Today, those who are too poor to travel pay taxes to support services for people who can afford to see the world. Taxes are one way in which government makes the poor poorer and the rich richer.

Q *Do libertarians believe that congressmen or senators should be volunteer positions? That would be asking a lot.*

A While libertarians don't have a formal position on whether or not our "public servants" should be volunteers, Switzerland has only a part-time national government. Some of the office holders also work other jobs to make ends meet.

A libertarian society would require even less national legislation than Switzerland. Indeed, a libertarian society might require no legislators at all!

Q *Most libertarians oppose the current income tax system. Is this because the system is too complicated and the IRS has a poor history, or because income taxes are inherently bad? What type of taxation system would be best? What type of taxation system would be best at the state and local levels?*

A It is true that the income tax is horrendously complicated, and also that the IRS has a long and ugly record of terrorizing and abusing people. That is not the reason that libertarians oppose the income tax system, though.

Simply, libertarians do not advocate the initiation of force, fraud, or theft to achieve social or political goals. If you refused to contribute to my favorite charity, and I took your money at gunpoint anyway, I'd be stealing from you. Similarly, if I vote for taxes to force you to contribute to that charity, I'm asking the government to take your money – at gunpoint, if necessary.

What is wrong for me as an individual, is wrong for a group of individuals acting through government. Wrong doesn't turn into right, just because the majority agrees to it. Minorities have no protection if they have to depend upon the majority for it.

As a result, libertarians believe that *all* taxation is theft, not just income tax. Libertarians believe that the services supported by taxes can be provided more economically and efficiently by user fees or via the private sector.

Q *I have read about proposals to eliminate the income tax and replace it with a consumption tax (national sales tax). To me this seems like a very good idea. I can't see a downside. Am I missing something? Do libertarians support this idea?*

A Libertarians recognize that taxation of any kind is theft and therefore do not support taxation. However, some dedicated libertarians have been working to replace the income tax with a consumption tax (often called the "Fair Tax,") like the one you've outlined.

Fair Tax supporters feel that people would feel the bite much more if everything that they bought came with a double-digit sales tax. Tax raises would be more visible and more unpopular for politicians to propose. The abuses perpetrated by the IRS would also end. Public support for abolishing taxes altogether would increase.

One danger that many libertarians see in proposing this switch is the possibility that we would end up with a national sales tax *and* an income tax. Why not simply get rid of the income tax and replace it with *nothing*, as Libertarian Party presidential candidate Harry Browne proposed in 1996 and 2000?

If all we did was to restrict government to its constitutional limits, we could provide for defense and other necessary functions with constitutionally permitted excise taxes. Next, libertarians could work on getting rid of those, too!

Q *I am bothered that some libertarians are advocating the idea of excise taxes to fund government. Isn't this just another form of force (making people pay more for things than they have to), and opening the door for yet more social engineering?*

A Yes, indeed! Excise taxes are theft, too.
Some libertarians advocate returning to the Constitution (and excise taxes) as a way to get closer to the no-tax ideal. However, a truly libertarian society wouldn't have any taxes at all!

Q *What is the libertarian response to handling the national debt?*

A The national debt represents loans to government secured by its willingness to tax (steal from) its citizens. Thus, some libertarians view buying government bonds as encouraging a thief and have no qualms about repudiating the debt. Others believe that government property (including over 40% of the U.S. landmass) should be liquidated to repay the debt, wholly or in part.

Restitution

Restitution is one of the early topics in *Short Answers* because it plays a pivotal role in libertarian solutions to environmental and other crimes.

Q *My only problem with libertarianism is that it pays no attention to prevention of initial force. In a free society, the government can only retaliate when force has already been initiated.*

A Studies[4] show that requiring aggressors to compensate their victims deters crime. Restitution is the most effective regulation of all!

Restitution is also just. Under this principle, a person who harms another is responsible for making whole the one who is harmed.

Q *What happens if someone steals in a libertarian society?*

A In a libertarian society, aggressors would be required to compensate their victims and pay for costs of their trial and apprehension. Studies[4] show that such restitution is one of the most effective deterrents known.

Q *So what happens if the thief refuses to pay? Is the victim out of luck?*

A Thieves unwilling to make payments towards a court-ordered judgment would most likely be placed in a work prison. In addition to compensating their victims, inmates would be required to pay the expensive costs of imprisonment. Most thieves would probably make compensation payments rather than risk such a huge increase in their liability and the loss of their liberty.

Q *Without taxes, where would the money come from to lock up the murderers and rapists?*

A Ultimately, the money would come from the murderers and rapists themselves. Prisoners could work off their room and board in the prison or pay for it out of their own resources.

Convicts who refused to work would end up with minimal accommodations or would have to depend upon the charity of others. To maximize profit, wardens would have incentive to train and motivate their captive workers.

Part of their sentence would likely include monetary payments to their victims as compensation. Historically, such prisons have not only spared the taxpayer, but have resulted in a high rate of rehabilitation.

Q *What will prevent prisons from using convicts as slave labor?*

A Prisons would be privately run in a libertarian society and would compete for inmates. Prisoners would choose the one offering the kind of work and environment they preferred. Normally, inmates would choose the institution that maximized their earnings and minimized their prison stay. If the inmates were mistreated or otherwise dissatisfied, they could transfer to another institution.

Work prisons that had the most productive and congenial environment would profit by attracting the most "customers." Work prisons that were shunned by inmates would go out of business.

Q *So if prisoners don't work, will they starve to death?*

A   Prisoners who don't work would depend on charity just as we, on the outside, must do if we don't work. Charitable individuals or groups might support non-working prisoners if they felt the circumstances warranted such compassion.

Some groups might only help prisoners who were at least trying to help themselves, even to the extent of paying part of their restitution. Other organizations might freely assist prisoners regardless of circumstances.

Q   *What could possibly motivate aggressors to keep on working if there was no chance that they could ever repay the debt to their victims?*

A   Aggressors making payments to their victims might be able to remain at liberty. By refusing to make such payments, they risk incarceration.

Q   *How can poor criminals with few skills pay the cost of incarceration and compensation?*

A   We usually assume that anyone who could make money working wouldn't bother stealing. We think that thieves couldn't pay their victims restitution. Historical evidence suggests differently. A saddle tree factory in St. Louis once employed inmates of the Missouri State Penitentiary. The prison was not only self-supporting; it made a profit![5] Almost any able-bodied person can do simple factory work.

Until 1980, Maine State's prison inmates were allowed to manufacture arts and crafts, making as much as $60,000 annually in year 2000 dollars.[6] In recent years, more than 70 companies have employed inmates from 16 states for telephone work, such as booking airline reservations.[7]

Obviously, many prisoners are capable of work and restitution; for-profit prisons have every incentive to train them to make high hourly wages, making them better suited to support themselves when released and less likely to turn to crime.

Today, many people are incarcerated for "crimes" in which there is no victim, such as drug possession. In a libertarian society the only people who will go to prison will be those who actually harm another person, and cannot work off their debt to their victim in any other way.

Restitution through productive work is the most successful rehabilitation known. Even if the victim can't be fully compensated, something is better than the nothing that they receive today. Also, repayment to the victim allows criminals to truly right their wrongs.

In addition, restitution is a more effective deterrent than prison. During informal surveys, inmates claimed that they much preferred jail time, which they saw as "time off," to restitution, which they saw as "work."

Q *So the thief goes free, while the victim must wait years for compensation?*

A Not necessarily. Insured victims would be compensated immediately, as with most insurance. The judgment against the thief would be collected by the insurance company instead. Of course, time payments are better than no payments at all, which is what most victims receive today.

Q *What would happen if the thief dies before the victim is fully compensated or the judgment is so big that the thief cannot pay it, even if he or she works for a lifetime?*

A The victim will receive at least partial compensation, more than what he or she would receive today.

Today, victims are robbed twice. Not only are they robbed by the thief, but they are taxed by their government for apprehending and jailing the thief.

Q *If the courts and police don't get full payment from an aggressor, who pays the bill?*

A The courts and police would probably write off bad debts, and factor them into their fees, just as businesses do today. Since the criminals pay these costs, *you* won't!

Q *Isn't it cruel and unusual punishment to make prisoners work?*

A Law-abiding citizens must work to provide their own food, clothing, and shelter. How can expecting the same from criminals be "cruel and unusual punishment?"

On the other hand, making innocent taxpayers or crime victims feed and clothe felons certainly seems "cruel and unusual" to me!

Q *Dr. Ruwart's proposal is an illegitimate first cousin to the civil forfeiture laws libertarians rightly oppose – laws that confiscate sums of cash not reported to the IRS, or to Customs, a car or home where illegal drugs have been found, a car from which the services of a prostitute may have been solicited, and more. The deprivation of liberty for months, for years, even for life, is surely punishment enough, even in a "country club" prison.*

A I doubt that victims of criminals would agree with you. Why should victims have to pay taxes to feed, clothe, and shelter those who harmed them? Why should criminals get a free ride at the further expense of their victims?

The focus of justice in a libertarian society is restoration of the victim, not punishment of the criminal. Full compensation, when possible, not only makes the victim whole, but gives the criminal a chance to truly balance the scales and start over.

Confiscation, incidentally, is taking the property of someone *not* convicted of criminal activity and is not even remotely related to restitution, which comes only after conviction.

Q *Libertarians should get real about criminals paying for costs of their incarceration, or effectively compensating their victims. How much compensation could Timothy McVeigh have made to pay the relatives of the people killed in Oklahoma City, and those who were injured?*

A For some crimes, especially murder, no compensation is ever adequate. In the case of McVeigh, this would be true even if he had killed only one person, and even if he had had millions of dollars in resources that could be seized for compensation. That's no reason that partial restitution shouldn't be made, however.

While nothing can compensate for the loss of a loved one, restitution may help the survivors afford counseling and other supportive measures in the aftermath. The victims and their families shouldn't have salt rubbed in their wounds by paying taxes to support someone who has killed a loved one as they do today.

Keeping Timothy McVeigh alive, and requiring him to work the rest of his life for his victims and their survivors (he was just 29 when convicted), might have provided a sense that at least some justice was being served.

Q *How does the amount of compensation get set in the case of a murderer of a retired individual without family? With no one to compensate, is there no consequence?*

A A person who harms another owes the victim compensation. If the victim has been killed, the claim to that compensation usually passes to the victim's heirs. Without apparent heirs, it's possible that a libertarian jury would direct the compensation towards a charity or group that the victim favored.

Although compensation is primarily awarded to restore the victim, studies show that restitution serves to rehabilitate the criminal as well. Thus, claims for compensation are likely to be enforced, even when the victims cannot personally receive them.

Q *Sounds pretty gruesome to me. Isn't there any mercy in a libertarian society?*

A In a libertarian society, any debt incurred by an aggressor represents a real injury or loss to the victim. Letting the aggressor off the hook simultaneously robs the victim of what is rightly due him or her. What could be more gruesome than that?

In a libertarian society, charitable organizations or sympathetic individuals, like yourself, might choose to pay the aggressor's debt to the victim, especially if the aggressor was truly repentant.

A victim might occasionally relieve an aggressor of their debt. Imagine that a drunk driver hits your car, killing your spouse. The driver is devastated by what he has done and never takes another drink after that fateful day. Instead, he often goes to schools to tell his story, begging the young people not to drink and drive. Might you consider his debt paid if you didn't need the money that the jury awarded you?

Q *What's to keep murderers and rapists who are already in prison from working just hard enough to pay for their food, but not hard enough to give their victims any compensation?*

A Prisoners would probably be given a percentage of their work credit for their own personal needs and the rest would go to their victims. Perhaps the victims would be paid a certain amount before the inmates received anything. Obviously, work prison payments could be structured to thwart both laziness and discouragement.

Q *Libertarians believe that the state's only legitimate job is to protect the rights of individuals. Does that give the state the right to use capital punishment – the death penalty? I do not believe in* *the death penalty. I think it is wrong to kill people regardless of what crimes they committed. But I wonder how libertarians answer this.*

A Libertarians differ in their attitude towards the death penalty. In the political realm, the Libertarian Party takes no formal stand on it.

Libertarians believe in compensation of the victim, not punishment. However, a murderer might be put to death if that was the compensation that the family wanted most.

Because of the finality of this compensation, guilt would most likely need to be unequivocal. The ability to determine guilt with DNA testing has indicated that a number of innocent people have been executed in the past. Some libertarians point to these mistakes as a reason not to give the state the authority to execute.

My personal belief is that a libertarian society might not outlaw capital "compensation," but execution would be rare.

Q *Do libertarians believe in capital punishment?*

A Libertarians believe in compensation of the victim, not punishment. Most victims and their families would probably prefer monetary compensation, not execution.

However, if an aggressor was not repentant or was unwilling to provide restitution, victims might ask for execution as compensation. The courts would then decide if execution of the aggressor was warranted.

Q *Dr. Ruwart, for perhaps the first time, I must disagree with you on one of your answers. Although I do agree that libertarians are split on the issue of capital punishment, I believe the philosophical position is clear: the state cannot take what it does not own! Under the libertarian core principle of self-ownership, one's life is one's own property. By what right can the state take possession of it?*

A I suspect that we have a misunderstanding rather than a disagreement.

You are correct in pointing out that the state cannot take possession of another's life. However, the victim(s) of an aggressor might be able to lay claim to that aggressor's life as compensation for injury.

For example, a child is tortured and murdered by an assailant, who shows no sign of repentance and is suspected to have committed such atrocities previously. In most libertarian societies, the parents would want the aggressor imprisoned indefinitely, in addition to any monetary compensation that they might request.

However, if the parents felt that they would only find solace in the murderer's death, a libertarian court might decide that the parents (not the state) do have a right to the killer's life as compensation for their child's murder. If the state actually handled the execution, it would be acting only as an agent for the parents.

That's just one theory. As you note, libertarians do indeed disagree over such questions regarding capital punishment.

Q *Timothy McVeigh was eventually executed. Should he have been made to pay the cost of his lethal injection? What a barbaric thought.*

A While I'm not an advocate of capital punishment, I would not be revolted by the idea of the criminal paying for his or her execution. Bombing a building that results in the killing and maiming of innocents is barbaric; making these victims or their families pay, via taxes, for the imprisonment or execution of the aggressor is even more so.

Q *Say that Timothy McVeigh had been released from prison and ordered to pay for the physical damage he caused. Where would he get a job? How much of his modest earnings would he be allowed to* *keep for food, clothing, and shelter? Would he be allowed to have a TV, or go to a movie?*

A Some well-known aggressors, if they are repentant, might be able to raise a great deal of money towards their judgments by writing books or sharing their story and change of heart on television. The amount that they could keep for themselves would probably be at the courts' discretion.

Q *If criminals only have to make restitution to their victims, how do they ever pay their debt to society?*

A Libertarians believe that aggressors owe their debt to their victims, not society. If the victim is made whole, isn't the debt fully paid?

Q *While I agree with the fundamentals of libertarianism, I am afraid that, at this stage of the human evolutionary process, most people couldn't handle complete freedom. How many people do you know who, when about to take a specific action, would stop and think whether or not their action would have an undesirable result for someone else?*

A People think about how their actions affect others when they experience the fallout. Libertarianism creates this link when those who harm others must make full restitution. Studies show that restitution is one of the best deterrents to crime.

Today, criminals are seldom caught because so much policing is focused on victimless crimes. Today, criminals go free after stealing, raping, and killing so that peaceful pot smokers can get mandatory minimums.

All of this would change in a libertarian society. People who harmed others would be deterred to a greater extent than they are today.

Don't expect perfection under *any* political system. Erring, after all, is human.

Q *It sounds like an aggressor could just declare bankruptcy in a libertarian society and get off without paying a dime or doing any time!*

A Bankruptcy is a grant of partial immunity which government gives to debtors at the expense of their creditors. A libertarian government would not have the power to waive a victim's right to restitution.

Q *How about corporations? Would they enjoy the limited liability that they have today?*

A Limited liability is a grant of partial immunity given to corporations by government. In a libertarian society, government could not waive a victim's right to restitution.

Q *If libertarianism were to become America's dominant political philosophy, what would be done to ensure that the powerful remain accountable to those that they may harm? Would corporations, for example, be banned? It seems to me there's something wrong with the idea that someone can cause tremendous harm (sometimes deliberately) and walk away relatively unscathed.*

A Restitution would be the norm in a libertarian society, even if compensation had to be made over time. Bankruptcy, for individuals or businesses, would not relieve the guilty of their duty to restore their victims. In a libertarian society, the state would be unable to grant a business limited liability, which is essentially what a corporate charter entails today.

Q *Surely libertarians would let people incorporate with limited liability and then let the consumers choose!*

A By including "Inc." in its title, a business could notify customers of the limited liability for its products' performance. Consumers could choose whether or not to buy such products.

However, if the corporation harmed its neighbors by polluting their soil, for example, liability limits are unlikely to apply unless the victims agreed to the pollution. Contrast that with the present system, where the government decrees pollution limits, in effect giving permission for a corporation to pollute *up to* the limits, regardless of the harmful consequences to others.

Q *I am helping Cambodia rewrite its corporation laws. Here's a place that desperately needs a shot in the arm economically, from corporations. Consequently, I was distressed by your comments on limited corporate liability.*

A Do you really want to protect foreign investors at the expense of Cambodia's environment and populace? Getting rid of taxes, regulations, and trade restrictions is the best way to give your economy a "shot in the arm." Look at how it helped Hong Kong!

Q *I am troubled by all of the big business scandals that have been happening lately. I have always been for privatization of government programs and such, but I'm concerned that the corporations are just as corrupt and badly managed as the government. How can we be assured that things will be any better with privatization?*

A Your concern is justified. Corporate owners are granted limited liability by the government. Consequently, owners (stockholders) don't oversee management as carefully as they otherwise would. Officers of a corporation can declare bankruptcy and the victims have no recourse.

Government has no right to "forgive" the wrongs that corporations or their officers do. Only the victims should be able to do that.

Imagine what would happen if government could not grant limited liability or bankruptcy. A person who defrauded others might have to spend their lifetime trying to compensate victims. Overnight we'd have a lot more owner oversight and a lot less fraud!

Q *One area I feel libertarians do not address as much as they should is the effect that corporations have as a "government entity." They receive billions in government subsidies, use the government to legislate their profits and stomp on their competition, and their internal policies toward their employees are the least of any democratic institution in our society – all at taxpayer's expense. Opening up a free market to this powerful lobby sounds scary. Any suggestions?*

A A free market is the *only* way to control corporations! As long as government has the power to regulate business, business will control government by funding the candidate who legislates in its favor. A free market thwarts lobbying by taking the power that corporations seek away from government.

For example, in a libertarian society, government could not give subsidies, legislate profits, or introduce legislation designed to favor big business as it does today. Today, when regulations are proposed, big business cries "Don't throw me in the briar patch!" More regulation means that their smaller competitors are forced out of business.

Free markets, by encouraging competition, would expand the economy by creating more jobs. Employees would have more choice and flexibility to move if they weren't treated well. Without the regulation that big business wants, employees could much more easily become their own bosses. Employers who didn't treat employees well might find themselves creating competitors!

Q *Libertarians seem to be against setting government standards and regulations for businesses and products, and instead rely upon lawsuits which depend upon showing harm in order to reimburse people hurt by pollution, faulty design of products, etc. Won't this after-the-fact continuing litigation create an even larger court load?*

A Restitution, even if enforced through court action, deters criminals and decreases the necessity of actually going to court. Japan, which has such a system in place, is the only industrialized nation that has seen a consistent decrease in violent crime since World War II.[8] Litigants normally come to a settlement before coming in front of the judge, so very little time is spent in court.

Because restoring the environment is so costly, the threat of having to right an environmental wrong would deter polluters just as the threat of restitution stops crimes of violence against people and property in Japan.

Q *Criminal defendants are routinely represented by public defenders whose services are often woefully inadequate compared to the resources that are available to the prosecution. Over 90% of these defendants plea bargain, even though some are innocent. In a libertarian society, however, they would not even have public defenders to turn to.*

A In a libertarian system, false accusers would often be liable for the defendants' attorney fees. Thus, defendants would be able to get top-notch law firms to represent them on contingency.

As you so rightly observe, a person in today's system can be bankrupted by false charges and pressured into confessing. Such a travesty would be much less frequent in a libertarian society.

Q *How would libertarians meet the public concern that there are too many frivolous liability suits?*

A If the loser had to pay the winner's costs in frivolous lawsuits, they would be much less common. Without this provision, someone can wrongfully accuse others and force them into bankruptcy with litigating costs. Indeed, this is one of the government's favorite tactics against individuals.

Q *What if someone harms another, but the victim is afraid to sue because he or she might have to pay the aggressor's legal bills if the jury didn't turn in a guilty verdict?*

A If the suit had a legitimate, rather than frivolous basis, it's likely that the jury would require each side to pay its own fees.

In a libertarian society, arbitrators could attempt to establish a mutually agreed upon settlement for a much lower cost than a trial. This economical alternative is ideal for situations where guilt is shared or not easy to establish.

Even if a trial was necessary, the cost would be substantially lower than it is today. In a libertarian society, you would not have to choose representation from state-licensed lawyers. As with most licensing laws, those governing attorneys drive up costs by limiting the number of practitioners. Representation would be much more affordable.

Q *In a libertarian court system, would there still be lawyers and judges, with the associated current procedural stuff (like subpoenas, discovery of documents, depositions, appeals to high courts, etc.), or would a libertarian court proceeding be fundamentally different, perhaps like mandatory mediation? Would jury service be mandatory, or just for those who want to do it? Any related information would be greatly appreciated.*

A Jury service is unlikely to be mandatory in a libertarian society, since justice would be based on compensation of the victim, rather than state-decreed punishment. Deciding not to serve on a jury creates no victim, and therefore would not be a crime. Unlike today, jurors might be compensated for their time, making it less onerous.

However, mutually satisfactory settlements, rather than the winner-take-all court battles of today, would be more likely when restitution was the goal. In some such instances, juries might not be necessary. The convoluted protocols currently in place would likely be replaced by more efficient and flexible ways of coming to agreement, like mediation and arbitration.

Q *Would you agree that the absence of a system of government police, courts, prisons and military would be a state of anarchy, and would bring intolerable chaos?*

A For eons, governments have persuaded us that without the protection of their "justice system," chaos would reign. However, police and courts are few in number; they can't control a populace in a high crime area where many people have no respect for property rights. They can only curb aggressors in a predominantly peaceful population. Indeed, the government "protection racket" usually creates more chaos through violation of property and personal rights than the so-called criminal element.

Chaos results from an absence of a respect for others and their property. For example, if you see something that belongs to me, and you can steal it without getting caught, would you? Probably not – and your decision would have nothing to do with the presence or absence of police, courts, etc.

A good historical example illustrating that respect for property comes before a justice system, not as a result of it, is the settling of the western United States. Because the West was only a territory, no governments, police, etc. existed. Yet, contrary to the portrayal by Hollywood, property rights were widely respected. Crime rates were actually higher in the more heavily governed eastern states than in the so-called "Wild West."

Why? The early settlers brought with them a firm commitment to peaceful behavior. They signed voluntary pacts among themselves before they even left the East as to how property would be allotted and how disputes would be settled. Miners got together and decided how claims would be enforced. If someone later decided that they didn't like these arrangements, they could simply execute their buy-out provisions.

In essence, the marketplace provided successful governing without government.[9] Peaceful people created their own justice system not to impose order upon an unruly populace, but to stop any deviations from the norm that they sought to preserve.

Q *Is there any inherent reason that a libertarian-style govern-ment could not be instituted between nations to bring justice to victims of physical force or fraud originating between these nations?*

A Today, international trading organizations have their own courts to deal with member disputes, because their members prefer peaceful resolution, rather than chaos. In a libertarian world, the marketplace is likely to provide such services as needed.

Q *Recently in Washington, store security guards, who were off-duty policemen, detained a teen because they suspected him of stealing the shirt he was wearing. The teen did own the shirt, and a lawsuit resulted. How would a similar situation be handled in a liber-tarian society?*

A Because of the possibility of error, most store owners would (and do) handle potential shop lifters as gently as possible. After all, store owners don't want to estrange a customer if they make a mistake! Since government agents generally can claim sover-eign immunity, they're not so gentle when making an accusation.

Most customers realize that shoplifting increases the cost of goods and are willing to submit to an occasional misdirected search to prevent thieves from getting away, especially when shop security is polite. Recently, my sister purchased earrings from one store, but the security tape wasn't removed during checkout. In a second store, these earrings set off an alarm. My sister emptied her purse to show security that she hadn't taken anything and the earrings came to light. The situation was resolved with courtesy, and my sister was not at all offended. Most inspections of innocent parties are resolved similarly in the private sector.

I suspect that the incident you described led to a lawsuit because our so-called "justice system" today imposes such a high price on any litigation that the store was likely to make a settlement just to avoid it. In my limited dealings with such suits, insurance companies find it more economical to settle even bogus claims rather than go to trial.

Q *Advocates of current hate crime legislation would have people receive more severe sentencing if they are convicted of a crime motivated by bigotry, racism, sexism, etc. What is the libertarian stance on this delicate issue? I consider myself politically libertarian, but I am interested to know what others think.*

A Libertarians believe that aggressors should make their victims whole again. For the most part, motivation is irrelevant. However, some victims might be less demanding if the harm done to them was accidental rather than intentional.

Q *How would a libertarian society deal with blackmail? Thinking of the blackmailer as a gossip offering the service of his silence for a fee, I cannot find any reason why it should be illegal in a libertarian society. Both parties receive something of value and the agreement is consensual.*

A The criteria for illegality in a libertarian society would be: "Does it threaten first-strike force, fraud, or theft?" For example, if I pay blackmail to someone who would otherwise beat me, they are using the threat of first-strike force to take my money, very much like a thief does. This would clearly be against libertarian law.

If I pay blackmail to someone so that they won't tell a true but embarrassing tale about me, I am not being threatened with first-strike force, fraud, or theft. Quite possibly, such "blackmail" might (depending upon the circumstances) be considered a private contract under libertarian law. If the blackmailer told his or her story anyway, I might be able to sue for contract violation!

If I pay blackmail to someone so that they won't lie about me, the situation is not as clear. Many libertarians consider slander of a person's reputation to be a violation of the non-aggression principle; others don't.

Q *In a libertarian society would Americans have inflicted genocide on the indigenous populations, as happened in the decades prior to the American Revolution?*

A Libertarian explorers would most likely have established peaceful relations with the indigenous populations. Indeed, most early settlers in North America tried to do exactly that.

Most intentional genocide occurred after the American Revolution by the U.S. government. Libertarians would not have called in the government military to drive native people from their lands or herd them into reservations as happened later in U.S. history.

Q *What laws can you repeal that will alter your country's history of crimes against humanity? What laws can you repeal that will recompense today's survivors of that history? Libertarian stress on freedom and rights rather than equality and responsibilities may eventually give you some political gains but cannot make the world a better place.*

A Unfortunately, many of the crimes against indigenous people happened so long ago that those who committed them are no longer available to compensate the victims. Stolen land is not even easy to return, since boundaries are often unclear. Descendants of those who may have taken the land improperly have made improvements (housing, etc.) for which they might legitimately claim compensation too. In other words, proper restitution would be difficult at best.

However, since the U.S. government, rather than individuals, was the prime "thief," perhaps an acceptable resolution would be to deed land now held by the U.S. government (about 40% of the U.S. landmass) to descendants of those whose rights were violated. Of course, just about every U.S. citizen could probably claim that government has damaged them in some way, so limiting restitution to Native Americans, for example, would be far from a perfect resolution.

Any time that compensation is delayed, its exact calculation becomes more difficult. Therefore, a justice system that swiftly sets compensation is mandatory to prevent such situations from arising. Until we have such a system, any claims for compensation are unlikely to be properly addressed, even with the best of intentions.

Q *In your writing you consistently claim that the only legitimate use of force is self-defense. While I agree that is a legitimate use of force, I believe one other exists. When someone violates another person in some way and is unwilling to make things right through restitution, as you call for, isn't it justifiable to use force to make sure the victim receives just compensation for his injury?*

A You are correct in interpreting restitution recovery as a proper use of defensive force. After all, if someone takes your TV, you can certainly use force to recover it if you aren't successful in stopping him or her. Such recovery would simply be an extension of the right to self-defense for yourself and your property.

The state could be your agent in such recovery, and the state should ideally recover payment for its own services from the aggressor as well. That way, innocent taxpayers don't have to pay for someone else's restitution.

Roads

S omehow, people have trouble imagining a world where government did not own and operate the roads. Here is some food for thought on that topic!

Q *How would roads be operated and financed in the ideal libertarian world?*

A Roads would probably be operated by companies charging tolls (highways), subscription fees (local roads), or condominium dues (neighborhood streets). Even today, some communities finance almost half of their roadways privately, saving themselves 50% or more.

Q *Wouldn't collecting a toll at each intersection be awfully cumbersome?*

A Too cumbersome! Road companies would design a system to avoid such hassle. You might pay a single annual fee, which the road companies would split, and be able to drive the roads much as you do today.

Alternatively, you might have a special tag put on your car that is electronically monitored as you pass the "tollbooth" without stopping or slowing down. Some toll roads, including ones in the area I live in, are using this system already. Customers are then billed monthly or quarterly for road usage.

Q *Couldn't someone buy up all the roads and then charge monopoly prices?*

A Probably not. First of all, most local roads would undoubtedly be owned by local neighborhoods through condominium associations. Even when roads are owned by businesses, profits will be greatest when price is low and volume is high, since road "inventory" remains fixed.

If roads are overpriced, customers will turn to carpooling, walking, bicycle riding, train commuting, flying and other alternatives. Road owners would be forced to lower prices once more to stay in business.

Q *You say that in a libertarian society streets would be privately owned and operated. Then could someone buy my street and tell me to move out of my house?*

A No. Homes are usually on property that is adjacent to, but not part of, the nearby roads.

In a libertarian society, most residential roads would likely be owned by an organization of residents, much like roads in a condo community are today. Even if the residents decided to sell the road to an operating company, they would most likely include clauses to protect their access.

Q *If roads were privatized, couldn't an owner of a small stretch of highway in the middle of nowhere charge exorbitant rates?*

A If someone owns and operates the only road in a particular area, the rates will probably be higher in the absence of competition. However, profits will start to dwindle if prices become exorbitant, because alternatives (e.g., flying, going the long way around, etc.) always exist. Since a road is a big capital investment, profits will probably be largest if the rates are kept low enough to get a steady stream of traffic. Thus, the scenario that you describe, while theoretically possible, is highly unlikely.

Q *Often there is only one road leading to a destination; in a true capitalist society, a business can limit service to anyone it chooses. What if for some reason I was banned from a private roadway? Would I need to find other means to arrive at my destination?*

A A roadway wouldn't turn away a paying customer except under the most extreme circumstances (e.g. reckless driving that endangered other customers). Knowing that, drivers would have every incentive to drive safely, because they might very well have difficulty finding other transportation. This isn't a "flaw" in libertarianism; it's an advantage!

Of course, we ban reckless drivers from the roadway today by taking away their license. Quite a few of them simply drive without one. In a libertarian society, reckless drivers would have a more difficult time getting back on the road.

Q *Even though independent companies may own the roads, one company may own the entire tracking system. This company could persuade, or pressure, all the road owners to start fining people. A cartel or monopoly could dominate this vital industry.*

A Since fining customers would be very unpopular, it's likely that the road companies would create their own tracking system if a competing one weren't available.

Q *Should there even be limits on speed? As long as no one is hit, there is no harm done. Would libertarians then only impose a penalty at the time of the collision?*

A Road owners would decide what speed limits (if any) would be set. Some might have no restrictions, like the European Autobahn. Others might have strict limits. Since safe travel is important to drivers, owners would most likely monitor and ban reckless drivers from their roadways. The marketplace would thereby impose "regulation" of its own, with emphasis on safety rather than speed.

Q *Is it permitted in a free society to drive a car while drunk, as long as you won't cause an accident?*

A Road owners would write the rules for drivers. Since owners would lose customers (and profits) if their roads were not safe, drunk driving might indeed be restricted.

Q *Should a driver whose negligent conduct happens to cause harm be treated more harshly than one whose similar conduct does* **not***?*

A A reckless driver is stopped when he or she poses a threat to others. In a libertarian society, the owner of the roads would decide whether to ban the driver from the road or practice a different sort of deterrent (e.g., a fine). Ideally, the deterrent is restitution or payment for the policing effort necessary to stop the threat of force.

If a reckless driver harms someone, however, the dynamics are different. Someone who threatens harm, but ultimately doesn't cause any, pays only for the cost of stopping their threat of force. However, if physical damage actually occurs, compensation for the victim's loss, as well as policing costs, are in order.

Q *If a careless motorist who kills several members of a family also dies, will there be no restitution because the responsible person is dead?*

A If the deceased driver was found to be at fault, his or her insurance or estate would be used to satisfy a judgment for compensation. Obviously, motorists would be wise to carry insurance that would cover any shortfall that might occur if they are hit by other drivers with minimal resources.

Q *Since roads today are **not** privately owned, should we vote for speed limits and laws against drunk driving?*

A My personal belief is that these laws do more harm than good. Instead, I'd prefer to see reckless or careless drivers pulled off the road, whether they are under the influence of alcohol, drugs, sleep loss, medication, or emotions that distract them from safe driving. The libertarian philosophy permits defensive measures when force is threatened (e.g., you can defend yourself against me if I point a gun at you but haven't fired yet). Reckless driving could qualify as the threat of force.

Q *Even though I feel that government should have almost no control over how people conduct their lives, I don't understand the problem with seat belts. It's proven that seat belts save lives. If making people wear seat belts will prevent millions of people from dying, isn't that one thing that should be enforced?*

A Although most people fare better if they are wearing seat belts in an accident, some fare worse. In addition, some data indicate that people drive more aggressively when forced to buckle up, killing more passengers, pedestrians, and cyclists.[10] It's not so clear that making people wear seat belts really prevents deaths overall.

However, let's assume, for the sake of discussion, that forcing people to wear seat belts saved lives. If we then force them to buckle up, for their own good, shouldn't we stop them from overeating too? After all, heart disease is the number one killer and overeating is a major contributor. Maybe we should force people to exercise, too.

Of course, all of this "enforcement" costs money. So we need to take money from the people we are trying to control. They won't give it to us voluntarily, so we need to expend more effort to fight them. That means we need to take even more money from them.

Eventually, those we are trying to control actually try to take over so that they can make us do things *their* way. We spend our time and money fighting each other instead of doing the things that enhance our lives.

Q *Seat belt laws for the driver make sense, because you are protecting other people's rights to life: passengers in the car, people in other cars, etc. because the driver theoretically will remain better in control in emergencies if wearing a seat belt.*

A Studies in both Britain and the U.S. repeatedly show that seat belt laws for drivers don't lower the traffic death toll.[10] Drivers forced to buckle up are protected, but more passengers, pedestrians, and cyclists are killed. Evidently, drivers forced to wear a seat belt drive more aggressively.

We should rejoice that forcing others, even for their own good or that of others, backfires. Otherwise, each of us would try to save our neighbors by bending them to our will. This is the prescription for eternal war!

Q *In certain kinds of traffic accidents, some people have been saved only because a seat belt was not used. What is the libertarian view of the government forcing people to use a seat belt just because the government hopes some people will be saved – while knowing at the same time that others will be more seriously injured or killed only because of such use?*

A Libertarians believe that choices should be made by those who must take the consequences. Every person who travels in an automobile must decide this important safety issue for themselves. I personally wear my seat belt religiously, since it has saved me from grave injury on more than one occasion.

Q *What do you think a free market road system would look like?*

A Historically, the market has a great deal to "say" about roads, since most of them were private in the early days of the United States.

There were some toll roads back then, just as there would undoubtedly be today. However, most roads were built and maintained by those who lived beside them. People who owned businesses, homes, and farms built roads for their own use and that of their customers or visitors, dividing the cost among themselves. In a libertarian society, I suspect that most business highways would operate this way too. Why scare away customers with a toll?

In St. Louis, neighborhoods are taking back their roads. Over 1,000 streets have been deeded back to separate neighborhood associations which were formed for that purpose. Those living on the road charge visitors nothing, but do restrict travel by closing off the street or expelling vagrants. Needless to say, crime is much lower on these private streets. Condo communities operate similarly except that their roads are built privately and remain private.

The market seems to prefer "free" access to privately owned neighborhood roads and commercial highways, with costs borne by those living beside it. Most likely toll roads would be the choice for longer distances.

In some states, private roadways charge premium prices during rush hour. This has encouraged carpooling and decreased traffic jams during peak hours, resulting in safer travel.

Q *Suppose Company A runs the "road police." When they stop another employee of Company A, they'd be likely to let him go with just a warning. But if they stopped employees of Company B, which A was competing with, there'd be a higher likelihood of an arrest/ticket/ whatever. Wouldn't this sort of unfairness result from private ownership of roads?*

A The "road police" would likely be employees of the company that owned and operated that particular roadway. Just as police protect fellow officers today, some favoritism might be shown to fellow employees. However, road police who protected their buddies instead of their customers would likely get fired, because management could not afford to lose customer confidence, business, and profit. Today's system allows unscrupulous police to get away with such cover-ups, because the system is driven by politics, not profit.

Road police under a libertarian system would certainly be less corrupt than they are today – but no system can guarantee perfection!

The Environment

T he combination of restitution and property rights provides superior environmental protection. For example, some environmental groups, such as the Kalamazoo Rainforest Action Committee, help native homesteaders to gain legal title to their land so that government cannot give it to corporate interests.

Q *How are we going to keep big business from polluting too much, if not by government regulation?*

A Restitution is an effective deterrent, especially to polluters. Restoration costs are monumental and polluters could spend the rest of their lives working to compensate their victims.

The process by which this "justice" is administered works best when all property is held privately. In Britain, for example, property owners successfully protect their river segments from upstream pollution by suing for restitution.[11] In the U.S., however, individuals are not allowed to sue polluters of public property, and the bureaucrats would rather not antagonize businesses that can contribute to their campaign chests by fining them for environmental violations.

Q *If business is not regulated, wouldn't the environment be destroyed?*

A Our greatest polluter is the government (i.e., U.S. military), not corporate America. Putting government in charge of protecting the environment is like asking the fox to guard the hen house.

The most polluted countries in the world are those where government had total control of the environment, such as Eastern Europe before the fall of the Berlin Wall. Government is just as dangerous to our environment as it is to the wealth of our nation – it is the proverbial wolf in sheep's clothing.

If your neighbor dumps garbage on your lawn, he or she should clean it up and compensate you for any damages. Similarly, if a business or government agency causes harm, they should make it right again. Today, restitution rarely happens. Businesses pay fines to the government, not to the victim; government polluters simply claim sovereign immunity and walk away. Regulation isn't working. We need to replace it with restitution.

Q *In a libertarian society, wouldn't polluters get away with destroying the environment?*

A Today, the biggest polluter of all – the U.S. military – literally gets away with murder. When courts found the military liable for illness and death after careless nuclear testing in Utah, the government claimed sovereign immunity and refused to pay damages. In a libertarian society, no one would be immune from the consequences of their actions, especially not a government charged with protecting us.

Libertarians believe that people and governments should right their wrongs by restoring, as much as possible, what they've damaged. Today, instead of making polluters pay, our government makes the taxpayers shoulder the burden. Sometimes it requires whoever buys a polluted property to bear the cost of the clean-up. If polluters don't pay for the damage they do, why should they stop polluting?

Q *How absolute are my property rights in a libertarian system? For example: I install a fish pond in my yard and stock it with trout. A corporation builds a coal-fired power plant 100 miles from my house. Because of their activity, traces of mercury show up in my fish. Do*

*my property rights include the right not to have my land contaminated
with poison?*

A Yes. You always have recourse if a person harms your property.
If someone dumps garbage on your lawn or mercury into your
pond, you have the right to: 1) full restoration of your property; or 2)
a settlement acceptable to you.

Q *It's true that one may sue if one's body or property is damaged by
pollution, but that hardly seems adequate. How could one prove
which company's pollution caused the illness? Even if this were feasible,
large corporations have the resources to drag litigation on almost indefinitely. They can often simply outlast their opposition.*

A Restitution isn't just a remedy; it's the most effective deterrent known. Few individuals or businesses will pollute when it
might result in a lifetime liability.

Obviously, to collect restitution, you need to prove your
case. You wouldn't want it any other way – especially if someone
accused you!

In a libertarian society, delaying tactics would backfire, because
the losing party could be liable for the winner's attorney's fees.

Q *In a libertarian society, who will be able to tell if a company
is dumping mercury into the soil or PCBs into the river? Who
would monitor businesses and governmental properties to make sure no
polluting is taking place?*

A In a libertarian society, property would be private, including
the waterways. Companies couldn't dump anything into the
rivers or neighboring land without permission of the owners. Such
permission might require the cost of periodic monitoring for excessive levels of contaminants.

If someone suspected a company was dumping without
permission, they could call in a monitor to check. They would then

sue the aberrant company and recover the cost of monitoring as well
as damages.

Of course, a company might secretly dump a toxin that seeps
into the water table or land without immediate overt consequences.
Local employees concerned with the safety of their own near-by
homes are the best watchdogs in such situations, even today.

Q *How would you deal with harmful pollution that is caused by
the combined actions of hundreds or even thousands of polluters
that could all claim that their small part could do no harm?*

A If a product polluted the air, victims would sue the product
maker(s), who in turn would pass the costs of restitution onto
the consumer. Higher prices would discourage use and decrease
pollution. The free market is not a free-for-all; it imposes its own
stringent regulation.

Q *How do libertarians plan to maintain a society where our
ecosystem is functional for this generation and those that come
after us?*

A Instead of putting our environment in the hands of bureaucrats, libertarians encourage private ownership. Owners profit
most when they harvest their forests sustainably; for example,
bureaucrats profit only when they sell out to special interests, such
as those wishing to clear-cut our national forests. In a libertarian
society, polluters must restore the property they've damaged. The
possibility of working off such onerous restitution effectively deters
most polluters.

Q *How would libertarians stop power plants from burning
polluting substances for fuel?*

A If a power plant uses fuel that causes harm, the victims could,
in a libertarian society, sue the power plant for damages.

Naturally, the power plant would pass this extra cost on to their consumers in the form of higher prices. Thus, polluting fuels would cost more than clean ones. Power plants and their customers would be encouraged by their pocketbooks to use non-polluting alternatives.

The marketplace almost magically adjusts costs to discourage pollution when those who harm others are expected to restore them. Since environmental "wrongs" are extremely expensive to rectify, a libertarian society would be one of the most environmentally sound in the world. Studies show that free countries are not only more wealthy than highly regulated ones, but that they also enjoy a cleaner environment.

Q *Do property rights give you the right to abuse land however you see fit?*

A Property rights actually prevent abuse. Polluting makes the land worth less. Thus, abusive owners are punished by the marketplace and caretakers are rewarded by higher land values.

Because this system works so well, private lands are generally cared for better than public ones. Private grazing ranges, for example, are better maintained than government-operated ones. Just as homeowners keep up their houses better than renters, landowners maintain their property better than bureaucratic administrators.

Q *If several large companies use covenants to permit the burning of large amounts of fossil fuels, what will protect the air we breathe?*

A Covenants can permit industrial development by mutual agreement, but they do not protect companies from their duty to compensate anyone whom they might harm. Any neighbor could successfully sue if noxious chemicals were leached into their soil, water, or air.

Q *Not all private owners will care for their property. What do we do with such people?*

A We needn't do anything. Only a very few people destroy what they own, and such foolish people won't own much. However, when bureaucrats make an error or deliberately sell out to special interests, large tracts of land or water are destroyed. To protect our environment, we must encourage private, rather than public, control.

Q *I believe every automobile driver unjustly destroys our urban environment, contaminates my air, and contributes to numerous health problems. Automobile manufacturers and drivers are certainly not in any position to make restitution.*

A In a libertarian society, roads would be privately owned. If neighbors complained of pollution, the road company might offer monetary compensation. If the neighbors found this acceptable, the cost would be passed on to the drivers in the form of higher user fees.

Most likely, however, the neighbors would want the pollution to stop. Since 80% of emissions' pollution is caused by 20% of the cars, the road company might deny access or charge much higher user fees to polluting vehicles. Given these alternatives, most owners would probably buy a newer car or get their emission system upgraded. Such measures would be used to decrease pollution until the neighbors were satisfied.

Q *Where would a libertarian fall with respect to laws outlawing smoking in bars and restaurants?*

A In a libertarian society, smoking policy would be set by the bar or restaurant owner. Customers would patronize the establishments that had the policy they preferred, much as they do today. For example, I avoid places that are smoke-filled, and opt for restaurants that are smoke-free or have separate accommodations for smokers and non-smokers. As a customer, I have no right to dictate smoking policy to restaurant owners any more than I have a right to dictate the color schemes to clothing manufacturers. However, I let both know my preferences by voting with my dollars to do business with them or their competitors.

Q *How would libertarians defend the rights of smokers, while protecting non-smokers from secondhand smoke?*

A In a libertarian society, all property would be privately owned. Each business establishment would set its own smoking policies. Some would undoubtedly ban smoking; some would permit it; some would segregate smokers and nonsmokers. Those who wished to avoid secondhand smoke could do so by patronizing the appropriate establishments. Those who wished to smoke could do likewise.

Q *In a libertarian society, if a person may assault me with secondhand tobacco smoke, may I then assault that person with my fists? If so, as an asthmatic, I would call that a "level playing field."*

A It depends. If you've invited someone to your home and reminded them of your "no smoking" rule, they certainly are purposefully damaging you if they smoke. On the other hand, if you go to a restaurant where the owner permits smoking, you're the one who's voluntarily put yourself in danger. If you punch out a smoker under those conditions, you would be guilty of assault in a libertarian society.

Q *I disagree with your recent column on smoking. Why is it up to the non-smoker to choose a smoke-free work environment or restaurant? Isn't this a case where a person's right to swing their arms (i.e., smoking) ends with the next person's nose (potential health risks and fouling the clothing of non-smokers)? Isn't it the smokers who are infringing on my right to be free of their smoke?*

A I, too, am a non-smoker who appreciates a smoke-free environment, so I know exactly where you are coming from.

Libertarians don't support government-mandated smoking bans in restaurants and bars, because these establishments are the property of the owners, not the patrons or the government. Only the owners have the right to determine whether smoking will be permitted.

Similarly, libertarians wouldn't outlaw smoking in residences so that non-smoking visitors wouldn't have to breathe the smoke of their hosts. In both cases, the owners decide what type of environment they will invest in; patrons and visitors are free to decide if they wish to expose themselves to that environment.

Q *If someone chooses not to breathe second-hand smoke, should it be the duty of a libertarian government to ban it in public places? Are smokers initiating force on non-smokers by forcing non-smokers to breathe their second-hand smoke in public places?*

A Public (government-owned) property, like courthouses and municipal buildings, poses special problems, because the "owners" (supposedly the entire citizenry, which include smokers and non-smokers), are unlikely to agree on whether or not to ban smoking there. Settling such disagreements is almost impossible. Such dilemmas support the libertarian notion that all property (or at the very least, as much as possible) should be private, and such decisions left to the owners. Clearly defined property rights solve many, many problems!

Q *In a libertarian society, who would own the air we breathe? Since there's no such thing as public property in a libertarian society, there must be an owner.*

A Currently the air that we breathe isn't either publicly owned or privately owned. When resources are abundant, no one bothers to acquire title *per se*. Since everyone has easy access to the resource, property rights are essentially valueless. I doubt that the status of air would change in a libertarian society.

Native Americans had difficulty with the notion of land ownership, probably because land was plentiful before white settlers arrived. In Europe, on the other hand, land was scarce and property rights were well-established. If the air ever became a scarce commodity, I would expect property rights to evolve.

Q *How would libertarians protect the right of planes to air space, while at the same time, avoiding bothersome noise?*

A Most new airports are built away from residential areas. Noise becomes a problem only when people choose to build houses in the surrounding area. Those who are bothered by the noise shouldn't build or buy around an airport.

Q *A nearby airport begins using the airspace over my house as part of its flight path. Do my property rights extend to the atmosphere?*

A Your rights extend to your body and property. At this point in time, atmosphere *per se* hasn't been considered valuable, so property rights for it have not been well-defined.

However, if noise pollution causes you (or your livestock) significant harm, it may violate your property rights. Let's examine some possibilities.

If you move next to an existing airport, you do so knowing that noise from the airport is part of your household package. The airport has, in essence, already established its right to use the air space by "homesteading" it. You would probably have recourse against the airport only if a new type of aircraft flying over your home caused new problems (e.g., windows breaking due to the type of noise, etc.).

If you live in a residential area, however, and a new airport opens, you have established your claim first. If the noise is mild, you might simply put up with it. If the noise keeps you from sleeping at night, you might ask the airport for compensation.

Today, most new airports are built outside of heavily populated areas so that anyone moving into the area will accept any noise – and the lower price of homes – as part of the package.

Q *My next-door neighbor builds a stadium in his backyard and begins hosting noisy concerts at volumes that make it impossible for me to sleep at night. Is this a violation of my property rights?*

A Most likely. The noise created by your neighbor is leaving his or her property and "polluting" yours in a manner causing you physical harm.

Nuisances in a libertarian society would often be dealt with through neighborhood covenants or condo associations. For example, at the time of home construction, developers in a particular area might attach restrictions to the deeds of properties not included under condo agreements. These restrictions on noise and other nuisances would be looked upon favorably by buyers who wanted to be sure that their neighbors would act in a particular way. Violations of these covenants could result in prosecution or activation of an arbitration clause.

The advantage of such agreements in that you know in advance what levels of noise your neighbors can have. Of course, if you have Vulcan-like hearing, you might still be annoyed by a neighbor's noise even though it is not loud enough to trigger the nuisance clause. In that case, you might need to use earplugs.

Without such pre-existing arrangements, resolution is obviously more difficult.

Q *Global warming is now widely accepted as a fact within the scientific community. What is not yet sorted out is the extent to which the planet will warm and the impact that it will have. What would libertarians do about this issue?*

A When our weather reporters can't get tomorrow's temperature right, it's difficult to believe that global warming can be accurately predicted, isn't it? (This sentence should be told lightly, as a joke, to elicit agreement.)

As you mentioned, we really don't know what the impact of global warming might be. High temperatures and CO_2 stimulate crop and other plant growth, so global warming could actually be good for us. Any action we take has to be based on the facts – and we just don't have those yet.

In a libertarian society, if a chemical such as CFC caused a problem, victims could sue the manufacturer for damages. The high cost of restitution would be passed on to CFC consumers, driving up the price. People would turn to cheaper alternatives and CFC production would be automatically curtailed.

People could sue before actual harm was done, as long as they could convince a judge or jury that CFCs actually posed a threat.

Q *How do we deal with global pollution?*

A Thankfully, most pollution does more local than international damage, thereby discouraging polluters. For example, governments try to prevent Chernobyl-type accidents because their local populace is put at greater risk than the international community. The country that polluted its oceans enough to cause global damage, for example, would destroy its own fishing first. The country that polluted the air enough to disturb other nations would asphyxiate its own population in the process. Thus, global pollution is usually accidental, so little can be done to prevent it.

(Asking the questioner for a specific problem would allow a more specific answer to be given.)

Q *What will a libertarian nation do in the unlikely event of pollution from another, non-libertarian country?*

A Such pollution would most likely be dealt with on an individual or local basis. For example, if Canadians polluted a local river which flowed into the U.S., the U.S. individuals who owned the downstream portion of the river would seek restitution from the Canadians. To maintain good international relations, the Canadian government would likely work with the U.S. victims.

If the Canadians refused to respond, the U.S. victims might feel better served by simply fixing the problem (e.g., putting up a dam in the U.S. so that all contaminated water was treated before flowing into the river bed). If the thieves just won't quit, you arm and alarm instead. The same process applies to pollution.

Alternatively, the U.S. victims could send in their own private police force to obtain restitution from the polluters. This last, very expensive, option would probably be used only on rare occasions when the pollution was great.

Q *If I walked into a restaurant to eat dinner and someone wasn't quick enough to cover themselves when they sneezed and I contracted the flu, what would prevent me from suing them for violating my basic right to stay healthy?*

In reality I wouldn't sue someone for doing that because common sense tells me they didn't get me sick on purpose but, theoretically, based on libertarian principles, why shouldn't I be able to sue them?

A The ability to obtain restitution depends upon being able to identify someone who caused you harm. In the case of common airborne diseases, such identification usually is difficult, if not impossible. How would you prove that the person sneezing in the restaurant was the one responsible for your flu?

As a society, we seem to accept that certain relatively harmless airborne pollutants, like cold viruses, are part of the natural environment rather than the responsibility of the carrier. Of course, the elderly and others with a compromised immune system may have fatal complications from contracting a simple cold. The current expectation is that sensitive individuals will protect themselves by staying home or wearing a protective breathing mask when they go out. My guess is that a libertarian society might adopt similar standards.

Q *Would libertarians protect the rain forests?*

A Libertarians would respect the homesteading rights of the native peoples, who generally use the rainforests sustainably. Any company that wished to harvest the forest would have to buy it first.

As owners, companies would have incentive to harvest sustainably. Today, companies simply pay a bribe to local governments who then evacuate the native people. The company clears the forest with little concern for the property's future worth. For a fictional rendition of this situation, check out the 1992 movie, *Medicine Man* with Sean Connery.

Q *I guess without the government to ban hunting of endangered species, lots of animals would quickly become extinct.*

A Just the opposite is true! In Kenya, for example, the sale of elephant products was banned. The elephant population decreased from 65,000 in 1979 to 19,000 in 1989. In Zimbabwe, however, where elephants could be owned and elephant products sold, the elephant population increased from 30,000 to 43,000 during the same time period.[12] People who are allowed to own animals and profit from their sale become fierce protectors, warding off poachers and other predators.

Commercializing a useful species takes it off the endangered list. The American buffalo is an example of how an endangered animal can be saved this way.

Q *How would libertarians protect sensitive environmental areas, such as breeding grounds for endangered species?*

A Instead of lobbying, conservation groups would use their money to buy and protect sensitive environmental areas. As an example, in Louisiana the Audubon Society manages Rainey Wildlife Sanctuary's marshland property ecologically, while using carefully placed natural gas wells and cattle grazing to produce income for future purchases.

The Nature Conservancy, National Wild Turkey Federation, Ducks Unlimited, Wings Over Wisconsin, and Trout Unlimited are among the many organizations that purchase and protect sensitive areas better than any bureaucrat could.

Q *How would you apply restitution to private property owners who may destroy endangered species in order to protect their crops or other material possessions? Who is the injured party? What value do you assign to non-commercial species?*

A Restitution would not apply in your example, since there is no injured (human) party. However, in a libertarian society, endangered species are unlikely to be destroyed. Instead of lobbying fickle politicians, conservationists would use their money to pay bounties for living specimens of endangered animals for relocation and breeding.

Q *I heard a scientist say that fish and other sea life in the North Atlantic are dying out very quickly and the effect on the world will be devastating if something isn't done. What, from a libertarian perspective, can be done? Can we own the oceans?*

A Although in theory oceans can be owned, historically only fishing or mineral rights to certain parts of the ocean have been claimed. Most countries claim their coastal waters, but actually enforce only the rights to fishing, drilling, etc.

In the first half of the 20th century, shrimp fishers along the Gulf coast formed an association and claimed homesteading rights to their ocean fisheries. The members agreed to limit their catches to fish sustainably. This system worked well until the government refused to recognize their claims. Without a stake in future catches, the shrimpers had no incentive to conserve.

Recognizing property rights of those who currently fish the North Atlantic will give them incentive to fish sustainably. After all, the fishing rights are worth little without the fish! Just as ownership encourages farmers to rotate crops and fertilize the soil, owners of fishing rights have every incentive to increase annual yield while maintaining the fertility of their oceanic "fields."

Q *Some species are going extinct in the oceans as a result of over-fishing and whaling. What would libertarians do?*

A Australia, British Columbia, Greenland, Iceland, the Netherlands, and New Zealand have increased their fish populations due to partial privatization of the ocean fisheries.[13] Basically, a government or private agency determines what the "sustainable catch" will be each year and the "deeds" (called "quotas") to these fish are allotted or sold to commercial fishing entities. If a company catches more fish than it "owns," it must purchase additional quotas from someone else. The price is determined by the market.

Historically, several ocean fisheries have been fully privatized, but governments have commandeered these "properties" much to the detriment of the fish population. Owners often improved the fisheries by sinking artificial reefs and by defending the property against poachers. Otherwise, boat traffic and other ocean use continued as usual.

As long as whales remain unowned, they will most likely be hunted to extinction. Bans don't really help since they attract poachers by driving up the price of whale products. Once whales are claimed as property by owners who profit from them, they will be protected from extinction.

For example, when Kenya banned the sale of elephant products, its herd dwindled from 65,000 to 19,000 within a decade. In neighboring Zimbabwe, where elephant products could be legally sold, the natives protected their "property," and the elephant population soared from 30,000 to 43,000 during the same time period.[12]

Q *I read recently that populations of bees and other pollinators are declining. I've heard that this could lead to increases in food prices. What would be a free market approach to such a problem?*

A I'm not sure that pollinator populations are declining, but let's assume that they are, for sake of discussing how the free market would handle such a situation.

Some pollinators, like bees, tend to stay in a particular area so that they can return to the hive. The most cost-efficient solution for farmers and others who are dependent upon pollinators might be to "grow their own." Depending upon the area involved, neighboring farmers might be able to pool their resources to establish a central location to maintain pollinators.

Of course, if the bee population were being poisoned by a particular chemical, the courts might entertain a suit by affected farmers, since they could demonstrate direct harm caused by the chemical pollution. Such a suit might be especially effective if farmers established their own hives and could demonstrate that the domestic bees, clearly private property, were being destroyed by the pollutant.

Because wild bees are normally not considered private property, they are, in effect, part of the commons. Assigning property rights to the commons is fraught with difficulties, which is one reason that libertarians advocate the conversion of the commons to private property to the greatest extent feasible.

Q *Under a libertarian government, shouldn't over-consumption be illegal? "Over-consumption" would imply taking more than one's fair share of the world's collective resources, therefore denying another citizen access to their share.... which we must understand would undeniably harm that individual.*

A A libertarian economy does prevent "over-consumption" by society as a whole. When resources are plentiful, prices are low. If resources become scarce, the price automatically goes up. People start conserving to save money and try to find other, less expensive substitutes.

Without government subsidies and interference, rising prices lower consumption as soon as depletion starts. Unfortunately, in today's world, governments use our tax dollars to subsidize over-consumption, such as wasteful irrigation and power use.

Q *Alternatively, since the earth is something which is passed down to future generations, isn't any destruction of the earth a direct threat to the existence – and thus, of course, the rights – of future human beings?*

A The best way to protect the earth is to honor property rights of individuals. People care for things they own and can sell later, but are not so careful about things they rent. If you go out West and compare grazing land owned by individuals with that administered by government, the benefit of individual ownership becomes apparent.

When I was a member of the Kalamazoo Rain Forest Action Committee, environmentalists recognized that helping the native people defend their property rights was the best protection the rain forests could have. The government is the biggest polluter and despoiler of our lands, yet we've been fooled into letting this fox guard our hen house.

Q *Wouldn't the poor be better off with public sharing of land than having it controlled by private (rich) owners or government?*

A If all land were publicly shared, who would settle disputes between people who wanted to use the same piece of land in different ways? Whether the decision-maker was an individual or group of individuals, control would rest in their hands, just as the control of government property today is in the hands of bureaucrats. Those who control government land profit most when they allow themselves to be bribed by the rich. The poor will still be left out in the cold, literally and figuratively.

The best way to empower the poor is to allow them to become rich – rich enough to buy land. This is easier than it seems, since most poverty today, even in the Third World, is a direct result of aggression-through-government. Minimum wage and licensing laws put the disadvantaged out of work, creating poverty by destroying jobs. (Chronic unemployment is the primary cause of poverty.[14]) When government aggression lessens, poverty decreases too.

In addition, most non-Western governments make it difficult to get clear land titles. Approximately 60-80% of such property is "extralegal," making it difficult to borrow against or transfer.[15] As a result, while the poor in these countries "hold" a great deal of land, they cannot easily use its full potential.

Q *Who should own the land? Nobody produced it, so shouldn't everyone have an equal chance to use it?*

A Most, if not all, of land's value comes from the use to which it is put. For example, when our ancestors wanted to farm, they had to clear the land to grow crops. Land was much more valuable after it was cleared. Those who worked to create this extra equity in the land should, naturally, own the improvements. To establish property rights on the improvements, these "homesteaders" took title to the land itself. Thus, ownership of land was earned. "Everyone" did not contribute equally to the land improvements, so "everyone" did not – and should not – have equal access to it.

Q *Libertarians like you often argue that private property ownership motivates people to be better stewards of Mother Earth. But this ignores the fact that some religious and/or cultural groups consider the earth to simply "exist," and that it should not be owned as any person's property. What about the rights and beliefs of those people?*

A   When land is plentiful and people few, there is no need for ownership because few conflicts arise. A viewpoint that the earth is unownable works well for both the people and the earth.

However, as population increases, some guidelines are necessary to decide who will have control or stewardship over particular tracts of land, water, etc., or the environment will suffer the abuse of the "tragedy of the commons." A wealth of data indicates that individual owners take better care of the earth, on average, than government or communal systems. Thus, the earth benefits from ownership as the best system of stewardship.

Many people, especially the poor, resist this conclusion because property is held by a privileged few in today's world. Government prevention of homesteading, property taxes, and zoning restrictions, coupled with laws that make it difficult for the poor to accumulate wealth, are responsible for skewed ownership. When these impediments to easy ownership of property are abolished, wealth and property distribution become more even. Earth "ownership" becomes a non-issue when ownership is within everyone's reach.

Q   *I'm very troubled by traditional libertarian responses to land-use questions. Land (or other natural resource) ownership tends to be a government-given privilege, more than an assertion of individual rights. As John Locke argued in his Second Treatise, one has a right to property with which one has mixed one's labor. But according to libertarian theory, how do people have the right to own land with which they are not mixing their labor? This is a huge problem in a world where land speculation is rampant, and many speculators own huge chunks of land that really don't "belong" to them in any sense of the word besides the legal one. Isn't some mechanism needed to prevent people from buying up huge amounts of land, at a terrific cost to everyone else who then is not able to touch that land?*

A   Locke defined property rights as he did to describe homesteading, a time-honored way of taking title to land. Today, governments ignore homesteading claims as they push native people out of their rain forest homes so that they can sell the land to specu-lators. Libertarian governments would do neither of these things, so speculators could only buy land from pre-existing owners/home-steaders, solving your concerns nicely.

Q *How would libertarians secure, for younger generations, the same access to land that previous generations had?*

A Younger generations do have the same access to land that previous generations did. They pay in the same coin – their labor. In today's world, people usually exchange their labor for currency, which they then exchange for land. The younger genera-tion has it relatively easy – backbreaking labor from sunrise to sunset is usually unnecessary today.

Q *Each of us is born onto this planet as a world citizen, and as a civilized society, we shouldn't be fighting over what is ours or not ours, as this planet belongs equally to every one of us.*

A We all live on the planet and have a stake in its well-being. History has shown us that the best way to protect every-one's interest is to respect the private property rights of individuals and groups.

For example, most rain forests are populated by native people who use them sustainably. In a libertarian society, these natives would be recognized as the owners of the rain forests and the forests would, in most cases, remain intact. Today's governments drive the natives from their homes and allow the highest corporate bidder to harvest them ruthlessly. Environmental groups fight this travesty by helping the native people gain recognition for their property rights.

Q *What should we do about the "tragedy of commons"?*

A "The tragedy of commons" occurs only when property is public. For example, public grazing land in the West is in poor condition because each person profits most when their cattle graze heavily. No one bothers to replenish the land, because they can't profit by caring for it.

In contrast, private grazing land is much better cared for. Private owners know that they will reuse the land, and so have incentive to care for it. The value of the land is maintained or even augmented when used sustainably. Thus, private owners are rewarded for caring for their land with higher property values. The solution to the "commons" problem is to do away with the "commons!"

Q *Given human nature I can see developers turning land around Yosemite and the Grand Canyon into housing developments that ruin the beauty of these places. Is there anything a libertarian society could do to stop this?*

A If national parks were sold to conservation groups, they'd get much better care than they do now. Government hasn't been a very good steward of our parks, contrary to popular opinion.

For example, earlier in its history, Yellowstone employees were encouraged to kill wolf, fox, lynx, marten and fisher because visitors enjoyed watching the deer, elk, and longhorn sheep that these species preyed upon. The expanding population of hoofed mammals destroyed the shrubs and berries that fed the bear population. As a result, bears began to invade camp sites, so park rangers had to start removing them. Now wolves are being reintroduced to Yellowstone to turn this cycle around.

Yellowstone may yet be saved, but other parks under bureaucratic stewardship haven't fared so well. Ravena Park in Seattle was established by a couple who wanted to protect the giant Douglas firs that grew in that area. Up to 10,000 people a day came to visit and attend the nature lectures, walk the trails and admire the majestic trees. The city eventually bought the park and made it public. Within 15 years, all the Douglas firs were gone. The bureaucrats overseeing the park could only profit by selling trees as cordwood, so that's what they did.[16]

These stories are not unique. People act in their own selfish interests. When they own a property, they profit most by caring for it. When they simply have bureaucratic oversight, they profit most from exploiting it.

A libertarian government recognizes this pattern and privatizes the environment. The owners profit when they protect it and are punished by losses when they don't. When government doesn't interfere, people do what's right in order to do what's best for themselves.

Q *I remember when the George W. Bush administration threatened to repeal regulations passed by the Clinton administration restricting development on some environmentally sensitive Alaskan land. What is a good, brief libertarian response to this?*

A Why spend time and money lobbying politicians who can't be counted upon? Isn't the environment more important than that? Just buy the property you want to protect and you'll be able to keep it just the way you want it. As the Nature Conservancy and other private foundations have discovered, you can readily get like-minded people to contribute to your cause and be proud property owners with you!

Q *What would libertarians do about the population crisis?*

A For centuries, pessimists have been claiming that we will be overrun with people and starvation will ensue. However, we've learned how to grow more food per acre and to build high-rises to give us more "space."

Some of the most densely populated areas in the world are the wealthiest. Hong Kong and Singapore have more people per square kilometer than India and China, for example.

Furthermore, as countries grow in freedom, they move from rural societies to technological ones. Children can earn their keep on a farm years before they can do so in industrial societies. Thus, a large family is a benefit in poorer societies, but a drain on family resources in developed countries. Consequently, as a country grows in freedom and wealth, the birth rate goes down, creating a natural balance.

Today, the birth rate in developed countries is not high enough to replace those who die. Consequently, developed societies keep growing primarily through immigration. Even in the Third World, birth rates are dropping, although they are still high enough to cause a net growth in the global population. As these countries become more industrialized, their birth rate will drop too and population levels will stabilize.

Q *As our population increases, as well as our speed and frequency of travel, the possibility of an epidemic is of increasing concern. Today, we require children attending school to have a base set of inoculations, and those who are world travelers are required by treaty to have a larger set. In addition, quarantines exist, not only for people, but animals, produce, etc. Having my body liquefied by the Ebola virus is not something I'd care to risk in pursuit of a libertarian society.*

A You needn't worry – a libertarian society is likely to be much safer and healthier than today's world!

First of all, medical advances would not be hamstrung by excessive regulation as they are today. Even former FDA Commissioner Donald Kennedy acknowledged, "…the pattern of intervention into science from a combination of local, state, and federal sources has moved from reasonable control to something close to chaotic strangulation." Better medical advances mean better overall health. Experts commonly attribute the decline of communicable diseases in industrialized nations to improved resistance to disease as much as to vaccines.

Reluctance to vaccinate today has a great deal to do with safety concerns. Some vaccines have elicited severe reactions, even death. As quality improves – and improvement will be most rapid in a libertarian society – more people will be vaccinated. Improvements will result in vaccines that protect against a wider range of disease.

The few people who still reject vaccines won't pose much of a threat in a population made resistant through vaccination and better health. Some schools, all of which would be private in a libertarian society, might still require vaccinations for their students.

Prosperity, which increases as a society becomes more libertarian, has been highly correlated with improved health. Knowledgeable economists claim that the best way to improve a population's health is to make it prosperous. Freedom makes us wealthier, thereby making us healthier. Pursuit of the libertarian way is a healthy choice!

Q *Given the importance that libertarians place on self-ownership and individual liberty, what would they do about such difficult public health cases as "Typhoid Mary" or other carriers of airborne communicable diseases?*

A In any society, asymptomatic disease carriers will spread infection. A libertarian society, however, has several advantages.

First and foremost, a libertarian country would enjoy considerable wealth. Wealthy societies tend to be healthier and thus, are more resistant to infection. Drug companies would develop vaccines or cures more rapidly without FDA interference. As an interim measure, antibodies isolated from resistant carriers might provide treatment. Because donors could be paid handsomely, people would have incentive to be tested and asymptomatic carriers would be identified.

Carriers could then take precautions not to spread the disease further, while profitably donating their blood for research.

Carriers who refused to take such precautions could conceivably be prosecuted for pollution. A more likely possibility is that they would be ostracized by the rest of the community. Such social censure has been found to be a powerful deterrent and can create an effective quarantine when all property is private.

During any epidemic, some people would isolate themselves or wear masks when they go out. Today, pregnant women who have not had measles, and elderly with respiratory problems, often take such precautions.

Deadly diseases spread by resistant asymptomatic carriers will always take their toll. In a libertarian society, this toll likely will be minimal.

Q *The debate over fluoridation of public water supplies has raged for 50 years. There is much scientific evidence showing that it can harm some groups of people (senior citizens, heart patients, kidney patients, among others).*

Given the conflicting safety information, and statistics that say it may or may not have real effect on cavities, and the fact that the target population (children ages 3–12) is only 4 % of all water consumers, what is the libertarian answer to mandatory fluoridation?

A In a libertarian society without utility monopolies mandated by law, each municipality would probably be served by more than one water company. Consumers would choose their service provider based, in part, on what they thought about the additives.

In small communities where competition provided few choices, consumers might buy bottled water, much as they do today. My bottled water provider offers spring water, distilled water, drinking water, and fluoridated water as options.

By eliminating the water monopoly, consumers might be able to get even more options piped into their home. Certainly, they would have more choice about additives than they do today.

National Defense

Most people think defense means a nuclear arsenal and a military presence throughout the world. Switzerland provides us with a modern-day model of the difference between having a strong defense and provoking the need for one.

Q *How would libertarians secure our national defense without taxes to fund a military?*

A Our best defense is to have no enemies. We turn enemies into friends by trading with them. Japan, the only nation to attack us in the 20th century, bombed Pearl Harbor because of our oil embargo. Trading with Japan has made our economies too interdependent for them to even dream of another attack.

Vietnam, where the U.S. fought a costly and ultimately failed war to stop Communism, is becoming a beacon of capitalism in Southeast Asia. Americans and others, peacefully trading with their Vietnamese counterparts, are doing more to "contain" Communism than bombs ever did.

To deal with any actual enemies, a libertarian military would probably be multi-layered and have several different sources of funding. Local militia might be volunteers or be supported by community fund-raising. Professional, full-time regiments might accept paid assignments in other countries as part of their training. The military might operate a business in peacetime that dovetails (excuse the pun!) with their defense function. Such efforts would likely be quite sufficient if we were not trying to police the world.

Q *How would libertarians pay for the military?*

A Defense in a free society would probably be more diverse, both in the scope and type of funding, than in our current system. Troops sent overseas to protect oil interests, for example, would be hired by the oil companies, who would include this cost in their prices to consumers. Vietnam-type action would be funded by activists enthusiastic enough to pay for it and would wither if that support waned. People excited about a Star Wars defense might buy stock in the company that develops the system and makes money from scientific spinoffs (e.g., satellites). Career military could train in combat and support themselves by selling their services to other countries on occasion. Volunteers could offer their time for clerical, training, medical or military duty.

Q *To protect our shipping on the high seas could be monumentally expensive. Who would shoulder this burden in a libertarian society? If left to the private sector, wouldn't U.S. import/export businesses be at a heavy disadvantage?*

A In a libertarian society, private shipping companies would hire their own escort as necessary. The cost of such protection would be passed on to consumers in the price of the product. Today, people who don't buy imports are unfairly taxed so that others can purchase imports at a lower price. Naturally, shippers might band together for cost-effectiveness and collectively hire protective escort.

Q *Clearly the presence of large professional militaries and the expensive equipment such as Stealth bombers and tanks that are present overseas would not allow us to have an army that consisted of citizens and their rifles.*

A Why not? Switzerland's defense is an army that primarily consists of every able-bodied man and their rifles. Even

Hitler refused to take on "the little porcupine" for fear he'd have to conquer each household individually. Switzerland stays neutral so that no one has incentive to attack. Before making assumptions about what our defense needs to look like, let's look to what works in the real world.

Q *During the Iran/Iraq war, there were several French companies that sold these nations weapons. Russians were doing the same just before the Gulf War. Shouldn't we have government controls to prevent such things from happening?*

A Government controls enable these sales to be made in the first place! Saddam Hussein rose to power with taxpayer-guaranteed loans from several Western governments, including the U.S.[17] In a very real sense, the money for the weapons came from us. When we later attacked Iraq, the joke was that we knew Saddam had weapons of mass destruction "because we have the receipts." Giving our government more power certainly won't solve the problems that they created in the first place!

In the name of national defense, our government arms terrorists such as Saddam Hussein, enforces embargoes that provoke attack (Pearl Harbor), and embroils us in other countries' civil wars (Nicaragua). The weapons companies are delighted to sell to the customers our government creates!

In a libertarian world, weapons dealers would sell little to dictators, since there would be no taxpayers to guarantee loans for that purpose.

Q *U.S. companies have recently been accused of selling military technology to China. In a free market, companies would have the right to sell to whomever they choose. How would libertarians assure that enemies of the U.S. would not be sold weapons and/or secrets they could use against us?*

A Most weapon sales by U.S. companies are financed directly or indirectly by the taxpayer. Thus, most of today's purchases wouldn't happen in a libertarian society. Indeed, the entire military-industrial complex would probably shrink dramatically if our country became libertarian.

Best of all, a libertarian country that traded freely with all nations and didn't try to police the world wouldn't have many enemies. Since free markets create great wealth and technology, any enemy would be outmatched, even if a U.S. weapons company would sell to them.

Today, our government routinely sells our secrets and weapons to hostile regimes (e.g. Stalin, Hussein, etc.) and we have little recourse. In a libertarian society, such sales would be made by private firms. An indignant public could bankrupt such companies by boycotts of the company and its stock.

Q *If a nation lets anyone hold any arm they pleased, what is to stop terrorist groups from stockpiling arms until they could take over the country, or to stop them from holding biological or nuclear weapons that would take us all hostage?*

A Terrorists *today* stockpile arms as they please, in spite of our gun control laws. Terrorists kill innocent people, in spite of our laws against murder. If we pass stricter weapons bans tomorrow, why would we expect terrorists to suddenly obey them?

People who operate outside the law aren't affected much by legal changes. Law-abiding citizens, however, deprived of their weapons by gun bans, are greatly affected. They become easy targets.

Terrorists usually attack unarmed civilians, even though their anger is most often directed at our government or its agencies (e.g., the CIA). Why? Government installations usually have armed security. If the average citizen was armed as well, terrorists would most likely back off.

When the city council of Kennesaw, Georgia, passed an ordinance requiring each household to keep a firearm, crime dropped

74%![18] Robbery and rape decreased 25% and 85% respectively in Orlando when the police publicized their program teaching women to use firearms.[19] Indeed, exhaustive studies have shown that even "rampage" shooters, who could be considered home-grown terrorists, are deterred by right-to-carry laws.[20]

The cause of terrorism – intervention by our government in the affairs of other sovereign nations – would be non-existent in a libertarian society. Switzerland, where virtually every household has military arms, has a foreign policy of non-intervention. As a result, Swiss citizens are rarely the target of terrorist attacks.

In summary, in a libertarian society, terrorists would have little reason to attack us. Even if they were so inclined, an armed citizenry would be better able to defend itself.

Q *How do libertarians address the issue of weapons of mass destruction? Every year the FBI intercepts people carrying large bombs, chemical and biological weapons, and occasionally nuclear material. Doesn't government have to have some power to keep the very dangerous people from causing disasters like Oklahoma City?*

A In a libertarian society, you (or your police) would be entitled to stop anyone who threatened you with a weapon of any kind. Most terrorists, however, don't announce their intentions. They can create weapons from the humblest of materials, making apprehension almost impossible.

Most terrorists are reacting to ill treatment (real or imagined) by our government. As government has grown, so has terrorism. Minimizing government, as libertarians suggest, might be the best way to discourage terrorists.

Q *In a libertarian society, individuals are free to do as they wish as long as their actions do not interfere with the liberty of others. Are they therefore free to possess thermonuclear weapons, or bio-engineered ones? Isn't the risk simply too high to allow individual liberty when the common liberty is more important?*

A   In a libertarian society, each of us has the right to defend
     ourselves against force or the threat of force. If I point a gun
at you, you needn't wait until I fire to disable me. If your neighbor
has a device that you feel threatened by, you (or your police) can
disable it as well.

However, your neighbor might decide to sue you for trespass.
If the jury is convinced that you acted without just cause, you might
have to pay your neighbor restitution. If the jury decides that your
neighbor's device did indeed pose a threat to you, your neighbor
might be compelled to get rid of it.

The U.S. government was convicted of harming Utah residents during nuclear tests. Nevertheless, the government claimed
sovereign immunity and refused to compensate the victims.[21]
Government, not freedom, is the real-life threat.

or...

A gun can be used by your neighbor for defense without
threatening you. However, nuclear bombs sitting in your neighbor's
backyard could pose a real threat, if their use will destroy you and
your property. Thus, a libertarian community might consider such
bombs to be a threat of force and act accordingly.

Obviously, anyone who truly meant to harm you wouldn't
advertise as he or she put their weapon together. Such a person
wouldn't be deterred by a law banning such a device either.

Q   *I want America to be superior in technology. Should the*
     government pay for any research and development? Only for
defense systems?

A   The government should stay out of research and development,
     since taxation is aggression. For the most part, computer tech-
nology has been developed without government interference and we
are, indeed, superior in this field. Maybe our bombers might function more effectively and efficiently without government too!

Q How would a libertarian society respond to a foreign request for military assistance?

A Individuals in a libertarian society could respond as they wished. Pacifists could decline to contribute. Activists could raise money to pay for sending troops overseas. Young people could volunteer for military service in that country. Non-combatants could volunteer their time to help with the paperwork and training that accompanies any war effort. Everyone could give or decline to give as they wished. Instead of Congress deciding what the American people would contribute, individuals would decide for themselves.

Q Should we intervene overseas if we can save lives?

A Naturally, when you, as an individual, feel that you can do good by supporting a fight, you should follow your conscience by supplying your own time, money, and effort. If you force your neighbor who feels differently to participate, however, you'll jeopardize your cause. After all, by using taxes to support the fight, you are first attacking your peaceful neighbors to save others from tyranny. You become the tyrant in order to save others from oppression. The contradiction should be obvious.

Many people applaud our entry into World War II as an example of how good (e.g., defeating Hitler) can come out of bad (e.g., taxes and the draft). With the advantage of historical hindsight, let's see if this is an accurate description of what happened.

Hitler offered to let the Jews leave Germany if other countries would accept them. Few nations would alter their immigration quotas, however. If you visit the Holocaust Museum in Washington D.C., you can see a picture of a shipload of Jews being turned away from U.S. shores. They eventually had to return to Europe, where most of them were killed. Without the aggression of immigration laws, we could have saved the Jews without spilling the precious blood of our young men.

Japan's attack on Pearl Harbor probably wouldn't have occurred without the aggression of a U.S. oil embargo. The lives of our servicemen might have been saved had we remained neutral.

The German resistance was already trying to assassinate Hitler by the time the U.S. entered the war, and probably would have succeeded eventually. Instead, the U.S. entered the war, took Stalin as an ally, and gave Stalin most of Eastern Europe afterwards. Stalin proceeded to kill millions, without offering to let them migrate elsewhere, making Hitler look benevolent in comparison. Those who survived these purges were forced to live in constant fear, poverty, and strife for decades. Did our aggression against our own neighbors to make war on tyrants save lives or take them? The Soviet body count, which greatly exceeds the German one, suggests that our aggression cost more lives than it saved.

Q *Would the government of a libertarian state believe in assisting the overthrow of a dictator who attempted to conquer the rest of the world?*

A Most modern tyrants, including Hitler and Saddam Hussein, built up their military with Western assistance, sometimes in the form of taxpayer-guaranteed loans. Without our help, they might have remained obscure footnotes in history. However, let's assume that a tyrant was able to become self-sustaining. In a libertarian nation, those who wanted to fight the oppressor would be free to raise support (money, time, volunteers, mercenaries) to protect the victims. Others in the same libertarian nation might choose to remain neutral and would not be obligated to contribute to this effort.

Naturally, the more successful a tyrant was in extending his or her reach, the more likely that freedom-loving people would rally in opposition. Since a modern libertarian society would likely be aware of its special heritage, many would see tyranny as a threat to be disposed of quickly. In the process, however, those who were pacifists or didn't feel threatened wouldn't be tyrannized themselves through taxation, the draft, and other forms of domestic aggression that usually accompany a war to free others.

Q *What theories of foreign policy would a true libertarian government practice?*

A A libertarian government would be non-interventionist in the fullest sense of the word. It would not impose duties, tariffs, or embargoes on trading between its citizenry and that of other nations. Such a policy would promote peace and stimulate trade, rather than being isolationist. Had the U.S. traded with Japan instead of instituting an oil embargo against it, the attack on Pearl Harbor might never have happened.

A libertarian government would not intervene in the affairs of other nations in a diplomatic or military fashion. Likewise, a libertarian government would not interfere if some of its citizens, as individuals or groups, voluntarily supported an overseas war.

In essence, a policy of non-intervention is a policy of non-aggression, not only toward other nations, but toward a government's own citizenry. Government intervention in foreign affairs invariably starts with the imposition of taxes and regulations on its own citizenry. War, like charity, begins at home.

Q *If you were walking down the street, and you saw a woman being threatened by a man with a knife, wouldn't it be morally acceptable to defend that woman by the use of force? You would not be initiating force – only using force to defend that woman's right to life. And if that is morally acceptable, then why isn't it moral for one nation to use military force in order to defend another nation?*

A It is moral to defend anyone, whether an individual or a nation, threatened by an aggressor. It is not moral to force innocent bystanders to help us in our quest. Nor is it moral to kill bystanders who are innocently obscuring access to the aggressor.

A nation that goes to war "defending another nation" usually commits both of these two immoral acts. It forces its own citizens to participate, even if they don't wish to do so (e.g., taxation). In the name of freedom for those abroad, we violate the freedoms of those at home.

Military action, especially bombing, kills innocent bystanders, but is dismissed as "collateral damage." We sacrifice the lives of the minority so that the majority may live better, contradicting our libertarian principles.

Our politicians tell us that we must choose between war with aggression and doing nothing to stop tyrants. To paraphrase Ayn Rand, this is akin to telling us our sexual choices are sadism and masochism.

Other choices are available. As libertarians, it is up to us to work together to envision non-aggressive solutions, rather than letting the war question divide us.

Q *Shouldn't we be willing to give up some liberties, as some politicians and media pundits have demanded, in order to fight terrorism in this time of crisis?*

A If the terrorists attacked the U.S. because they "hate freedom," aren't we playing right into their hands by giving up our liberties?

Giving up our liberties won't give us security – indeed, the opposite is true. If passengers, or even just the pilots, had had the liberty to carry airplane-safe weapons, the 9-11 terrorists would have had to face a plane full of armed opposition. If the unarmed passengers on one flight were able to thwart the terrorists and cause them to crash into an empty field, imagine how effective *armed* passengers would have been. Indeed, gun-toting passengers might have been considered too difficult to control and the 9-11 events might not have happened at all!

Every time we give up our liberties, Americans lose their lives. By accepting the War on Drugs, the American people gave up their freedom to ingest the recreational substances of their choice. Instead of saving lives, the War on Drugs kills over 10,000 Americans each year, the equivalent of two repetitions of 9-11 for the last several decades.[22]

Americans gave up their liberty to choose their own medicines through FDA regulation of new pharmaceuticals. These laws have caused the death of 10,000-100,000 Americans each year for the past several decades, an annual toll 2-20 times greater than the 9-11 tragedy.[23]

Would we have more deaths if we refused to give up these freedoms? No – the numbers reported here are the deaths above and beyond the lives that these regulations save. As government expenditures (and regulations) increase, liberty, wealth creation (as estimated by per capita GDP), and citizen longevity go down.[24]

Less liberty ultimately means less life.

Q *Why do some libertarians think we shouldn't have attacked Afghanistan? We were only defending ourselves!*

A Sadly, we may have actually started the fight. Bin Laden's stated reasons for his action against the U.S. included stationing U.S. troops in Islamic countries, U.S. trade sanctions against Iraq, and U.S. aid to Israel.[25] If we were a libertarian country, bin Laden probably wouldn't have had these "excuses" to attack us since we would have no troops stationed in the Middle East, no embargoes, and no foreign aid to Israel. Our tax dollars wouldn't have been used to "grow" bin Laden, his network, and the Taliban in times past. As a result, he might not have been strong enough to arrange the 9-11 hits, as he is alleged to have done. Perhaps we are simply reaping as we have sown; 9-11 may have been "blowback" from past U.S. policies.

Regardless of whether or not that is the case, you are absolutely correct in your contention that we have a right to defend ourselves. We have a right to go after those who have harmed us. Indeed, we should.

What we should not do, in my opinion, is use the actions of terrorists to justify killing innocents ourselves. That's what those responsible for 9-11 did. They couldn't get at the masterminds behind our unenlightened foreign policy, so they took their frustration out on others.

In spite of our "targeting," we have killed innocent Afghanis, destroyed their livelihood, and turned thousands into refugees, many of whom literally starved to death. Now our tax dollars go to rebuild Afghanistan. However, no one has interviewed each displaced Afghani and reimbursed him or her for the value of the business or family members lost.

Our real loss isn't financial, though. The innocents we harmed hate us. They will be the new recruits for terrorists like bin Laden, the new suicide bombers. Terrorists are created, not born. If we defend ourselves by becoming aggressors ourselves, we will simply create more enemies. The cycle will simply repeat itself. This is not effective defense.

In Arnold Schwarzenegger's movie, *Collateral Damage*, the terrorist who kills Arnold's character's son and daughter asks (I'm paraphrasing), "What makes you so different from me? You're a killer too – or you want to be. You want to kill me!" Arnold answers, "The difference is that I'm only going to kill *you*!"

Collateral Damage is hardly realty, but the philosophical point is worth pondering. In our quest for justice, how many innocents is it OK to kill, how much property is it OK to destroy, how many people can we sentence to starvation, before we become terrorists, too? When does collateral damage become terrorism?

Q *I agree that the world would be a much better place if we could all just "get along." But what do you do when there are people dedicated to your annihilation?*

A You can destroy them, deter them, or win them over. In real life, the first is often attempted, but rarely accomplished. Indeed, the backlash from the attempt is often worse than the original threat. Our "War on Terror" may fall into this category.

Deterrence buys time, sometimes enough time for an enemy to self-destruct (e.g., the "Cold War" and the Soviet Union).

Winning over the enemy is the preferred solution, since it creates allies and is the least costly, both in dollars and lives. Free trade is a great peacemaking vehicle, since it intertwines economies and makes war unthinkable.

The military-industrial complex has incentives to discourage such peacemaking and does so by telling us that our enemies can't be reasoned with. Perhaps this is why President Dwight D. Eisenhower warned us that "we must guard against the acquisition of unwarranted influence" by this group.

Q *What do you, as a libertarian, think of the 9-11 terrorist attacks? What should libertarians do?*

A Libertarians believe that physical force is justified only in self-defense and only against those who are directly responsible. The attack on the World Trade Center cannot be considered anything but aggression. In any such attack, we should seek out the perpetrators before they can kill again. In our passion for justice, however, we must take care that we do not harm innocents, or we too, shall be among the guilty.

The scope, length of preparation, and suicidal resolve of the 9-11 perpetrators suggests extreme anger, frustration and vengeance. If we wish to stop future attacks, we would be wise to investigate the motivation behind them.

Most likely, our foreign policy is perceived, rightly or wrongly, as a threat that must be countered with desperate action. Libertarians could greatly contribute to homeland safety by seeking such information, educating the American public, and suggesting appropriate changes.

Seeking to understand the motives of an enemy is what any good military commander must do. It does not excuse enemy actions, as some tried to maintain in the wake of 9-11. Understanding enemy motivations can help us prevent future attacks and thereby save innocent lives.

Q *How would a libertarian government react to a 9-11?*

A The actions of a libertarian government would be designed to protect its citizens from further attacks. These might include:

1. Encouraging its citizenry (especially pilots) to learn the proper use of firearms and other defense tactics (e.g., personal combat skills). Criminals (and terrorists) are deterred when their intended victims are likely to fight back.[26]

2. Investigating the motivation behind the attacks in the hopes of defusing it. People must have a compelling reason to train years for a suicide mission. Take away the motivation, and terrorism dies a quiet death. For example, the Al Qaeda leadership said that tax-supported aid to Israel, the embargo/blockade of Iraq, and U.S. support for corrupt rulers in the Middle East impelled the attacks. While a truly libertarian government wouldn't have done those things in the first place, it would certainly want to find out if other actions had been misconstrued and used as an excuse for terrorist acts.

3. Making sure that its policy doesn't feed the monster. As with Saddam Hussein, bin Laden was armed and equipped by the U.S. and other Western nations when he was thought to be of use. President Bush gave the Taliban – which sheltered Al Qaeda in Afghanistan – 43 million taxpayer dollars in May 2001, just months before the 9-11 attack. The *LA Times* claimed that this made the U.S. the Taliban's largest financial backer. Although a truly libertarian government wouldn't have taxpayer dollars to give to such unworthy causes, it would want to be sure that its policies did not indirectly aid and abet the terrorists.

4. Finding out who is responsible and going after them personally. Publish evidence against the perpetrators so that the whole world can judge it. Compelling evidence will unite law-loving nations. When going after the guilty, a libertarian government would not use tactics that endanger innocents. Using Letters of Marque and Reprisal, as authorized by our Constitution, would virtually eliminate collateral damage.

Bombing Afghani cities, or firing Predator drone missiles into compounds housing innocent men, women and children along with suspected terrorists, is bound to result in civilian casualties. This only breeds more hatred. Terrorists are made, not born. The most effective way to stop terrorism is to stop creating the conditions under which it breeds. What good does it do to kill today's terrorist if, in the process, we inspire many more?

Q *Dr. Ruwart, people do not back terrorism or become terrorists just because they are angry; they do so because they think the terrorism will work. Following your policies would tell them they are right.*

Edmund Burke said that all that is necessary for evil to triumph is for men of good will to do nothing. In the face of great evil, you advocate doing nothing to combat it.

A On the contrary, I have advocated doing a great many things.[27] I'll summarize some of them that you may have missed in past columns:

First, stop taking the aggressive actions which give so many Arabs and Muslims reason to hate us. Second, stop the foreign aid that empowered both Osama bin Laden and Saddam Hussein, so that we create no new tyrants.

Third, end the War on Drugs so that the FBI can focus its attention on following up on reports of terrorists. At least two flight schools called the FBI before 9-11 to report that Arab students wanted to learn how to fly jets, but not land or take off. Had the FBI followed up, 9-11 might never have happened.

Fourth, trade with all nations, rather than embargo them as we did with Iraq, so our economies become entwined. We wouldn't go to war again with Japan, our World War II enemy, largely because we've become trading partners.

Fifth, stop loaning or gifting tax money to other nations (e.g., Iraq and Afghanistan) for the purchase of weapons. This single policy will do more for disarmament than all the negotiations thus far.

Sixth, protect our oil interests abroad with private security, rather than the American military. Private security profits most by preventing conflicts, so it is less likely to do things that aggravate tensions in the Middle East. We would also conserve more oil if its true cost was passed on to consumers.

Seventh, encourage our citizens to report unusual activity, as the flight schools mentioned above did. Encourage Americans to arm themselves. Terrorists like to prey on helpless hostages, not ones that can fight back.

Eighth, ask the Immigration and Naturalization Service (INS) to focus on tracking terrorists and aggressors, rather than going after peaceful produce pickers. The alleged lead hijacker of 9-11, Mohamed Atta, entered the U.S. three times after he had violated his visa by taking flying lessons. Had our immigration officials stayed focused on real threats, 9-11 might never have happened.

Ninth, encourage private "bounty hunters" to track down terrorists, just as they tracked down Nazis after World War II.

While we might legitimately disagree on and debate the best non-aggressive options for dealing with terrorists, bombing is only one of many. Indeed, CIA veterans, in an October 7, 2002 letter to the Senate Intelligence Committee, noted that: "It is our view that an invasion of Iraq would ensure overflowing recruitment centers for terrorists into the indefinite future. Far from eliminating the threat, it would enhance it exponentially."

Should we pursue a foreign policy that encourages terrorists? I'm sure that we both agree that the answer to that question is "No!" What makes foreign policy discussions so polarized is often the lack of solid, hardcore information. We should constantly seek out the best sources for information, and share them with others, so that we can all better find the truth that will set us free – and keep us that way.

Q *President Bush aggressively advocated for – and used – military force in response to the September 11 terrorist attacks. What do you see as a proper response from our government toward the terrorist attackers and Saddam Hussein?*

A Bombing only creates more terrorists by giving victims and their families a reason to hate us. Since we can't possibly kill all the terrorists by bombing them, a better defense is to de-motivate them.

Terrorists claim that they are reacting to U.S. aggression. Osama bin Laden, for example, believed that our embargo on Iraq killed hundreds of thousands of innocents. Sadly, according to independent observers, that's exactly what it did. Since the embargo hurt the Iraqi people, rather than Saddam, we should have ended it.

If we withdraw our troops from the Middle East (another bin Laden complaint), we'd stop paying five times as much to protect our oil as we do to buy it.[28] Let the oil companies hire less expensive private security and pass on the costs to consumers to encourage conservation.

Stop tax-supported aid to Israel (and all other foreign governments, of course). Those who want to help Israel can do so through private means. Since private charity is cheaper to administer by a factor of 2-3, the Israelis may end up with just as much, or even more, aid. However, the American taxpayer is less likely to be the target of terrorist wrath.

Instead of funding the Homeland Security bureaucracy, we can encourage our pilots and populace to arm themselves. Terrorists target people who can't fight back. Had our pilots been armed on 9-11, the Twin Towers might still be standing.

Instead of chasing peaceful drug users, our domestic law enforcers can follow up on tips from citizens. For example, *two* private pilot training schools, one in Minnesota and one in Arizona, told the FBI that men from the Middle East wanted to learn how to fly jets, but not land or take off. Had the FBI followed up, they would probably have been led to the ring of 9-11 hijackers.

Instead of turning away Mexican agricultural workers, our immigration officials could focus on keeping track of known terrorists. The alleged lead hijacker of 9-11, Mohamed Atta, entered the U.S. three times after he had violated his visa by taking flying lessons. Had our immigration officials stayed focused on real threats, 9-11 might never have happened.

If we didn't use tax dollars to empower dictators like Saddam Hussein, we wouldn't need to worry about them later. We gave Saddam biological and chemical weapons to attack Iran's Ayatollah Khomeini.

The bottom line is this: by sticking to our libertarian principles, we are better able to protect ourselves from those who have none.

Q *Don't you agree that the only way to defeat terrorism is to enforce democracy and human rights all over the world, and to support all the people who are peacefully struggling in their own countries in the face of persecution, misery and death from their own governments?*

A Terrorism is not something that can be rooted out and destroyed by force, as the U.S. is trying to do. Terrorists are not a separate species that we can make extinct by intensively hunting them down. Some terrorists, probably most of them, are made, not born. If we don't understand how they are created, our efforts to kill them may actually create more of the same. Indeed, we may become terrorists ourselves. Certainly, the poor Afghans whose possessions and families are destroyed by U.S. bombing must think of us as such. What is terrorism but a willingness to sacrifice innocents to gain our own ends, however noble they may be?

Q *Wouldn't you agree that America existing as a democracy is not a sin? In these circumstances, Americans would be wise to avoid* *the trap of being paralyzed by guilt from past mistakes. America should especially avoid any temptations to further isolationism.*

A "Democracy" or "majority rule" is another way of saying "minority persecution." Libertarians believe that majorities shouldn't rule minorities and minorities shouldn't rule majorities. We believe that everyone should rule themselves as long as they don't steal from, assault, or defraud others. Libertarians don't believe in isolationist tactics like embargoes or tariffs, either, because these actions stop people from voluntarily trading together – at gunpoint, if necessary.

Rather than wasting time and effort feeling guilty about past mistakes, we should simply not repeat them again. If our mistakes harmed others, we should make things right again to the extent possible.

Q *I am an Italian supporter of libertarianism. I worry that most American libertarians seem to favor isolationism, to avoid being involved in world troubles. This happened prior to World War II, but apparently the lesson was not fully understood. I believe even the current terrorism crisis can be blamed on a lack of U.S. intervention in world politics, not an excess of it.*

I think that the motivation behind the Sept. 11 attacks is clear. Simply the fact that America exists is a threat to militant Islamic fundamentalists, and to governments that are bloody dictatorships and have total disregard for their own citizens' lives and rights.

A I have heard the news media echo your certainty on the terrorists' motivations, but frankly, I see little hard evidence for this viewpoint. On the other hand, bin Laden, the presumed mastermind, claimed that the crimes of the U.S. include, but are not limited to: stationing troops in his native Saudi Arabia; intervention against Muslims throughout the world; sanctions against Iraq, Syria, Sudan, Libya, and Iran; and support to Israel.[25]

These seem like concrete complaints against U.S. intervention (military troops, embargo, tax-supported aid), not a concern with threats to fundamentalist beliefs. However, non-intervention (as seemingly called for by bin Laden) is not the same as isolationism. For example, libertarians wouldn't impose embargoes, as the U.S. government does now, so trading with all nations would occur. Trading is neither interventionist nor isolationist. Indeed, it's quite neighborly and interactive.

Q *How can I show support for the military if I disagree with the war they are fighting? How can libertarians show support for our troops when they don't believe in taxes?*

A I personally don't support the idea of a tax-supported military, but I do applaud the sincere efforts of our men and women in uniform who are courageously willing to lay down their lives to defend us. As a libertarian, I support them by speaking out against military action that endangers their lives without increasing our security. The best support we can give our troops is not to put them in harm's way unless it's absolutely necessary.

Q *Speaking of the troops, an 18-year-old can fight in a war and die for his/her country but that person can't drink until they are 21. I want to know why there are age restrictions on alcohol, tobacco, and gambling. I know legislators say that the reason for this is because they want to protect the youth, but there has to be more of a reason than that. I don't understand that.*

A I'll tell you the reason, but you won't – and shouldn't – like it. Today, adolescents are considered too young to handle tobacco, alcohol and gambling. In my day, they were considered too young to vote even while they died in Vietnam – supposedly to protect that right. In reality, they were the sacrificial lambs offered up to promote special interest agendas. The recent conflicts in the Middle East are more of the same.

Since young is not the same as stupid, our youth are not told the true reason for their military service. Instead, they're proclaimed to be heroes and heroines who fight to preserve freedom overseas. Of course, freedom, like charity, must begin at home.

The laws are very consistent in their disdain for our young people – and their lives. That's why so many from Generation X and the Millennials are becoming libertarians!

Q *Let us assume that tomorrow, we wake up in a true libertarian society. How do we protect ourselves from foreign threats? Specifically, how would a libertarian society prevent a terrorist from putting a nuclear device in the back of a truck and detonating it in an American city? We would still have to contend with specific groups that desire revenge from our previous actions.*

It seems to me that the only way to prevent terrorist activities such as these is to have intelligence agents throughout the world gathering information. Obviously, to do this would in some way require that property rights of citizens from other nations be violated (theft of information, etc.).

A If we somehow, overnight, elected a libertarian Congress and President, they would quickly withdraw our troops from foreign soil and end support to tyrannical dictators. Most terrorists are seeking these very ends when they strike, so presumably they'd have little motivation to attack. Vengeful acts, could, after all, encourage the libertarian government to re-think its stand on nonintervention. Terrorists would have nothing to gain and everything to lose by continuing their attacks.

Even a world-wide surveillance system such as you describe would be inadequate to locate terrorists before they strike. Realistically, prevention is the only workable cure in this arena.

Our government plays up the threat of foreign attack and terrorism as a reason to steal our liberties. The "karma" that the U.S. will reap for its past misdeeds won't come from foreigners, except in a minor way. By giving our government the power to aggress against other nations, we've also given it the power to aggress against us – and it certainly does!

We pay approximately 50% of our income in taxes; our assets can be confiscated without trial; our young people spend years in prison for the crime of trying to feel good with drugs; we are denied new pharmaceuticals and inexpensive remedies because of the FDA; our greatest polluter, the U.S. military, continues to poison our land, water, and air. The true price of violating the rights of foreigners is empowering our government to violate ours!

Q *Many of our veterans have permanent disabilities that directly interfere with their ability to compete vocationally with their non-veteran counterparts. I believe that an immediate increase in all disability compensation rates is justified by the sacrifices these veterans have made for their country.*

How do libertarians plan to deal with the support of these consequences of our wars and other military actions? Will you just cut off funds and hospital care for the nation's disabled veterans?

A In a libertarian society, military personnel would have compensation that was guaranteed by written contract. Their fate would no longer depend upon political whim.

Today's veterans aren't the only ones at risk. Our young people, for example, even by the most optimistic calculations, will be lucky to recover what they put into Social Security, let alone get any type of return on it. Indeed, anyone who pays taxes is unlikely to recover the full benefit of their "investment" in government.

The solution isn't to debate which group is more deserving. The solution is to change the system so that everyone gets what they've earned. That's the libertarian way!

Q *I've suffered a back injury serving in the U.S. military. Do you think I deserve monetary compensation from the government?*

A In a libertarian society, your contract with the military would determine whether or not you get compensation for injuries. Without such a contract, your benefits depend on bureaucratic whim.

Individuals on the government payroll can render an important service, e.g., defending the nation or teaching in a public university. Unfortunately, their compensation is derived from taxes, taken from their neighbors – at gunpoint, if necessary. Many libertarians move into the private sector to avoid the moral dilemma that obviously results.

Some libertarians believe that any benefits they get from the government are a recovery of their stolen tax dollars. Some libertarians believe that any money taken from the taxpayer represents ill-gotten gains.

Obviously, in a libertarian society, you wouldn't face this dilemma, since taxation would be an abuse of the past, much like slavery. Until then, you must let your conscience be your guide.

Q *What is the libertarian view on the U.S. Department of Veterans Affairs? Do libertarians support tax dollars going to help our nation's veterans with health care and other services, including disability benefits? Or is that also considered pork-barrel spending by libertarians?*

A In a libertarian society, military personnel would have compensation that was guaranteed by written contract. Funding these benefits wouldn't depend upon taxation of future generations, as it is today. Instead, the benefits would be supplied by annuity-like funds that would grow over time. Thus veterans' benefits wouldn't become the political football that they are today.

Some libertarians do indeed support the use of tax dollars to fulfill promises to veterans, retirees, and others. Unfortunately, government has promised so much to so many that the only way these promises could actually be completely fulfilled under the current system would be to inflate the currency, which essentially imposes additional "taxes" upon us all. The promised benefits are diluted accordingly.

Some libertarians have suggested selling off government assets, such as its 40% of the U.S. landmass, in order to attempt to fulfill these promises. I personally prefer this solution.

However, I suspect that none of us will ever see more than a fraction of what the government has promised us. The government operates a Ponzi scheme by spending today what has been promised for tomorrow. Because we, as a nation, have gone along with this Ponzi scheme, we will all eventually suffer the consequences.

Very few politicians will ever share this unpleasant truth with you, because they fear you'll lose your faith and trust in them. However, the truth does set you free to take another path and work to create a libertarian society!

Q *I believe we shouldn't be forced to participate in some kind of National Service. However, some of my friends say we owe some duty to our country for being born here and living here. What about a citizen's duty to country?*

A If "doing our duty" is equated to providing "service," who decides what is service and what is not? If young Steve Jobs had been forced into some type of National Service instead of being left alone to tinker in his garage, he might never have invented the personal computer. The resulting increases in everyone's standard of living would have been lost or delayed because of a bureaucrat's uninformed decision about what was good for the country.

Freedom is what is good for a nation, especially one that wants to help its poor. More freedom means more wealth creation and less poverty. Government interference, even well-intended, backfires.

Most people give generously of their time and money if this is the voluntary custom. For example, tipping is not mandatory, but almost everyone does it. Before government got involved in social welfare, almost everyone helped a less fortunate neighbor individually or as part of a formal organization, because that was the custom.

You were either a charity case or a provider of charity; few people wanted to be in the former group.

To return to this way of charitable thinking, the government should stop forcing people to "give at the office" through taxation and resist the temptation to force people into service. Doing so will only create resentment towards those in need, leaving little sympathy for the poor when their "help" disappears in the shifting political tides.

Q *In a libertarian society, the U.S. military would be scaled down. By doing this, won't the U.S. be putting itself at risk should it face a country with a larger military that is aggressive towards the U.S.?*

A Although it's likely that we'd have a smaller military in a libertarian society, we'd probably have a much more efficient one.

Navy Seal Commander Richard Marcinko was asked by his superiors to infiltrate key U.S. Naval bases with a handful of colleagues. Commanders of the target installations were given notice that Marcinko's raiders were coming. Nevertheless, with only seven men, Marcinko planted dummy demolition charges on nuclear submarines, captured the women and children living on base, and even gained access to Air Force One as it was being refueled! The Commanders complained that Marcinko had cheated by coming in by water or other "back doors" that they hadn't prepared for.[29] Wouldn't you want to fire such "commanders"?

Our military is a subsidized monopoly that has trouble protecting us on our home turf. Like most government services, it costs much and delivers little, wasting the energy and lives of our brave soldiers. This isn't the fault of our soldiers. It's due to politics and the inevitable inefficiency of government. Our soldiers deserve better and so do we!

Q *What is the libertarian stance on foreign relations? Example: Should we be involved in the situation between Israel and Palestine? Also, should we be involved in the United Nations?*

A Most libertarians believe that, as a nation, we should not be involved in the United Nations or the defense of foreign countries, since such entanglements involve taxation and other aggression.

Libertarians also believe that, as individuals, we can help whomever we want. Thus, in a libertarian nation, both sides in a conflict could ask us to volunteer money, time, and even military service. Those who felt the cause was worthy might choose one of these options.

Q *What's your stand on U.S. membership and participation in the United Nations?*

A The United Nations has many of the same features as coercive government. First of all, most of its resources come from forcible taxation, rather than voluntary contributions. Secondly, it forcibly imposes its collective will on individual nations at times. Thirdly, the UN, through a number of strategies, seeks to usurp the sovereignty of its member states. Thus, most libertarians believe that the US should withdraw from the UN.

Q *Dr. Ruwart, you wrote: "... most of [the UN's] resources come from forcible taxation, rather than voluntary contributions."*
This is completely wrong. No United Nations body is funded through taxation, and that in fact is prohibited by US law. The budget for the United Nations' peacekeeping efforts worldwide is less than that of the police department of New York City – look it up! Every dollar the UN gets is from contributions paid by member governments – and they are for all intents and purposes voluntary!

A You are correct in stating that member governments contribute to the UN voluntarily, but the money that is "contributed" ultimately comes from taxes levied on its citizens. These taxes are not voluntary for the citizens. If they refuse to pay because they don't wish to "contribute" to the UN, the taxes will be taken at gunpoint, if necessary. Libertarians generally consider taxation to be coercion, not volunteerism.

UN officials and influential policymakers in various countries keep floating the idea of a direct tax on the world's people, to fight "climate change" or provide food aid, etc. This bad idea could become a reality one day if member governments go along with it.

Q *You wrote: "The UN, through a number of strategies, seeks to usurp the sovereignty of its nation states." I would expect to hear this from someone in the "black helicopter" crowd, trying to stir up fear and suspicion without evidence, but I am surprised to read such a blanket statement from Dr. Ruwart. The only sovereignty we should be concerned about is that of the individual.*

A I agree that the "only sovereignty we should be concerned about is that of the individual." Let's look at how the United Nations interacts with its member nations and the sovereignty of its individuals.

In 1995, U.S. soldiers overseas were asked to don the United Nations beret and insignia and report to a foreign military commander. The U.S. was "contributing" soldiers to the UN. These soldiers, who had voluntarily enlisted to serve in the U.S. military, were not asked if they were willing to be the fighting arm of the UN.

To appreciate the significance of this "transfer," note the words of the new commander, General Jehu Engstrom. He claimed: "...a non-American officer or non-NATO officer has never before had command of an American battalion abroad." One soldier, Michael New, who had been decorated for service during a Persian Gulf deployment, believed that donning the new uniform was a violation of his oath to serve the United States and its Constitution. When his commanding officers were not able to satisfactorily reassure him, he respectfully requested a transfer to a non-UN unit.

Instead, Michael New was dishonorably discharged. His individual sovereignty and choice of allegiance was not respected. In essence, U.S. soldiers who voluntarily enlist to serve in the U.S.

military are being drafted into the UN army, sometimes against their will.[30]

Almost by definition, the UN threatens U.S. sovereignty and that of other countries. Attorney Herbert W. Titus explains:

"It is commonly assumed that the Charter of the United Nations is a treaty. It is not. Instead, the Charter of the United Nations is a constitution. As such, it is illegitimate, having created a supranational government, deriving its powers not from the consent of the governed (the people of the United States of America and peoples of other member nations) but from the consent of the peoples' government officials who have no authority to bind either the American people nor any other nation's people to any terms of the Charter of the United Nations."[31]

Our individual sovereignty is certainly threatened when we can be bound to a contract without our express consent.

Q *You wrote: "Thus, most libertarians believe that the U.S. should withdraw from the UN." But staying firmly engaged at the United Nations protects American interests by making sure our points of view are voiced and incorporated into whatever decisions are made. But if you would rather have a UN in which American voices are not included...*

A The libertarian view on sovereignty is that the individual is sovereign. By definition, any international governance detracts from the individual's sovereignty. "Governance" is another way of saying that the peaceful individual is forced – at gunpoint, if necessary – to do things he or she doesn't want to do. The more governance we have, the less sovereignty we have. Ultimately, this loss of sovereignty leads most libertarians to oppose the UN.

I use the qualifier "most" because some libertarians, like yourself, feel that it is better to have an influential seat at the table than not to participate. My personal suspicion is that, without our support, there would be no table at all.

Q *How do libertarians view the World Trade Organization, and the existence of the United Nations and its involvement in so many countries' affairs?*

A International organizations, such as the ones you name, are usually supported directly or indirectly by taxes (legalized theft), which are repugnant to libertarians. Often, these organizations forcibly interfere in the affairs of nations. Since libertarians oppose the use of force except in self-defense, they abhor such actions as well.

Let me hasten to add that some international organizations are voluntarily funded and purely humanitarian. With these, libertarians have no quarrel.

Money and Banking

C urrency expansion through government's deficit spending takes from the poor and gives to the rich.

Q *Wasn't the Great Depression caused by too little government regulation?*

A Most economists believe that the Great Depression was primarily a result of the Federal Reserve's manipulation of the national currency. Had the government not interfered with the banking industry by giving the Fed a monopoly on money, the Depression might have never occurred. Too much government, not too little, was the culprit.

Q *How will libertarian government deal with the tremendous hold that the international bankers have upon the world political/economic system?*

A Bankers are powerful because they have a monopoly on creation of a country's money supply and because they are not held personally liable if their bank becomes insolvent. Libertarian governments would not give bankers these advantages.

In the early 1800s, Scotland had a banking system similar to what a libertarian country might have. Banks each had their own currency, backed by gold. They collectively operated a clearinghouse so that each customer could use their bank notes freely. If a bank started over-inflating, it was punished by the clearinghouse, which refused to take the inflated money at face value.

Since owners were personally liable for depositors' funds, banks rarely inflated dangerously anyway. When an occasional bank went under, the depositors were reimbursed by other banks seeking their business.

Q *You point out that Scotland used a free market banking system in the first half of the nineteen century, but at that time Scotland was a small agrarian society, not readily comparable to even the industrialized United States of the late nineteenth century.*

A Canada had a banking system more like Scotland's during the Great Depression. Consequently, Canadians lost only about 3% of what U.S. citizens did.

Free banking systems can easily adapt to changing conditions, because they don't have to get permission from bureaucrats to implement reforms. Highly regulated banking systems depend upon legislation and bureaucracy. Which do you think adapts better?

Q *I don't like big government, but I see no other way to control the amount of money than a central bank especially in an industrial nation. The Federal Reserve is the only department of the government I know of that actually makes a significant profit.*

A First of all, the Federal Reserve is a private banking organization, which has been given a legal monopoly on our currency by the same government that promises to protect us from monopolies. When the Fed manipulates the currency supply, the whole country suffers, as it did in the Great Depression.

Q *I was wondering what the libertarian stance is with regards to the Federal Reserve. On one hand, it is an institution that is somewhat independent of the government (like a private business)* *and it generates profits from check collection that go to the Treasury and lower taxes. It also seems to have prevented another great depression. On the other hand, it is a regulator that forces banks to follow certain procedures. Are there aspects of the Fed that libertarians would change, would they propose an alternative, or do they like it?*

A The Federal Reserve is a private institution that has been given a monopoly on the money supply by our government. The member banks of the Federal Reserve are corporations, who enjoy limited liability due to government decree.

The Federal Reserve actually contributed to the Great Depression, because it permitted banks to reduce reserves. The devastating inflation that results from expanding the money supply outweighs any positive benefit derived from check collection.

In a libertarian society, an institution like the Federal Reserve would lose its monopoly status and its members would lose their limited liability. The Fed would have great incentive to lower its expansion of the money supply as a result. This new, libertarian, Federal Reserve would be more like a clearinghouse for member banks, than an instrument for economic control.

Q *In the 1800s, the U.S. suffered recessions and depressions too, so I don't see that the Fed has made things worse.*

A During the 1800s, the U.S. had a regulated banking system but without a central bank. Regulations varied by state, but most required banks to use government bonds as part of their reserve. Before maturity, these bonds were often liquidated at a loss. Thus, the banks went under when faced with unusually high demands from depositors. Deflation caused by the resulting contraction in the money supply was rapid and destructive, just as deflation was during the Great Depression.

The Great Depression was more severe than the ones in the 1800s (hence the name "Great"). In addition, the Fed has made greater inflation possible, something that cannot happen as readily without a central bank. Today's dollar buys about 3% of what it did in 1900. This is why inflation is sometimes referred to as the "invisible tax." Money that we earn and save steadily deteriorates due to the Fed's expansion of the money supply faster than the U.S. increase in productivity.

Q *How would a libertarian government institute a gold standard?*

A A libertarian government wouldn't need to institute a gold standard. No laws would force people to use paper money, so competition in currency would begin. People would turn to the money which kept its value best, most likely gold.

Q *Would a libertarian government take responsibility for converting the gold into coins, ensuring the accuracy of their weights and purity?*

A They probably wouldn't have to. Private mints would most likely use a professional organization to certify their coins in order to insure weights and purity. Clearing houses would refuse to give banks full credit if they accepted coins from disreputable mints, so the good money would drive out the bad.

Q *Would it be necessary for banks to ship gold every time two individuals engaged in commerce?*

A No. Historically, banks have cooperated in establishing clearing houses so that individual transfers are unnecessary. Today, this mechanism is in place for paper currency as well.

Q *Won't a gold standard cause deflation as the economy grows? Isn't this harmful? Isn't mild inflation good? How can the gold supply adjust to changes in wealth creation?*

A Rapid deflation caused by contracting the money supply can be destructive, just as deflation was during the Great Depression. Some deflation, however, occurs when the production of goods and services becomes so efficient that prices drop, much as the price of computing power drops rapidly today. This type of deflation, like cheaper computing power, is obviously a boost to the economy, not a detriment.

When deflation is caused by the failure of the increase in the supply of gold to keep pace with the increase in the size of the economy, gold becomes relatively more valuable, creating incentive to produce more. Mining generally continues until the balance between prices (including mining costs) and gold supply is restored.

Today's inflation is caused by the Fed expanding the money supply faster than wealth creation. The new money goes first to the bankers and politicians. These groups essentially pass "GO" on the MONOPOLY™ game of life before the rest of us and enjoy the ability to command more resources as a result.

Most of us get the higher prices that result from this inflation before we get the trickle-down benefits of the new money. That's why inflation is sometimes referred to as an invisible tax on consumers. Every decade, we lose approximately half the purchasing power that we would have otherwise had. Can you imagine what your life style would be if this buying power had not been taken from you?

Q *Suppose there were two islands unaware of each other's existence. Both used gold as their currency, but one had ten times as much as the other. Once they do discover each other, wouldn't the inhabitants in the island with less gold suddenly find themselves at a major disadvantage economically?*

A Not necessarily. If the island with less gold had a higher production capacity, it would trade goods for gold and both islands would benefit.

Q *If the government prints money at the rate of economic growth and removes money at the rate of economic decline, wouldn't the value of money be more stable than the price of gold?*

A Governments claim to do just as you've suggested, but to the best of my knowledge, they've inflated the currency relative to the economy without exception. Because of the mechanism by which this inflation is accomplished, buying power is shifted from the poor to the rich. Government aggression always hurts the disadvantaged the most.

Q *I am against the gold standard because it gets the government in the business of hoarding gold. Gold is a useful natural resource for such things as electrical conductors. Why would we need to back money by gold? Paper money is just a medium for exchange. Money represents what the people accept it to be worth.*

A People prefer gold because it is not only a medium for exchange, but has intrinsic value. Overnight, people can lose faith in paper money and it can become worthless. Gold can fluctuate in value, but historically these variations are small compared to the volatility of paper. Governments can easily manipulate the paper money supply by simple decree; gold cannot so easily be inflated.

Jobs and Wealth Creation

J obs, and the wealth they create, are limited primarily by government interference. Without it, poverty as we know it today, would cease to exist.

Q *What will libertarians do when the population outstrips the number of jobs?*

A In a libertarian society, job growth is not limited by taxes and regulations as it is today. In a free market, job creation is not limited at all. Since there is always another need or desire to be met, there is always the potential of fulfilling it (i.e., a job).

The population of the U.S. in its early years grew extremely rapidly due to massive immigration. If jobs grew linearly during this exponential population explosion, many people would have starved. In fact, the opposite occurred. Immigrants to the U.S. fared much better than their European counterparts.

Job creation exploded along with the population. In Europe, the guilds restricted who could work; in the U.S., jobs weren't destroyed this way. Without government interference, supply rises to meet the demand.

In a libertarian society, job and wealth creation are virtually unlimited. The poor benefit the most because they are the ones disenfranchised by legal restrictions.

Q *If we privatize government institutions, where will these millions of people whose jobs are wrapped up solely in bureaucracy and red tape find work?*

A Most will find employment in the expanding private sector. We should expect at least an eight-fold expansion of the economy as we get rid of the excessive regulation that stifles its growth.[33] Many who are currently unemployed will find jobs easier to get and less red tape stopping them from starting their own businesses!

In a free market, jobs are limitless. Someone always has a need that someone else can fulfill. Taxes and regulation decrease job creation and cause unemployment by outlawing someone's service to another.

The New York taxicab industry is a prime example of this. The number of licenses for taxis hasn't changed since before World War II. As a result, they cost over \$700,000 (as of 2011).[33] People who turn their cars into cabs become outlaws. Without this kind of aggression-through-government, unemployment – even of ex-bureaucrats – would be very low.

Q *I am a Libertarian running for my State House of Representatives, and I have a question for you. Unions: good or not?*

A Unions can be useful go-betweens between employers and employees, and would probably exist in a libertarian society. However, union members would be prosecuted for assault or property destruction in pursuit of their goals, unlike today. Furthermore, unless forbidden by contract, employers could hire replacements for striking workers.

Unions *per se* are fine organizations; many promote a professionalism that their members take pride in. However, when unions violate the non-aggression principle, directly or through legislation, they become the exploiters.

A free market produces an economic boom, where labor is in high demand. Wages and benefits rise. Thus, the avowed goal of most unions is met by a society with more liberty.

Q *I am curious about the libertarian viewpoint on collective bargaining and trade unions.*

A Libertarians believe that workers should be free to organize, bargain, and strike for better wages and conditions. Employers should also be free to hire new employees who are willing to work under existing wages and conditions. Each side is free to do as it pleases as long as they don't defraud, steal from, or assault each other.

Today, most employers are legally prevented from hiring new workers during the strike. Union violence is often ignored. Thus, unions have the edge in any negotiation and union wages are usually artificially high. Businesses on the edge go under and the disadvantaged workers lose their jobs to subsidize the union members.

Q *Without regulation, wouldn't wages stabilize at subsistence levels?*

A Just the opposite! In a free economy, wages increase, so few workers stay at subsistence levels. Relative to the rest of the world, the U.S. has less regulation and high wages. That's why 90% of our workforce makes more than minimum wage, even though no law requires employers to pay more.[34]

Q *What good does it do a poor person to work if they just get stuck in a sweat shop?*

A In a libertarian economy, a worker would stay in a "sweat shop" only long enough to get a skill, experience, or better understanding of the business culture. For example, a seamstress can work for herself with few start-up costs. However, in regulated economies, the law might require an expensive license or forbid a person to use their home for commercial purposes. In a libertarian society, no such barriers would exist.

Q *If you take away minimum wages, businesses can pay whatever small amount they want and keep the rest for profit.*

A If businesses can pay what they want, why do 90-95% of today's workers in the U.S. make more than the minimum wage? The answer: supply and demand applies to employees as well as products. If a business doesn't pay a person what he or she is worth, they go to a new employer or start their own business. In a libertarian society, with its expanded economy, such moves will be much easier than they are today.

Minimum wage laws actually destroy entry-level positions for the unskilled. Black economist Walter Williams believes that the minimum wage laws are the single most important factor in keeping young blacks out of the job market.[38] The next time Congress considers raising the minimum wage, look in your newspaper for an estimate of the number of jobs that will be lost – potential training jobs for the disadvantaged.

Q *Libertarians say the minimum wage will cause unemployment because fewer employers will be willing to hire at costs above what an unskilled worker is worth. Yet one of my professors said that when the minimum wage was first initiated, despite what Republicans and libertarians said would happen, unemployment went down. This also was the result after Eisenhower raised the minimum wage in the 1950s. So, was my professor mistaken, or is the claim that the minimum wage causes unemployment simply libertarian rhetoric?*

A Exhaustive studies, many of which are cited in Chapter 3 of *Healing Our World*, show conclusively that minimum wage laws decrease employment. However, total employment is a composite of many factors, only one of which is minimum wage. The employment figures that your professor was looking at would have likely been even higher without minimum wage laws.

Minimum wage laws affect minorities, disabled, and otherwise disadvantaged workers the most. Therefore, looking at employment statistics for these groups give a better picture of their true impact. Figure 3.1 in *Healing* shows employment of young black men was similar to that of young white men in 1950, but decreased dramatically as the minimum wage laws grew to cover more jobs in the next 30 years.

When the next minimum wage hike is under consideration, scan your newspapers. The correlation between unemployment and minimum wage levels is so well known that newspapers usually give estimates of the number of jobs that will be lost.

Q *I'm a college student. My professor asked me a question and I need a clear answer. I understand that the minimum wage leads to unemployment, and this is clearly reason enough to not have it. However, doesn't increasing the minimum wage at least force businesses to invest in technology that they otherwise wouldn't have, thus improving productivity?*

A Your professor is only looking at one side of the equation. Technology can only increase productivity of employed workers. Any such increase would be more than offset by the zero productivity of workers who lost their jobs due to minimum wage.

Of course, if investing in technology was indeed more productive (i.e., profitable) than hiring people, businesses, which are greedy for profit, would mechanize. When businesses find it more productive to hire workers, and minimum wage prevents this, productivity obviously goes down, not up.

Technology is often more productive than manual labor, but not always. The marketplace knows best. Bureaucrats have no way of knowing.

Q *If taxes were dramatically reduced wouldn't free market forces reduce wages accordingly? Would people really have more of their own money to give to charity, or would competition force them to eventually accept lower wages? I think market forces (competition) would reduce actual wages and people would have less money to spend and would be unable to give more money to charity or answer the other needs that are currently being taken care of by the government.*

A Whenever taxes have been reduced in the past, the economy has boomed, the demand for labor has gone up, and wages have increased. Supply and demand determine wages.

In addition, wealth creation would increase immensely without government interference, so that every dollar could buy more. Studies suggest that we could have 8 times as many goods and services without government.[32] Our poor would be wealthy compared to their current state!

Another way to look at it is in terms of waste. Government wastes half of what it takes in due to inefficiency. The burdensome regulations that government imposes on businesses may cost employers a needless 30-40%. Thus, we could probably have all the services government now provides for a fraction of their current cost. With such great savings, we would indeed have more to give to the poor!

Q *During the Industrial Revolution, huge businesses gained a monopoly in their respective markets, and paid workers far less than they deserved. Why wouldn't this happen again in a libertarian-style free market?*

A Wages, like prices, are a result of supply and demand in a free market.

During the Industrial Revolution, many farm workers, who tired of the long hours, dangerous conditions, and uncertain income, came to the cities for industrial jobs. Since wealth creation at that time was inefficient, both agricultural and industrial jobs gave little compensation by today's standards and could be viewed by modern economists as "exploitive." Wages – and working conditions – gradually improved over time as we learned how to create wealth more efficiently.

If an employer pays too little, employees simply go to work elsewhere or go into business for themselves. Historically, employers have tried to collude to pay workers "slave wages," but such attempts never succeed for long.[36] The employer who pays a bit more gets the best workers, produces wealth most efficiently, and makes more money. Consequently, employers pay over 90% of the adult work force more than the minimum wage, even though no government regulation demands that they do so.

Q *Have you people ever studied history? One hundred years ago sweat shops and factories working child laborers over 18 hours a day were commonplace – and will be again without child labor laws!*

A History does indeed remind us that child sweat-shop labor was common in the 1800s. History also shows us why.

In the 1800s, wealth was created slowly. Most of the population, children included, spent the better part of their lives working just to survive. Childhood, as we know it today, didn't exist for most people. In rural areas, even children of four or five years had chores to do. Their very survival often depended upon their contribution to the family's earnings.

Eventually, industrialization helped us to create wealth rapidly. Eighteen-hour days, the rural standard, gradually turned into today's 8-hour standard with adults becoming the family's sole support. A non-working childhood, as we know it today, was born.

An interim step in this transition was the 10-12 hour factory day for both children and adults. We won't return to this situation unless we limit the creation of wealth. Studies show that the greatest single factor limiting wealth creation today is government intervention in the economy.[37] The poverty of the Third World is directly attributable to this government intervention. Children in these poor nations often must prostitute themselves just to survive. Business has been so strangled by government that sweat shops, benign by comparison, frequently aren't an option.

Q *How much is our labor really worth?*

A We know what we are worth (in a financial sense) to others by how much others are willing to pay us to do a job. If we have skills that are in demand because few people have them, we are paid more. If we have skills that many people have and few people need, we are paid less. In a free market, how much people are willing to pay us acts as a barometer indicating which skills are highly valued.

Q *You say that training can be gotten through apprenticing or on-the-job-training. But you link these training opportunities to living in a libertarian society. Why do you think that only a libertarian society would provide these opportunities? Why, for example, do the minimum wage laws preclude offering jobs at training wages?*

If a business wants to offer a position with an initial training period and candidate evaluation at the end of it, what's stopping them from doing so? As long as the terms of the training, wage level and requirements for passing the evaluation are clear at the start of employment, what can government do to stop them?

Unfortunately, the government has effectively outlawed on-the-job training and apprenticeships through the minimum wage and licensing laws.

For example, I used to rehabilitate low income housing in Michigan. A young man who lived down the street came and asked me if he could work for $2/hr. He was disabled, but he figured he could convince me of his worth and learn what was needed. Even if he couldn't do enough to get a raise, maybe he could get a work reference. After all, people are sometimes afraid to hire the handicapped. He didn't drive, so a job he could walk to was very appealing.

I was willing to help him get some training and experience at that price. However, the minimum wage was almost twice that, so I didn't dare. If I had to pay minimum wage for unskilled labor, why not get someone without problems? Many disadvantaged individuals lose any chance to work their way up the ladder because they can't make themselves attractive to employers.

Similarly, licensing laws have destroyed apprenticeships. Young people aspiring to be plumbers could once apprentice to learn their craft. Today, government demands that they jump through a series of regulatory hoops to get a license, without which they can't legally provide their services.

As a result, many minority plumbers simply operate outside the law. Licensing laws also destroy self-employment opportunities for many. In New York City, taxi licenses go for more than $700,000 today,[33] effectively keeping the disadvantaged from using their automobiles to earn their living.

Can businesses attempt to get around the regulations today? Certainly, and you're right to encourage it. However, they will be greatly crippled by the existing system, and for most, the price will be prohibitory.

Can we eliminate these restrictions without having a libertarian society? In theory, it's possible, but the special interests that benefit from these laws will simply put them back in place. We need to outlaw government interference in business – a very libertarian approach!

Q *Have you read **The Grapes of Wrath** by John Steinbeck? I know it's fiction, but it's how I feel big business would treat workers and even consumers in a libertarian society. The heroes in **Atlas Shrugged** do not reflect reality. We don't have capitalists like them, we have greed! I hope I'm wrong. I love the libertarian stands on social issues, but the economic side worries me a lot.*

P.S. I moved from borderline centrist/left liberal/libertarian into the Libertarian area of the Quiz's Diamond Chart, so reading the Advocates' FAQ and newsletter must be affecting me a bit!

A Glad to hear that you're moving in our direction!

Greed is indeed rampant among us; that's precisely why libertarians advocate a free market! In a free market, we all deal with each other voluntarily. In a regulated market, the bureaucrats dictate – at gunpoint, if necessary – who we can deal with.

For example, until recently, local phone service was provided by a single company, which was given a monopoly by government. The cost was high and going up every year. The monopoly started when

AT&T convinced government to stop competitors – at gunpoint, if necessary.

On the other hand, long-distance service became competitive in the 1980s. The cost dropped and is still going down. I remember the days when AT&T had a monopoly on long-distance service as well. Prices were much higher than they were just a few months after the Justice Department finally allowed competition again. Free markets keep the quality up and the prices down.[38]

Please continue to inquire further into these issues. You will happily find that liberty works for both economic and social issues!

Q *Libertarians say that if government would just quit interfering with business, a new era of prosperity for all would dawn, because smart business people looking to make a buck would eagerly provide for every need. But where are all these smart business people hiding? It seems to me that everywhere I look, I see business people who wouldn't recognize an opportunity if it bit them on the nose. It does not seem likely that the business community will suddenly get smarter if government interference stops.*

A Many of the smart business people are hiding in the slums where government regulation has put them. Would-be cab drivers are out of work because they can't afford the government license (over $700,000 in New York City).[33] One woman that I know personally was stopped by the city government from sewing curtains in her home, even though no customers came to her apartment. Another woman was forbidden to use her apartment for child care, even though her landlady approved. Both women are now on welfare.

Today, many businesses can get away with poor service and wasteful practices, because those who are willing to work for a smaller profit are thwarted by government regulations. When people who are used to managing on a shoe-string get into business, they are usually efficient and eager to please. Just as in the early days of our country, the humblest workers become the best entrepreneurs.

Q *Historically, businesses have exploited human and natural resources until forced by law to stop. Even if the market becomes aware of abuses, it may not act or be able to act soon enough. And there are always those who will buy something no matter who or what it destroys. We have laws to protect us from tyrants, why not tycoons? Even now our rights in the workplace are like those of serfs in a feudal society. For some, the option of quitting is not there.*

A In a libertarian society, the option most likely *would* be there. Today, jobs are limited by government licensing and minimum wage laws. Without such regulation, jobs would be plentiful. Self-employment would be easier and more affordable. The unfettered marketplace is the only way to protect workers from exploitation.

Discrimination

W hen speaking to college students, I often hold up a copy of black economist Walter Williams' *The State Against Blacks* as easy-to-read documentation on the real root of discrimination – government!

Q *How does a libertarian address civil rights issues? Would there be laws prohibiting discrimination by businesses?*

A In a libertarian society, businesses could refuse service to individuals for any reason. However, they would be punished by losing the profit that they otherwise would have made. This feedback is so powerful, that even in the post-Civil War South, segregation could only be maintained when governments made integration (serving blacks and whites in the same establishment) a crime.[39]

If integration could only be stopped by outlawing it in the post-Civil War South, surely today it would take place readily without government mandates. If some individuals, black or white, wished to maintain some separateness, why should we force them together?

In a libertarian society, laws enforcing segregation could never have been passed in the first place. Slavery would never have been legal. In short, if the U.S. had been a totally libertarian society, Africans would never have been enslaved and given second-class status. Government creates conditions that foster racial prejudice, then creates backlash and further prejudice by forcing people together.

Q *I know that quotas are not in accord with the libertarian philosophy, but sometimes I think they might be helpful.*

A Quotas require expensive enforcement, which in turn, results in higher taxes and/or inflation. As a result, jobs are lost, primarily for those at the low end of the ladder (i.e., blacks, handicapped, etc.). Thus, for every disadvantaged person who might get hired because of quotas, several other disadvantaged people will lose their jobs. Like most aggression, quotas hurt the very people they are supposed to help.

Q *Why is it that libertarians are always quoting Thomas Jefferson as one of the leaders of individual freedom? Didn't he own slaves?*

A For the most part, Thomas Jefferson understood and articulated the libertarian ideal, but applied it initially only to his own race and sex. Many people of Jefferson's day believed that blacks and women were not true equals of white males. Later in life, Jefferson apparently realized his error.

For most us, libertarianism is more of an evolution than a complete and immediate change in perspective. Our culture is so steeped in aggression that full realization takes a while.

The implications of liberty reach out to impact our lives beyond the political. Libertarianism is a journey of transformation as we come to recognize its impact on our emotional and spiritual growth as well.

Q *How would a libertarian system deal with discrimination in a private business?*

A Just as we choose the people we want in our homes, we should be able to choose the people we want to serve in business. We should be able to choose to date people of the opposite or same sex as we choose. Such discrimination is a common and accepted facet of everyday life based on our preferences or prejudices.

Wholesale discrimination, which can be very destructive, usually occurs only through legislation. For example, after the Civil

War, whites ran ads in local newspapers suggesting that blacks shouldn't be hired, except at very low wages. Smart landowners soon found that if they disregarded this advice and paid their black workers well, they always had help when harvest time came around. Discrimination was too costly, so many people swallowed their prejudice in favor of their pocketbooks.

Enraged Southern bigots struck back by passing licensing laws that required trades people to pass literacy tests and have apprenticeships before hire. Even if a black person could perform the job, they could not legally be hired.[40]

Merchants began serving black customers, rather than turn away profit. Once again, the bigots turned to the government and passed laws prohibiting intermingling of blacks and whites in eating and other establishments. Since whites had more money and brought in more business, merchants naturally chose to exclude blacks.

In a libertarian society, the bigots would not have been able to pass these laws, many of which (e.g., licensing laws) are still hurting minorities by increasing the cost of entry into a profession. Indeed, the worst forms of discrimination are legal today but would not be so in a libertarian society.

Q *What laws would libertarians pass to get rid of discrimination in this country?*

A Libertarians would get rid of the laws that are the hidden roots of discrimination. First, adoption would be privatized so that interracial adoption would no longer be discouraged. Today, many white families are not permitted to adopt a minority infant, and so go oversees to Korea or China instead. Historically, interracial adoption has been the quickest, most effective means of integration.

In his book, *The State Against Blacks*, black economist Walter Williams notes that "the minimum wage law is one of the major causes of spiraling unemployment among young blacks." Minimum wage laws would be abolished to end such discrimination.

Licensing laws, many of which were first put into place to prohibit minorities from entering into the professions, would be ended.

Affirmative action and quotas employ a few token minorities while destroying the jobs of many more disadvantaged. In a libertarian nation, such laws would be abolished.

Discrimination will only end when we do away with the laws that create most of it.

Q *African-Americans suffer disproportionately from poverty in America. How do you propose to stop that?*

A Studies show that most poverty is created by government. When government regulates the workplace, the poor are left without jobs.[41]

Government regulations discriminate against minorities and the poor. Minorities know that "the system" is against them, but few understand the mechanism by which the system keeps them down. As a result, they are frustrated and racial hatred is exacerbated.

In a libertarian society, these minorities wouldn't be denied jobs through government regulation and would be able to partake in the American dream. Racial hatred would subside, if not fade entirely. Today, minorities thrown out of work by government regulation turn to the libertarian Institute for Justice (www.ij.org) for help.

Q *In a libertarian society where everything from housing, to health care, to education, to adoption, is privatized, how would the minority population – namely anyone not white, male, straight, and Christian – be guaranteed equal rights?*

For example, being a lesbian, I am afraid that a Catholic hospital (the only one for miles in my small town) will be allowed to deny me treatment, even for a broken bone, just because I'm gay. Personally, I'm of the opinion that if you can't be a doctor to everyone, maybe you should have chosen a different line of work.

A Your concern, a legitimate one, is that some service providers, for example, doctors or hospitals affiliated with some religious denominations, might refuse to treat gay people in a libertarian society. Sadly, they might, even though Christ regularly healed those who did not live by society's norms and were therefore called "sinners."

However, in a libertarian society, we wouldn't have today's morass of medical regulations which limit the number of health care practitioners and facilities. Instead of a single hospital in your neighborhood, you'd likely have more and better facilities to choose from. Most would probably do their best to help anyone who walked through their doors.

Prejudice doesn't end by legal decree. Indeed, people become more resentful towards groups that they are forced to tolerate, associate with, or treat. Consequently, laws which seem to protect minorities often harm them instead.

You suggest that perhaps a doctor who won't treat everyone shouldn't be a doctor. But legalizing that opinion opens the door to legalizing others such as "if you aren't marrying to procreate, you shouldn't be allowed to wed." Where would that leave the gay community?

Of course, in a libertarian society, laws discriminating against gay people would not exist. For instance, same-sex couples find themselves facing the same laws against intermarriage as blacks and whites once did. In a libertarian society, marriage would be a private contract between two willing individuals who could set the terms to suit themselves.

Too often, we want freedom of choice, but we don't want others to have it. We can only have freedom if we are willing to give it to others. Ironically, when we honor our neighbors' choices, they are much more likely to honor ours.

Q *Shouldn't a person have an inalienable right to rent an apartment or be employed regardless of sex preferences, etc.?*

A Anyone providing a service should not be forced, as they often are today, to take customers they don't want. Historically, while individual service providers might discriminate, customers don't usually have trouble finding willing vendors. That's why southern governments, for example, found it necessary to prohibit restaurants from serving both whites and blacks. Most businesses would rather overcome their prejudices than lose profitable customers.

As a personal example, I was a landlady in Michigan for 15 years. I found that many property owners did not want to rent to welfare recipients and low-income individuals because the rents were often uncollectable and they tended, as a group, to be more destructive of the premises. In spite of this, I saw an opportunity for profit and started specializing in rentals for low-income individuals. Potential profit drives service providers to work with such people in spite of the disincentives. Therefore, you can rest assured that prejudice will be very difficult to maintain where the government does not penalize service providers who do serve customers who aren't "mainstream."

The moral of the story is that the best way to get rid of prejudice is to honor our neighbors' choices, not try to enforce ours via government.

Q *If I own a gym or health club and want to hire people who appear to be physically fit, people who are overweight or otherwise appear unfit would have a case for a lawsuit against me.*

Suppose I owned an apartment and didn't want to rent my property to people whose sexual or religious lifestyles I don't support. Where are the lines drawn concerning rights in a libertarian view?

A In a libertarian society, the person who owns the fitness center or apartment complex decides whom to hire or service. In a libertarian society, your business is just as much your castle as your home is – you decide who comes and goes.

Discrimination is part of life. Heterosexuals discriminate against romantic involvement with same-sex individuals;

homosexuals discriminate against romantic involvement with opposite-sex individuals. What kind of society would we have if these lovers were forbidden by law to discriminate?

A worker has no "right" to a job created by someone else. The job only exists because of the person who created it. The job is therefore the property of the creator and he or she decides who it has been created for. The same applies to an apartment rental as well.

Helping the Poor

After ten years of rehabilitating low income housing, I had many anecdotes to make the case for liberty. Become active in your local community so that you too can speak from experience!

Q *Libertarians want to cut taxes for welfare. Don't you care if the poor starve?*

A I think that the poor deserve *more* than welfare; they deserve the chance to become wealthy. History proves that only liberty – not government handouts – can give them that chance.

About two-thirds of our welfare dollars, enough for each family of four to receive $50,000 annually, goes to the middle class social workers who administer these programs. On the other hand, two-thirds of each privately donated dollar goes to the needy.[42] Anyone who advocates welfare taxes is lobbying for subsidies for the well-to-do.

Welfare breaks up families by paying teens to get pregnant and by paying mothers to desert the father of their children. Welfare is a major force in the destruction of family values in minority households.

or, for Christians...

Christ always asked his followers to give to the poor, but never demanded it or forced anyone. Shouldn't we follow His example when trying to help others?

Q *Don't we have a duty to help the poor?*

A We certainly do have a duty to get rid of the minimum wage laws that prevent the poor from being paid for on-the-job training. We certainly do have a duty to get rid of licensing laws that make the poor pay up to $700,000 for a taxicab license.[43] In short, we must stop supporting laws that keep the poor out of the job market.

Q *What makes you so sure that people would help the poor if they weren't forced to do so through taxation?*

A We needn't worry that people wouldn't help the unfortunate in a libertarian society. If you value volunteer labor at minimum wage, private organizations today still provide twice as much help as public ones, in spite of the high taxes for social services. If people are willing to help the poor now, wouldn't they be even more likely to give generously when they were taxed less?

Q *In a libertarian society wouldn't disabled folks and single parents be living in the gutter and eating out of garbage cans?*

A Just the opposite! Studies confirm that free societies are the wealthiest and that their disadvantaged fare best. Contrary to popular opinion, free societies have the most even distribution of wealth. If these facts seem counter-intuitive, just ask yourself whether you'd prefer to be disadvantaged in a wealthy and relatively free society, like the U.S., or in a poor and highly regulated one, like Zimbabwe.

Government taxes and regulations generally hurt those that they are intended to help. The disadvantaged are least able to cope with such aggression from government and suffer the most from it, contrary to popular opinion. What a cruel betrayal for those with so much to cope with already!

Q *How would the handicapped fare in a libertarian society?*

A The handicapped would be less so in a free society. Without regulation, medical advances would skyrocket, giving these people new hope. Because of these advances, fewer of the handicapped would be disabled. Those still in need would receive more help than they do today, because society would be wealthier and fewer people would be poor.

Q *Your statement that in a libertarian society the "few still in need would receive more help than they do today because society would be wealthier" seems idealistic.*
     I don't wish to insult you but I will give you my honest reaction: when I read your phrase "the handicapped would be less so in a free society" it sickened me. Sure, there will always be medical advances. But as the sun rises in the morning there always will be infirmity and disabilities in this world.

A My reply wasn't flip; I've been in medical research for 25 years and am well aware of the impact of regulation on innovation. We have the medical knowledge today to stop many crippling birth defects and diabetic amputations, for example, but this information is rarely shared, because of FDA and other regulations. Research in medical devices, including ones that assist the handicapped, has been restricted in recent years as well.
     Naturally, not all disabilities would disappear in a libertarian world. However, in a wealthier world, people have more to give to others. In a world with fewer disabled and greater wealth, more money will be available to help smaller numbers of people. Assuming that human nature stays constant, this translates into more help per person.

Q *In a libertarian society what would happen to people who are mentally or physically unable to work (or perhaps unable to do skilled work due to disability), and who have no families to support* *them? Right now there are a number of people completely dependent on government in this way. Private charities, unlike government, cannot support totally disabled people in the long term.*

A Before government welfare, private charities owned and operated hospitals, orphanages, and mental institutions. Government simply took over this private sector function and does it poorly in comparison. Two-thirds of each tax dollar targeted for helping the disadvantaged goes to the middle-class administrators; over two-thirds of private donations actually reach the people that we're trying to help.[42] When people aren't forced to give to wasteful government welfare programs, they'll have more to give to efficient private charities.

Q *And on the same subject: What if private charities all just decide to close down? The massive influx of people expecting long-term aid from private organizations caused by recent welfare reform is already causing problems. This would be much more of a problem in a libertarian society. How would it be handled?*

A Because private charities are many and diverse, there's little risk that they'd all shut down for any reason. However, centralized government funding can easily be cut or eliminated by a handful of politicians, virtually overnight. When this happens, many needy people are displaced while the private sector races to catch up.

The needy are best served by those who care enough to volunteer time and money. They don't need the further abuse of being treated like a political football.

Q *I sit now as a quadriplegic in a power wheelchair. I have returned to work as a programmer and do not expect the government to take care of me. However, I'm lucky I was a programmer and not a carpenter.*

Before the Americans with Disabilities Act (ADA), buildings were routinely built without access to wheelchairs. That's a point I know

*firsthand and not debatable in my world. A business that loses wheel-
chair customers loses only a tiny amount of revenue. Those in wheelchairs, however, lose the dignity of being able to be as independent as
possible. Sure, large businesses such as Wal-Mart might still try to be
accessible. But the mall on the corner with only five or fifteen businesses
will find it economically convenient to only build for the vast majority of
their customers. Unless the human species has become significantly more
sensitive since 1992, I need only point to those malls built prior to that
date as proof of my point.*

A You are quite right. In a libertarian society, small businesses
probably wouldn't install wheelchair access. When I visited
Canada recently, some places didn't have access either. One of our
party was in a wheelchair. A couple of guys from our group simply
carried him wherever he wanted to go.

The question to ask yourself is this: Would you go to your
neighborhood businesses, gun in hand, and threaten them unless they
installed wheelchair access? Probably not. You most likely recognize
that a disability doesn't give anyone that right. Yet, if you support
ADA, you're asking your government to point that gun for you.

For some businesses just barely making it, such a demand
from government can cause them to shut down. Jobs are lost, prices
for competitive products rise, and everyone loses. The handicapped
pay a high price for those ramps, since they are hurt the most in a
market with high prices and high unemployment. To be sure, having
someone carry you over the threshold isn't always romantic, but at
least it's not violent.

Q *In response to all the questions about disability, you missed the
opportunity to point out that in a libertarian world, insurance
to cover those losses would be more readily available and affordable for
the following reasons: Insurance companies wouldn't have to pay outra-
geous punitive damage claims, nor would they incur the costs of legal
defense under a "loser pays" system. Consumers would be more likely to*

ensure that they were insured, rather than operate under the false sense of security that "the government will take care of me."

A Good point! You are correct; more people would be appropriately insured in a libertarian society.

For the disabled wanting to work, employment would be easier to get. Because of the Americans with Disabilities Act (ADA), many employers hesitate to hire the disabled, who might require extra concessions and are more difficult to fire if they don't work out. Consequently, employment of the disabled plummeted after passage of the ADA.[44]

Q *What is the libertarian solution for those who truly cannot help themselves, i.e. the very old, the disabled, etc., who have no family? Who takes care of them if all of government is paid for with "user fees?" Do we just let people starve?*

A On the contrary, countries with the most liberty care for their disadvantaged the best. Without the government restrictions that keep the disadvantaged out of the marketplace (e.g., licensing, minimum wage), many more people are employed. Because more people work, more wealth is created. Indeed, the U.S. became the richest nation on earth because it allowed many more of its poor to work.

Libertarians would provide charity for those not able to support themselves through private organizations, which deliver about ⅔ of every charitable dollar to the intended recipient. Most governments today spend two-thirds of each dollar on the social service bureaucracy instead.[42] Thus, the same charitable service would be provided in a libertarian society for a fraction of the cost!

We needn't worry that people wouldn't help the unfortunate in a libertarian society. If you value volunteer labor at minimum wage, private organizations today still provide twice as much help as public ones, in spite of the high taxes for social services. In a libertarian society, you could eliminate government help and part of the private charity sector and still provide more to the poor.

Q *Without government regulation, the gap between the rich and poor will widen. How can the Libertarian Party call itself the "Party of Principle" and yet advocate this?*

A Countries with less government intervention are more prosperous and have the most even distribution of wealth.[45] That's why a libertarian society would have fewer people in need of help. Let's get to the root cause of poverty and rip it out!

The poor fare better in free markets because entry into the workforce is easier. Many Europeans immigrated to the U.S. to escape the guilds and trade restrictions that kept them out of the labor market. Because the U.S. allowed its poor to work, it became the wealthiest nation on earth. Even the poor in the U.S. are better off than the middle class of less affluent nations.

Q *Separate studies from Harvard and Berkeley have both shown that increased income inequality worsens social problems including crime, bad health, bad education, etc. How would a libertarian society deal with the problem of income inequality?*

A Studies also show that free societies have a more even distribution of wealth than less free ones.[45] In other words, a libertarian society would "solve" the problem of inequality by having less of it in the first place. Any political attempts at redistribution inhibit the entire society's wealth creation, resulting in less for everyone.

Q *If somebody is injured and needs help, it is your legal duty to help him. How would a libertarian society handle this issue, and how would that affect victims?*

A People who are cold-hearted enough to refuse help to a bleeding stranger certainly aren't going to change their behavior because of the law! If anything, such people will make an even faster getaway, so that no one will be able to make positive identification of them.

It's very difficult, if not impossible, to force people to help each other. You cannot create a caring society at gunpoint, even when the gun is wielded by government. You can only succeed in teaching violence. Maybe that's why we have injured people who don't get help!

The great care-givers of history (e.g., Christ, Mother Teresa) taught by example. They did not force others to be "good Samaritans." Perhaps we can learn from their example.

Q *From what I'm reading, libertarians believe that all taxes should be eliminated as well as minimum wages, tariffs and farm subsidies. What about those who cannot afford needed services?*

A A libertarian society would enjoy more jobs and prosperity than we do today, so fewer people would be unemployed or poor. Services provided by the private sector instead of the government cost, on average, half as much. Only a few people in a libertarian society would have difficulty paying for services that they need.

In the prosperous libertarian society, private charity could easily help these unfortunates. After all, ⅔ of every private charity dollar goes to the needy, while only ⅓ of our tax dollar earmarked for welfare does.[42] Middle-class social workers and other administrators receive most of the taxes intended for the poor.

Q *Like many others in the United States today, I'm sick of governmental intervention in my personal life. Yet I question the libertarian stance concerning voluntary, charitable care of the less fortunate in our society. Most people are self-centered, rapacious, concerned primarily with their own self-aggrandizement. Thus my question: libertarianism and social care, a dichotomy?*

A Of course people are selfish! Libertarianism channels this selfishness to the service of others and gives the disadvantaged their best chance at becoming wealthy themselves.

In a free market, for example, you buy from the person who gives you the best quality for the lowest price. Since the poor are hungriest for your business, traditionally they will offer you the best deal. In serving you, they serve themselves.

Established businesses hate this kind of competition, so they go to the government and ask for regulations which cost so much to satisfy that they drive out their less affluent competitors. The existing businesses are, of course, "grandfathered" in.

I had a tenant who got caught in this trap. She provided child care in her apartment, which was fine with me. However, the city regulators shut her down because the apartment didn't meet their burdensome regulations, which did nothing to improve service. As a direct result, she ended up on welfare.

Our regulated economy creates poverty, then graciously offers welfare to those it has disenfranchised. In a free market, we'd have fewer poor, since most poverty today is created by government through regulations.[46]

Q *I agree with the majority of libertarian principles. I firmly believe in social and, above all, economic liberty. But when I try to argue this philosophy to others, they label it as "greedy." How do I answer these people without sounding miserly myself? I give to charity. Actually, I give more generously then my non-libertarian friends. Does not wanting to give my money to a government bureaucracy make me a Scrooge?*

A When your friends equate resistance to giving your money to the government to being a Scrooge, try helping them discover how they really feel. If they won the lottery and wanted to give 10% to charity, would they donate the money to private charities or government welfare programs? When they say "private charities" (as almost all will), ask them why. Let them make your arguments for you!

Q *What should we do with irresponsible people? You know, those who didn't save for retirement, or the ones in the hospitals with drug problems and diseases. Let 'em starve?*

A A libertarian society rewards responsibility; a welfare state punishes it through taxation. Thus, a libertarian society teaches responsibility so that people learn to make good decisions for themselves, instead of poor ones.

In addition, instead of being forced to contribute to wasteful government programs like Social Security, people in a libertarian society could contribute to private retirement plans. Unlike Social Security, these grow with time, instead of steadily eroding.

Those who didn't save for retirement would be able to continue working since a libertarian society would have no mandatory retirement age. For many people, continued employment is an attractive option, especially since retirement is associated with a greater mortality rate.

In summary, a libertarian culture would encourage responsibility and greatly lower the number of people in need. The greater wealth of a libertarian society means that more resources would be available to aid the few remaining unfortunates. A libertarian society provides the best "safety net" of all and is the last place where you would expect to find starvation.

Q *I am just learning about libertarianism and I have one question: what is the libertarian stance on support to low-income divorced women with children who might pursue education and need some support during this period? I do agree with Jeffersonian/libertarian values, but also realize we live in a modern world where families are often torn asunder, and some women (and hence some families) fall through and self-destruct. I see government support in that instance as* *good, but I see government in most every other area as negative and evil. Please consider this question.*

A Many charitable causes are worthy of our support. However, libertarians believe that this support works best when it is given through private, rather than public means. About ⅔ of every tax dollar that goes to social services funds the welfare bureaucracy instead of going to the needy recipients. Public aid, therefore, is very wasteful.[42]

On the other hand, private charities get ⅔ of each dollar to those we wish to help. If you won the lottery tomorrow and wanted to give 10% to help the women you describe, wouldn't you give it to a private charity that served this group rather than to an equivalent government program?

Q *The libertarian solutions you provide are fine if we can tolerate the failure of those we leave behind. Can we watch them grow sick, die, and live in wretched Third World conditions? I think not. Until someone learns how to hide these human failures, the world you want to see will never come. It may be logical, desirable and doable, but it will never come.*

A If you've followed my column, you should be aware that a libertarian world would be a prosperous one with a more even distribution of wealth than we have now. In a libertarian country or world, fewer people will be left behind than they are today.

Q *What is the libertarian position on unrestricted pregnancies by those that can't afford them? A whole host of social problems are caused by parents who can't afford to support their children, including overcrowded classrooms, jails filled with criminals of all levels, reductions in benefits to others, and more. And these children in turn repeat the cycle when they become of age.*

A Years ago, when I rented housing to low income tenants, young unwed teens would frankly tell me that their pregnancy helped them to establish their own household. One mother of three even advised me to quit my day job so that I could get on welfare and enjoy life!

When you subsidize anything, you get more of it. Paying teens even a pittance to have more children encourages them to do so. By the time they are old enough to vote, they finally realize that they will always be poor unless they can get into the work force. By then, however, it is almost too late. Unless a relative helps out, child care costs are prohibitive for someone starting in an entry level job. They find themselves forever stuck in the "Poverty Trap."

In contrast, when welfare programs stop paying women to have children, pregnancies plummet. A libertarian society wouldn't have taxpayer-guaranteed programs to reward those who had children that they couldn't afford, so fewer would. Unlike government, liberty rewards, and thus encourages, responsible behavior. Parents, children and society as a whole would benefit enormously.

Q *In every human endeavor that has been measured, humanity shows a distribution of talent, ability, error, height, weight, intellectual capacity, etc., that follows the traditional bell-shaped curve. So, then, my question: How do libertarians, with their "pull yourself up by your boot straps" outlook, propose to deal with those on the left side of the curve? To blithely say that "privatization of welfare," private charity, and so on will take care of these more unfortunate folks is simply "pie in the sky" thinking.*

A Libertarian societies will be wealthier than other countries because the poor are given the opportunity to work. European immigrants, for example, came to the U.S. to escape the guilds and trade restrictions that kept them out of the labor market. Thus, the first thing a libertarian society does to help the "left side" is to shift as many people as possible further into the middle. Because almost everyone is better off in a libertarian society, more charity is available for the few who cannot support themselves.

When help is given privately, approximately ⅔ of each charitable dollar gets to a worthy recipient. Only ⅓ of each tax welfare dollar reaches the poor; most of the money goes to pay the salaries of the social workers. In addition, welfare harms the poor by discouraging them from entering the work force.[46] After ten years of personally working with welfare recipients, I can attest that the system does the poor more harm than good.

Q *I agree with most libertarian views, but how would a libertarian society solve the present income gap? In a libertarian society, wouldn't the rich just get richer?*

A The rich would get richer, but the poor would make even bigger gains. Most poverty today is caused by government regulations which especially penalize the poor.

Studies clearly show that government intrusion in the economy decreases a country's wealth creation. Countries with more wealth creation (i.e., those that are closest to the libertarian ideal) have a more even distribution of wealth. In other words, the poor become less so in a libertarian society.

When the Statue of Liberty was erected, government was the acknowledged enemy of the poor. Lady Liberty asked for the poor, the wretched refuse, the masses, not the wealthy or skilled. Why? Because everyone understood that the poor prospered best when government didn't put them out of their jobs with excessive regulation. In the 1800s, for example, guild membership was required in Europe to work in certain occupations and the poor had a difficult time qualifying.

For examples of how today's poor and minorities are put out of business by government and defended pro bono by libertarians, visit the Institute for Justice's Web site at www.ij.org. You'll see living proof that liberty, not government, is the true friend of the poor.

Q *Libertarianism is all very well, but what about our collective responsibility to those less fortunate? Is there not a danger that* *libertarianism will degenerate into individual greed and selfishness, and a disregard for others and the environment? Never forget that the great majority of humanity lives in conditions of desperate poverty.*

A The libertarian principle of non-aggression shows profound respect for our neighbors. We tolerate behavior that might even be repugnant to us by refusing to forcibly bend our neighbors to our will, even through government. Why would you think that such extraordinary respect would degenerate into greed and selfishness?

Societies that practice this respect, tolerance, and high regard for their neighbors (and their property) have the cleanest environments. When everything is individually owned and respected, damage to the environment is minimal. In contrast, where people or governments don't respect others' property, the environment (property) suffers. On the whole, owners take better care of their little piece of the environment than bureaucrats do.

Libertarian societies also create immense wealth primarily because their poor are not excluded from the labor market. Studies show that the closer a country is to the libertarian ideal, the more even is its distribution of wealth (i.e., the poor are better off). Thus, a libertarian society does very well by its poor automatically.

In countries with the desperate poverty that you speak of, government regulations make it difficult for a poor person to become affluent. Land and jobs can only be had by those wealthy enough to jump the regulatory hurdles. Eliminating the cause of poverty (i.e., government barriers to working) is the best help that we can give to the unfortunate.

Q *I recently visited the Philippines. I spent my time in and around Manila. There was very little government involvement in most people's lives. You could put up a shanty just about anywhere you wanted. Isn't this a case where the government could have improved everyone's lives by restricting freedom?*

A In the Philippines, as in many underdeveloped nations, government rarely grants title to the lands homesteaded by the populace. People have squatted on the land, traded and sold it, all without what we would call "clear and legal title." About 57% of the land in the Philippines is in this legal limbo.[47] Consequently, people don't put much money into their homes. They can't get mortgages or loans for improvements because they can't use the land as collateral.

People can gain formal title only after jumping through a morass of bureaucratic hoops for several years. The few who persevere and manage to gain clear title then convert their cardboard shanties into better homes. Where formal and informal communities exist side-by-side, this difference is clearly seen. Rather than enforce building codes, government should make the process for formalizing title easier.

Enforcing building codes will only create homelessness. Even in the United States, about half of the homelessness is caused by building restrictions, rent control, and zoning regulations that drive up the cost of housing.[48] When housing prices go up, people end up in the streets, not in better homes.

Forcing employers to pay workers more encourages employers to mechanize, decreasing the number of jobs. Consequently, countries with the highest level of unionization also have the most unemployment.[49] The most skilled workers get higher wages; the less skilled end up with no wages at all!

You truly seem to care about the Third World poor. That's great! I hope this will help you discover what works – and what doesn't work – to improve living conditions.

Abortion

When campaigning, I would state my personal position (pro-rights), but advise my listeners that some libertarians of good conscience think differently.

Q *I am pro-life. I'm curious to know if other libertarians hold this view, or if I am alone on this.*

A You are not alone. Just as in other parties and organizations, the abortion issue is hotly debated among libertarians.

In general, libertarians are split into three camps, all believing that their view best expresses the non-aggression principle.

The group which identifies with the "pro-life" viewpoint feels that a couple engaging in sexual relations should be responsible for the results of their actions. If a child is conceived who cannot fend for himself, the parents are responsible for caring for him until he can. Abortion is viewed as murder of an innocent.

The predominant "pro-choice" viewpoint is backed by principled arguments as well. Libertarians believe that no one should be forced to support another. If a woman has chosen to gift a fetus with life, it does not necessarily follow that she is obligated to continue to support it with her body, especially if that support threatens the woman's life. A woman's body is her property, to do with as she wishes.

Libertarians of this persuasion generally believe that parents do not have a legal duty to support their offspring, although most parents gladly do so. Obviously, children's rights are a related and unresolved issue between these two viewpoints.

Another perspective, which I call "pro-rights," is that the fetus, by definition, is part of the woman's body as long as it cannot be sustained outside of her: "Her body, her choice."

However, once the fetus could live outside the mother, pro-rights libertarians argue that a live birth, rather than an abortion, is the proper method for a woman to exercise property rights over her body. Just as you would ask a trespasser to leave, rather than blast him or her away without warning, so too should a woman evict a fetus in the least forceful way possible. Those wishing to adopt the newborn could then assume the costs of caring for the premature infant and become its legal guardian.

Q *Even though I'm pro-choice, I think that abortions are abhorrent. Is there anything that libertarians can do to stop them?*

A If we truly want to stop abortion, we must make abortion obsolete. Because of its increased wealth and tolerance, a libertarian society is best equipped to do that.

Libertarians advocate changes that support a woman in continuing an unwanted pregnancy. A prospective mother has more options in a society that encourages, rather than discourages, interracial adoption, honors contracts between prospective parents and surrogate mothers, and enjoys the increased prosperity that makes children more affordable. A libertarian society is best equipped to fund research in more effective contraception and in the ability to transfer a fetus to a willing mother. All of these advancements make abortion a less attractive and less necessary option. Few, if any, doctors will be willing to end a life when doing so becomes unnecessary.

If people on both sides of the abortion question would give the same amount of time, money, and effort as they do to political lobbying to promoting the changes described above, abortion would indeed quickly become obsolete.

Q *In a libertarian government would a woman be able to have an abortion any time as long as the umbilical cord is still connected?*

A Abortion is a controversial subject in our society and among libertarians. The Libertarian Party platform, for example, acknowledges that principled arguments can be made for either side. If you have strong feelings on the matter, join the debate!

Let me share my personal beliefs on the matter. Remember that not all libertarians, pro-choice or otherwise, think this way.

Since the embryo in the early stages of pregnancy can't live outside its mother, it is truly part of her body and not a separate individual. During this time period, a woman having an abortion is exercising property rights over her body, not killing a being separate from herself. She is the individual with rights. The embryo, at this point in time, is not an individual.

Once a fetus is old enough to live outside the womb, the woman is still under no moral obligation to carry the child to term. Just as she can invite people to her house, change her mind, and ask them to leave, she can invite an embryo to grow inside of her body, change her mind, and "ask" it to leave. However, if her unwanted guests don't leave immediately, she wouldn't just pull out a gun and shoot them. That would be (excuse the pun) "overkill." Libertarians believe in using only the amount of force necessary to defend one's self and property. Going farther turns defenders into aggressors and puts them in the wrong.

Abortion at this latter stage of pregnancy is, in my opinion, overkill, because the fetus can now live outside the mother.

Instead of abortion, delivery could be induced and adoptive parents could take over the time and expense of nurturing the infant. When technology enables any embryo or fetus to grow outside the mother into a healthy infant, abortion will become obsolete. A libertarian society makes medical advances and adoptions easier and quicker, enabling this day to come much faster.

Q *Dr. Ruwart, I just wanted to thank you for putting the link to the Libertarians For Life page (www.l4l.org) on your short answer on abortion. There are a lot of us out here who disagree with your position on abortion and still stay devoted libertarians. I just wanted* *to share my appreciation for your openness to different positions on the issue and your willingness to share the other side of this issue.*

A I appreciate your response as well. No one likes the idea of abortion; we all look forward to the day when it is obsolete.

Abortion is such a heated issue that our emotions often get in the way of understanding the other side. Without that understanding, we can't present our own point of view in a way that has merit to our "opponents." Instead of discussing until we come to resolution, we start name-calling and fighting, making enemies instead of friends.

You obviously understand this. By responding positively, you've set an example for all of us to follow. When we are talking and sharing, instead of snarling and hissing, we increase the chances of finding a resolution that we can all support.

All libertarians use the non-aggression principle as their yardstick of behavior. However, the application of that principle is not always crystal clear on every issue. It's a real-life challenge. How do we as libertarians proceed?

My preference is to honor libertarians who disagree with me on the abortion issue (or any others). Very few libertarians agree on everything. I am delighted to engage in respectful discussion. I thank you especially for setting an example for us! My fervent hope is that somehow, some way, we can find unity in this diversity.

Family Values and Children's Rights

C hildren's rights are still a hotly debated issue among libertarians. Feel free to contribute!

Q *Do children have rights in libertarian society?*

A Since we are born with our rights, children have the same rights (and responsibilities) as adults. Normally, however, they can only exercise them with the help of a loving parent or guardian because they are physically incapable of doing so during their early years.

For example, young people have the responsibility to support themselves, but parents usually do this job for a couple decades. In return, parents expect children to accept the ground rules for living in the family unit and the consequences of violating them (e.g., "You'll be grounded if you don't come home on time").

Q *What if parents don't want to support their children? Are they obligated to do so in a libertarian society? Can the government force them to do so?*

A Not all libertarians agree on the answers to these questions. Some believe that bringing children into the world comes with an obligation to care for them until they can support themselves. This may be a life-long commitment, especially if the children are physically or mentally unable to support themselves.

Others believe that giving the gift of life does not obligate parents to support that life. However, once a child is born, killing it is a violation of the non-aggression principle. Consequently, parents who didn't want a child would most likely be expected to give it to an adoption agency so that it could be placed with people who would lovingly provide for it.

Q *How would children be protected from abusive parents in a libertarian society? Let's keep in mind the fact that abuse is often done in the manner calculated to avoid detection, so the probable cause necessary for criminal prosecutions may be very difficult to establish.*

A Abused children could ask friends or relatives to take them in. Unlike today, children would not be considered property of their parents or the state. If they wanted to live with a more caring adult, their wishes would be respected more frequently.

In the case of an abused infant, a concerned neighbor or relative could assume temporary guardianship. If necessary, they could petition the court on the child's behalf.

Children who won't admit to abuse or who are kept hidden will have a difficult time, whether in today's society or a libertarian one. However, libertarian societies are more likely to be neighborly, so abuses might be more readily detected.

Q *Are children treated special, so that society would have to create laws that restrict children's access to items such as cigarettes and pornography, or are there no such laws and all such decisions are left up to the parent?*

A A libertarian society would not have laws that discriminate on the basis of age. Parents who were concerned about sales to minors, however, should be able to convince store owners to establish their own age requirement. After all, the parents are generally better customers than the children! Businesses tend to favor the wishes of their best clientele.

Owners who actively encouraged sales of cigarettes or pornography to minors could be effectively boycotted in communities that felt strongly about such issues.

Q *Should children be allowed to work, vote, marry, have sex, drive, own a gun, have the right to enter into contracts, etc.?*

A Libertarians acknowledge that children have rights, such as the ones you've enumerated, but often disagree as to how they apply. In practice, children's rights are limited by their inability to take responsibility for their choices. For example, a child who wishes to work, but can't convince his or her parents to provide the necessary transportation, will be unable to exercise that right.

Q *How do you determine when children are ready to enter into contracts? Will the laws specify the age of majority? Would parents decide? The child?*

A In practice, you would decide if the child was old enough to enter into a contract with you. Is the child willing and able to provide the contracted service to you? If so, what kind of recourse would you expect from the courts if the child refuses to provide the contracted service?

The age of majority for marriage, work, etc., is most often established by custom of the society and will vary with the individual's circumstances rather than being dictated by law.

Q *What about orphanages and adoptions in a libertarian society? Will they be privately funded? If so, who will regulate these businesses to make sure the children are taken care of?*

A Orphanages and adoption agencies would be run privately in a libertarian society, as they were in the past. The needless suffering caused by the political agenda of today's institutions would finally come to an end.

For example, many affluent white couples who want a baby would gladly take one of the many disadvantaged black infants – even "crack" babies. For years, government policy, however, dictated that black babies shouldn't be adopted by white couples.[50] Instead, the children ended up in foster homes while their frustrated would-be parents imported a child from Korea or China!

Traditionally, government-run adoption centers have looked unfavorably on single individuals and middle-aged couples wishing to adopt. In today's society, where single parents are common and many women delay child-bearing until their forties, it seems especially cruel to deny a child a home on such grounds.

In a libertarian society, without these bureaucratic roadblocks, more children would be adopted than ever before. Agencies would probably be paid directly by the adoptive parents. Agencies which could show that their adoptees end up in happy and healthy families would be most likely to be given custody by courts or unwed mothers. Orphanages and adoption agencies in a libertarian society, therefore, would only survive if they did their jobs well.

In recent years, the courts have allowed children to be torn from their homes because of suspected drug use by their caregivers. When the parents are not formally charged, they don't even have the opportunity to prove their innocence. Whatever the lifestyle of the parents, most children who suffer no direct abuse are better off in their own family. Why rip them from their home only to place them then in a succession of foster care homes?

Q *Would same sex couples be allowed to adopt in a libertarian society?*

A Each adoption agency would probably set its own standards for prospective families. There would be no legal barriers, however, so agencies or mothers wishing to give up their children for adoption could choose the people they felt would provide the best home.

Q *What would be your short answer to Elian Gonzalez being seized at 5:15am by INS agents? He was the young Cuban boy living with relatives in Miami, who was sent back to Cuba (from where he had recently escaped) due to a custody claim by his father. Am I the only person to be terrified by this?*

A You certainly aren't the only person who's terrified! If the government wanted Elian, they could take the matter to court just as you or I would have to do in a custody dispute.

Forcibly kidnapping Elian was bad enough, but terrorizing him with storm troopers at 5am doesn't suggest compassion for his plight. The government claimed it was trying to save the abused children at Waco too, but their means – tanks, tear gas, and machine guns – created a horrifying end for those innocents.

Actions speak louder than words. What do our government's actions say?

Q *Why do so many "good" kids turn "bad"?*

A I'm not aware of any official research in this area, but I do have some ideas of my own, if that would help you.

We teach our children the non-aggression principle of libertarianism when they interact with their playmates. "Don't hit, don't steal, don't lie," we tell them. "Don't be the first to start a fight. If no one hits, steals, or lies first, there can be no fights."

However, on the societal level, we teach aggression. Our children are forced, by law, to go to school, take certain subjects, attend for a specified number of days per year for a specified period of years. The parents are forced, by law, to pay the taxes to support them, even if their children go to private schools.

In school, children are taught that stealing is OK as long as the majority thinks it's for a good cause and the process is called "taxation." Children are taught that it's OK to break your word as long as it's a "campaign promise." Finally, children learn that it's OK to kill those who have done you no harm (e.g., Afghan peasants) as long as you do it while hunting bad guys like bin Laden.

Is it any wonder that our children get confused?

Q *Would the state be involved in marriage anymore, such as marriage licenses?*

A No. Marriage licenses were first instituted, at least in the U.S., to keep couples of different races from marrying. Why should the state have anything to say about whom you spend your life with?

Q *Would polygamy be legal in a libertarian society?*

A The state would no longer regulate marriage or define what constituted a family in a libertarian society. Any structure that was agreed to by all the participants would be possible.

Q *How would same sex marriages be treated by insurance companies in a libertarian society?*

A Each insurance company would define what structures it recognized for its purposes. Families could shop around to find the insurance arrangement that suited them best.

Q *How would a libertarian society insure that a divorced mother would receive adequate financial support from deadbeat dads without resorting to force like that used today?*

A In a libertarian society, couples would probably have marriage contracts that specified the duties of each, including financial support of any offspring. If one partner violated their contract, the other could sue for compliance. Force might still be required if the violator refused to pay up. However, when people agree ahead of time as to what their responsibilities are, they are more likely to live up to them.

Today, however, no one really knows what they're committing to when they marry. The judge and the current state laws determine what is owed and by whom. People rarely feel responsible for commitments that they haven't agreed to ahead of time. Fathers probably feel especially discriminated against, since they have a more difficult time getting custody and a harder time getting child support if they do.

In summary, a marriage contract would do much to eliminate the "deadbeat dad" syndrome.

Q *I think your answer to the child support/deadbeat dad question leaves something to be desired.*

Even in a libertarian world some things are presumed. When you marry, you promise to "love, honor, and obey." So it's a bit vague, but the parties agreed and, given the nature of the relationship, that promise should be construed broadly. More to the point, however, when the parties have children, they each implicitly agree to support the child. This is presumed as a necessary and proper consequence of the reproductive acts the parties took. Wouldn't you agree? To suggest that nobody really knows what they are agreeing to in a marriage is not a satisfactory libertarian position, especially when it comes to children.

A Yes, it *is* unsatisfactory that no one really knows what they are agreeing to when they marry. In a libertarian society, instead of a one-size-fits-all marriage, defined after the fact, a marriage contract could be individually tailored to a couple's needs.

I use the phrase "defined after the fact" because the jurisdiction in which a couple divorces decides what couples actually agreed to when they married. A divorcing couple is subject to the laws of the state they divorce in, not the laws of the state that they marry in. In some states, all separately owned property becomes joint after marriage; in others, couples can retain property that was theirs prior to marriage. Some states rarely will give men custody of their children; in others, they have equal footing with their spouses.

State laws are themselves subject to judicial interpretation. Even if the couple agrees between themselves what their commitment entails, the law may tell them differently. The courts often disregard prenuptial agreements instead of enforcing them.

My divorce in the mid-70s illustrates this uncertainty. My soon-to-be-ex and I agreed on a property settlement, hired a single attorney, and asked the court to rubber-stamp our divorce. Instead, the judge counseled my husband that the laws of the state entitled him to alimony and encouraged him to sue for it! He never even asked my husband if we had considered my higher income in our settlement.

Since my husband was a man of integrity, he declined the judge's invitation. However, the judge did not give up easily. He continued to badger my husband, who gained my respect in his steadfast refusal to substitute the state's viewpoint for our own.

However, many couples in the throes of divorce find that legally eviscerating their soon-to-be ex is an irresistible temptation. The spouse on the receiving end feels betrayed and not morally obligated to comply.

Q *Are you also meaning to say that, without a written contract, the guy is off the hook for support? His act of having the child with his wife (and vice-versa) is the same as a promise to support the child, to follow through with a responsibility that is presumed in the act of reproducing children.*

A I'm saying that without a contract, misunderstandings about what has been agreed to are almost inevitable. The subsequent arguments cause animosity and often result in a refusal to abide by a court-ordered settlement which is viewed as unfair. By having issues like custody, support levels, etc., discussed and agreed to in writing before marital problems arise, the chances that the settlement will be viewed as fair and binding are increased.

We wouldn't dream of going into business with someone else without a written partnership agreement, because we know that we'd be asking for trouble. However, we enter into the more serious business of procreating without even a word about supporting offspring, and perhaps a promise "to love, honor, and obey" our spouse, depending upon whether the marriage is secular or religious. What has been promised is strictly a matter of opinion.

Q *Like most people, I want to live my life as I see fit, with consideration of others' right to do so. My question is, do libertarians esteem the traditional family and its supposed values over alternative lifestyles? Will single people continue to be discriminated against?*

A Libertarians honor all lifestyles. People of one way of life should not be sacrificed to others or ask that others be sacrificed to them. This live-and-let-live approach allows everyone to pursue their happiness in peace, whether they are "traditional" or "non-traditional" with regard to family, marriage, or lifestyle. This is certainly better than continuing to fight culture wars in the political realm, where different sides attempt to force their values on others.

As to your question about single people: One way singles are discriminated against is through the tax code. Since libertarians believe that taxation is immoral, this form of discrimination would surely end!

Animal Rights

A nimal Rights advocates ask us to consider "What is the proper code of conduct between species?"

Q *Do libertarians believe that animals are property and have no rights?*

A The libertarian philosophy only addresses relations between human beings. However, our predominant cultural norm is that animals are property. If you accept this cultural norm, then libertarianism allows owners sole discretion over that property.

If you're one of the people who are challenging this cultural belief, and think that animals are more than property, a consistent paradigm is needed. Please feel free to offer one. I have so far failed to come across a satisfactory philosophy of animal/human interaction.

Q *What is the situation with abuse of animals? If we allow someone to purchase or raise dogs, does that give them the right to abuse them for amusement?*

A I certainly wouldn't want to live in a society where animals were mistreated. In a libertarian society, a person who abused their animals would most likely be visited by concerned neighbors. If the abuser showed no remorse, the neighbors might ostracize the abuser, refusing to associate or do business with him or her.

If the abuse continued, the neighbors might attempt to rescue the suffering animals. If the abuser sued, a libertarian jury would have to decide if he or she was due compensation.

If compensation was awarded to the abuser, the rescuers might gladly pay it as a cost of saving the animals. Such compensation might allow the abuser to save face, but the public exposure would likely dissuade him or her from purchasing more animals to abuse.

Animals might gain a semblance of rights in a libertarian society if juries failed to award abusers compensation for the rescued animals. Failure to award compensation would essentially be a verdict of "not property."

Such a recognition of rights has precedent. Prior to the Civil War, even in the North, it was illegal to help slaves escape from their owners. However, juries often acknowledged the rights of escaped slaves and those who assisted them by returning a verdict of "not guilty" when they were tried. It is conceivable that the same thing could happen in respect to animals in the future.

The War on Drugs

Libertarians should be proud of their stand on the Drug War; only re-legalization will keep the pushers out of schools.

Q *We need to outlaw drugs to protect our children.*

A To save our children, we need to get drugs out of our schools. The only way to do that is to take the profit out through re-legalization. You don't see pushers selling tobacco and alcohol in the schools because there isn't the profit margin that prohibition brings. If we're serious about saving our kids, we have to stop the pushers by slashing their profits.

The War on Drugs can't even keep drugs out of our well-guarded prisons. How can we be so naive as to think it can keep them out of our schools?

Q *If we legalize drugs, won't more people turn to crime to fund their drug addiction?*

A Making drugs illegal drives up their prices a hundred-fold, so addicts must steal to support their habit. People rarely steal to buy alcohol or cigarettes, even though these substances are addictive too. Decriminalizing drugs will end the stealing and make our streets safer.

Q *If we legalize drugs, won't more people die?*

A The War on Drugs is killing more people than the drugs themselves. Contaminated needles are the number one cause of AIDS transmission in the U.S. Almost 80% of drug related deaths wouldn't occur if users had access to standardized doses and purity.[51]

Q *Doesn't keeping drugs illegal save lives?*

A No! The war on drugs kills more people than the drugs themselves.

Approximately 7,000 people die each year from drug overdose. However, 80% of these drug deaths (about 5,600) are due to impurities and other factors that would not be present in legal preparations.

Because needle sales are banned, shared needles have become the primary mode of AIDS transmission in the U.S. (approximately 3,500 new cases/year). The turf wars over drug territory result in gang shootings in which innocents (1,600 annually) are killed. Because drug prohibition makes the price of drugs almost 100 times higher than they otherwise would be, addicts rob to support their habit, killing many of their victims in the process (about 750 each year).

Thus, the death toll caused by the War on Drugs (5600+3500+1600+750=11,450) is about 8 times higher than it would be if drugs were legal (20% of 7000=1400/year). Since almost one out of eight people in the U.S. use illegal drugs regularly, the whole population would have to use them in a legal setting for the death toll to be as high as it is under drug prohibition.

These estimates are consistent with the death toll per capita from drugs in Amsterdam, which does not prosecute users. Only an average of 60 people per year are killed by drugs in a population 20 times less than that of the U.S.[52]

Q *We have to keep drugs illegal or else we will have a society of deadbeats!*

A It hasn't happened in the Netherlands or Portugal, where drug users aren't prosecuted, why would you expect it to happen here? Before hard drugs were outlawed earlier in this century, U.S. pharmacies sold opiates openly and addiction was not a problem. Real-life experience should reassure you on this point.

Q *If drugs are legalized, won't a lot more people start using them, creating societal havoc?*

A In the Netherlands, where marijuana is legal and hard drug users are not prosecuted, addiction is declining among the population as a whole, especially among youngsters.[53] Most likely, pushers left the schools once the immense profit, a by-product of drug prohibition, was gone.

Many people in our society are addicted to alcohol, yet we wisely treat alcoholism as a disease. As a result, drinking has gone down in the last several decades, not up. Because of its dangers, alcohol is shunned by many people and used carefully by most others. History suggests that people will treat re-legalized drugs in the same manner.

Q *We have to ban drugs because they are so harmful.*

A Alcohol and tobacco are both more addictive and more dangerous than marijuana or other street drugs. While only 7,000 people a year die from drug overdoses, over 100,000 per year die from alcohol-related causes and over 300,000 per year die from tobacco.[52]

Q *In addition to the Drug War, we should ban tobacco and alcohol as well.*

A We tried to ban alcohol and it didn't work (Prohibition). Outlawing something that people want doesn't stop them from getting it. The only way to protect people from themselves is to show them a better way. Every dollar we spend on the Drug War is a dollar that enriches the dealers instead of educating the drug users.

Overeating kills more people with cardiovascular disease than alcohol, drugs, or tobacco. Should we pass a law to monitor the caloric intake of each person or should we spread the word about the dangers of weight gain?

Q *We don't need medical marijuana because the active ingredient, THC, is already available by prescription.*

A THC is available in oral form in discrete doses. While smoking allows the dose to be adjusted exactly as the individual needs it, pills can result in overdose or underdose. In addition, large amounts of THC must be taken for the drug to be effective orally. These large doses can irritate the stomach and cause vomiting. In patients taking THC for nausea, such a side effect can be self-defeating.

My sister Martie was vomiting constantly from the cancer that blocked her gut, yet her doctor refused her request for such a prescription. Doctors are discouraged by the paperwork and the justification that THC prescriptions require by law.

Patients who do persuade their doctor to prescribe THC will spend an average of six hundred dollars per month for the drug instead of the pennies it would cost them to grow their own marijuana.

Q *Marijuana should not be legalized for medical use because it will lead to harder drugs.*

A We offer our terminally ill patients all the addictive narcotics they want, so why forbid them the use of marijuana to fight the pain that narcotics can't soothe? Should we throw little old ladies in jail because they dare to use marijuana to prevent the blindness of glaucoma? Should we let our cancer patients quit chemotherapy because the nausea and vomiting are unbearable without marijuana? Where is our compassion and our sense of perspective? How can we be so cruel?

Q *It seems to me that if you decriminalize drug usage and do end the drug war, drug kingpins aren't just going to sit idly by. How can we keep the peace and protect people from drug violence and gang warfare after drugs are decriminalized?*

A When alcohol Prohibition ended, the gang wars ended, too. The Mafia focused on other illegal activities when re-legalization took the profit out of booze. Crime decreased dramatically and so did the need for police.

When we end drug prohibition, we can expect the pushers to fade quietly away also. When we re-legalize drugs, we'll take away the black market profit that attracts the criminal element. Drug wars will stop because they won't be worth winning. People won't need to steal to support their habit because legalization lowers prices. Just as with alcohol Prohibition, crime will decrease dramatically, freeing up 50% of our police and judicial resources, which are now consumed by drug prohibition.

Q *In a newly libertarian society where marijuana and other now-illegal drugs were once again legal, what would happen to the huge numbers of imprisoned citizens in prison for simple possession, distribution or other non-violent drug-related crimes?*

A Libertarians would free such people, who never should have been sent to prison in the first place. Most Libertarian Party presidential candidates, for example, have pledged to release peaceful individuals who are in prison for so-called "victimless crime" laws as one of their first official acts. In many cases, the only "crime" these individuals committed was trying to feel good through a chemical high. They are victims of government oppression.

Those who are addicted to drugs and are unable to hold down a job or function well in society need our help, not a jail cell. In a libertarian society, people with a substance abuse problem would be able to get the help they need without the fear of being incarcerated.

Q *Imagine a drug, let's call it "murdercycline," that creates in those who ingest it a strong desire to murder another human being. Yep, it's obviously imaginary – so far – but the question is nevertheless valid: Should it be legal?*

A Obviously, taking "murdercycline" must have benefits, since few people would risk a murder charge otherwise. In a libertarian society, a person who wanted these benefits might only take such a drug after having a friend tie them up or otherwise confine them.

Alcohol presents us with a similar problem. If we want to get giddy, we ask someone else to drive. If we take certain medicines, we avoid driving as well.

People who don't care if they harm others or who just don't think about consequences aren't stopped by laws banning alcohol or other drugs. Only a society that encourages responsibility at every turn has a chance of enlightening such people before they harm others.

Q *A friend of mine broke free of his addiction and has turned his life around. But his wife continued to take drugs, telling him that if he loved her he would continue also. She spent the family's money on drugs, leaving the kids hungry and dirty. In order to protect the kids and himself, my friend divorced his wife.*

My question is, how would this have turned out if the father went before a judge and claimed he wanted to end his wife's child custody and visitation rights because she's doing something that's legal?

A If the drug in question had been alcohol, a legal "recreational" drug, your story and its outcome would likely be the same. Indeed, alcohol is a much bigger problem than all the illegal drugs put together. About 7,000 people die every year from drug overdose, but 100,000 from alcohol-related causes. The number of families destroyed by alcohol are likewise more numerous than those destroyed directly by illegal drugs (as opposed to indirectly through the War on Drugs). With alcohol, however, people can admit to their problem before it overcomes them and get help without risking imprisonment.

A knee-jerk reaction to these numbers might be "Let's outlaw alcohol, too." Prohibition was tried earlier in the 20th century and failed to help the problem, just as the War on Drugs is failing today.

Q *I am leaning toward libertarianism, but I am concerned about the ramifications of free drug use. I am an executive in a transportation company (school buses, motor coaches) and I shudder to think what would happen if my school bus drivers came to work still high from marijuana or crack or cocaine.*

A As an employer, you could, in a libertarian society, require your employees to abstain from alcohol, drugs, etc., before coming to work. Airlines today have such requirements for alcohol, even though it is completely legal, to make sure that pilots are sober. Naturally, their insurance rates and accident rates would go up without this requirement, so it's in the airlines' best interest to have it.

Q *I believe that many young people are attracted to selling drugs because of the money that's involved. They see one neighbor working hard at a fast food place for minimum wage while another neighbor, involved in the drug trade, has plenty of money and drives a flashy car. That lifestyle draws them in. Do you agree?*

A I suspect you are right. According to a 2003 survey reported by the U.S. Department of Health and Human Services' Substance Abuse and Mental Health Services Administration, more than 900,000 teenagers sell drugs.

For disadvantaged youth especially, the drug trade may well be the most accessible and lucrative profession open to them. The government adds to the economic woes of these kids by giving them poor educations in government schools, and then destroying hundreds of thousands of entry-level jobs through job-killing policies like minimum wage laws.

In contrast, we rarely see kids selling alcohol because it's legal, if only for adults. Because drugs are illegal, a lucrative black market in drugs exists. Criminals are happy to offer kids a chance to make money selling drugs.

Today's War on Drugs is just repeating the mistakes of 1920s-era alcohol Prohibition on a far larger scale. If we want to get one million kids out of the drug trade, the only way to do that is to end the War on Drugs, just as America ended the horrors of alcohol Prohibition by repealing it in 1933.

Assisted Suicide

O n this issue, I speak from personal experience. My sister, Martie, was Dr. Kevorkian's fourteenth patient. After hundreds of radio and TV shows, I found the following questions to be the most frequently asked.

Q *Suicide is against God's law and should be banned, whether it's assisted or not!*

A At least one of Dr. Kevorkian's patients, Martie Ruwart, felt that he was sent to her by God to ease her suffering. Obviously, each person's attitude depends on their religious beliefs. Outlawing assisted suicide, therefore, compromises the separation between church and state that we hold dear. If you value freedom of worship, you must honor your neighbor's choice in this matter or set a precedent for religious persecution.

And, if you are Christian, remember Christ told us to love our neighbor and judge not lest we be judged. Doesn't this mean that we should honor the free will of others? What if the physician assisting terminally ill patients in their suicide has been sent by God to relieve their suffering? How would we justify ourselves?

Q *Legalizing assisted suicide just prepares the way for legalizing euthanasia of "unwanted" people, such as the elderly and handicapped.*

A The choice to leave this world should always be the choice of the individual or their designee, never the choice of the doctor or government. The doctor's only choice is whether or not he or she will assist.

Because a patient cannot choose their own path today, some doctors, in the name of compassion, are making that choice for the terminally ill, usually without consulting the family. Legalizing assisted suicide puts the decision back into the hands of the person most affected by that decision and their loved ones.

Q *If assisted suicide is legalized, won't every depressed teenager be able to take it as an easy way out?*

A Oftentimes, teenagers commit suicide because no one takes them seriously. When they talk about depression and death, their family tells them that these feelings will pass or admonishes them for even considering suicide.

In an assisted suicide clinic, such comments would be taken seriously. The teenager would be steered towards counseling that he or she might otherwise not have gotten.

Thus, if teenagers had a place to go where they would be taken seriously, their suicide rate might actually go down. Few physicians would risk their reputation by assisting the suicide of the depressed teenager, so increased teen suicide is highly unlikely.

Q *If we legalize physician-assisted suicide, some people who might have had a miraculous recovery could kill themselves before that happened. In other words, more people would die than otherwise would.*

A Just the opposite is true! Eighty percent of our health care resources are spent in the last few weeks of our life. A terminally-ill person who commits suicide frees these resources for others. Since our health care resources are strained, releasing them might make the difference between life or death for someone on the edge. Terminally ill individuals who leave this life earlier may actually save those whose life depends on a little extra time and insight from their health care providers. If you've ever had a terminally ill loved one, you know that end-of-life care is rationed because it's such a great strain on health care resources.

Consumer Protection

C onsumer legislation literally protects us to death. Ironically, without it, we'd live longer, healthier lives.

Q *Is it true that in a free society, preventative government regulation is always wrong, no matter what the consequences (death, etc.) will be?*

A The intent of government regulation is often to prevent problems, but history shows that the opposite usually happens. The government force used in consumer protection legislation, for example, creates a backlash that is usually more problematic than the original concern.

Q *There is a growing problem with herbal remedies such as ginseng. Many of the most popular products have no ginseng content. What would be the libertarian way to handle this?*

A In a libertarian society, consumers could buy from a firm with quality assurance in the form of independent certification. Consumers could sue companies for fraud if they were sold ginseng products without ginseng.

Today, companies often provide certified analysis of their products on request. You can then deal with manufacturers who consistently make quality products.

Q *What would the libertarians replace the FAA with and how would they keep the skies safe for air travel?*

A Airlines lose money when lives are lost. Their stock plummets. They face lawsuits from victims or their families and loss of business from frightened consumers. Airlines therefore have great incentive to avoid safety problems. They have nothing to gain and everything to lose by killing their customers.

Private groups would likely evaluate each airline and make suggestions for safety improvement. Airlines would probably pay for inspections in the hopes of getting the "Seal of Approval" from such organizations. Prudent consumers would fly only airlines that received high safety ratings; without such certification, an airline would be unlikely to survive.

Examples of highly effective private inspection groups abound. One well-known example: most electric devices you purchase will have the famous UL stamp of approval, the symbol that indicates the product has been evaluated as safe by Underwriters Laboratories, a private organization funded by insurance companies.

As with the safety of the aircraft themselves, responsibility for screening passengers for possible threats should rest with the airlines instead of the Transportation Safety Administration (TSA), as they have the greatest incentive to prevent actual would-be terrorists or hijackers from boarding their planes. If the airlines were in charge, we likely wouldn't have to put up with the groping we currently get from the TSA.

Q *What is the libertarian answer to the government stepping out of the air traffic control business?*

A As featured in a recent John Stossel special, the Canadian government has already taken the libertarian path and privatized their air traffic control system. As a result, the antiquated "paper passing" system of notifying other air traffic controllers of problems has been replaced by computers. Because the private system is more efficient, Canadian airports handle more planes with fewer delays and no compromise in safety.

The Federal Aviation Agency (FAA), on the other hand, simply blames the airlines rather than their own misplaced emphasis when something goes wrong. As a result, the FAA focuses on making sure that their check lists are followed, rather than coming up with safety innovations themselves. Perhaps that's why airline safety has improved along with the partial deregulation that began a couple decades ago in the U.S.

Q *How do I convince my fellow mental health professionals that licensure would prove ineffective and costly?*

A States that have the strictest licensing laws for electricians also have the greatest number of accidental electrocutions.[54] As requirements for a license go up, so does the cost. The poor either do without or try to do things themselves.

Certification, on the other hand, evaluates service providers, but lets the consumer decide. Certification increases the quantity and quality of service delivered, while decreasing the cost.

In the health fields, we are all patients before we are providers. Doesn't it make sense to give ourselves the best care by avoiding licensure and promoting certification?

Q *How can libertarianism work when people and companies are so determined to put their own gains ahead of the rest of society? What is to control the profiteers and price gougers in a libertarian society?*

A In a libertarian society, consumers rule. If a company tries to overcharge their customers, their competitors can offer consumers a better deal. People choose the businesses that serve them best. Profit follows service.

To avoid this regulation by the consumers, many companies have tried to secretly fix prices. However, these "cartels" invariably fail because whichever company violates the agreement first – and gives consumers the best deal – wins the business. Thus, the free market is self-regulating.

In California, regulations required utilities to sell their generating plants and buy only from a single state-administered source. This monopoly, mistakenly referred to as "deregulation," has made competition illegal. If consumers are displeased, they cannot vote with their dollars and take their business to another company without encountering the same problems.

In summary, the aggression of state regulation allows greedy companies to exploit consumers by destroying freedom of choice. In a libertarian society, companies can only serve their own greed by giving their customers a better deal than a competitor would. That's what makes "service with a smile" possible.

Q *What is the libertarian solution to the problem of corporate power and corporate welfare? The politicians have been bought; they are not about to stop giving the big corporations whatever they want.*

A As long as government has the power to regulate business, corporations will "buy" our legislators at the consumers' expense. Big business knows this; as a result, most "consumer protection" legislation is introduced by the very people it's intended to regulate: the businesses themselves.

The only real hope for citizens and consumers is to take away government's power to regulate business, so that wealthy corporations can't "buy" that power any more. The consumers then vote with each purchasing dollar for the business that serves them best.

Government is the servant of the wealthy and powerful, but masquerades as the friend of the little guy. When we agree to violate the rights of business owners, we empower those we seek to regulate. What goes around, comes around.

Q *If we privatize federal programs, who will be handed the reins of these immense institutions? Will they simply go to the highest* *bidder? Who could afford to buy, for example, the U.S. Post Office? And who gets the revenue?*

A Many private firms, such as the ones now delivering overnight mail, would gladly bid for the Post Office. They could finance the purchase by assuming some of the national debt, which is in the form of long-term notes. Perhaps they would simply get a loan like many of us do when we buy a home. They could also sell stock or issue bonds to cover the purchase. Post offices have been privatized successfully in other countries, such as New Zealand, so why not in the U.S.?

Q *Aren't monopolies a problem in a free market economy?*

A Monopolies are very rare in the free market, contrary to popular dogma. For example, Rockefeller's Standard Oil gained 85% of the market for a couple years, but found that the only way he could keep competitors from gaining ground was to maintain low prices. Even then, competitors took more than half of his market share in just a few years.

AT&T, on the other hand, asked the government to give it a monopoly to put its many competitors out of business. For all his greed, Rockefeller could only dominate the marketplace by giving the customer a good deal. Until the government reversed its policy on long distance service in 1984, AT&T was able to charge monopoly prices. Government intervention is usually necessary to make monopolies possible.[55]

Q *Isn't some regulation necessary to ensure competition in telecommunications?*

A In the late 1800s, Bell Telephone had a monopoly in the telephone industry. When its patents expired, the independents took half of Bell's market in barely a decade. To compensate for their smaller size, the independents served individuals rather than businesses, and started to interconnect. That's when Bell Telephone, now AT&T, asked the government to "regulate" the industry, so it could enjoy a monopoly once more. After a half-century of AT&T monopoly, MCI successfully challenged it in the marketplace and in the courts.

The moral of this story is that a monopoly – in telecommunications or any other industry – is virtually impossible to maintain in the free market and the "little guy" can compete and grow by serving a niche market. Deregulation in telecommunications has given us more competition in this sector than any time in the previous century, along with lower prices and better service.

Q *When you eat in a restaurant, you expect the food to be prepared in a clean environment. So we ask the government to send inspectors to force the owner to clean its place. In a libertarian society, how can someone protect himself against hidden threats to his health?*

A Restaurant owners who can assure customers that their establishments are clean and healthful will prosper. Thus, they are likely to band together and set standards (and inspections) through their own professional organization. The organization's "Seal of Approval" would be proudly displayed by restaurants that met its high standards. Concerned consumers would patronize only certified establishments.

Studies show that voluntary certification, instead of mandatory inspections, increases the delivery of high quality, inexpensive service to the customer. Certification is win-win for both service providers and consumers.

Q *How does a libertarian address the issue of city housing codes ordinances and fire safety laws, considering the fact that one's negligent neighbor may pose a very real threat to the safety of one's family and possessions?*

A In a libertarian society (and today in many locales), insurance companies would charge higher rates in neighborhoods where houses were poorly maintained. When people can lower their rates substantially by making electrical and other repairs, they often will do so.

Q *If you free the business community from government regulations, how do you keep business people from appointing themselves as an aristocracy, and turning America into a feudal state?*

A In a libertarian society, you, the consumer, control businesses by voting to buy or not buy their products. You vote to keep them in business or shut them down. You eliminate the "bad guys" by purchasing only from the "good guys."

In today's society, government regulates some companies out of business, leaving a monopoly (like most local utility companies) or a cartel (like the banking industry). Limiting your choices limits your control.

Government doesn't keep business in check; government keeps big business big.

Q *Like you, I want to live in a free society. However, I am just as concerned about big business as big brother, maybe more so.*

A Business only has two ways to get big: by serving customers better than the competition or by getting Big Brother to regulate their competition out of business. Keeping government out of the marketplace keeps business in its true service role.

Q *In a libertarian society, how much regulation would there be on recreational and pharmaceutical drugs? Next to none? Would manufacturers have to show that a drug is pure, or safe for human consumption? What if recreational drugs became significantly stronger? Would the libertarian stance be the same?*

A In a libertarian society, manufacturers would have to compensate victims whom they defrauded. Obviously, selling someone a different amount of drug than advertised falls into this category. Claiming that a drug was pure when it was not would also be fraudulent.

Killing customers is bad for business; companies don't profit by selling something that harms people. Before the FDA (Food and Drug Administration), companies took great pride in their brand names and advertised their safety record to attract customers.

Without the FDA, companies that produced drugs (either recreational or medicinal) would likely seek third-party certification. Independent companies would test products for a fee and give their seal of approval if products met their standards. Discriminating customers would buy only drugs which carried such a seal.

Those who couldn't wait for the seal (for example, patients suffering from terminal disease) would still have access to new drugs. Today, AIDS and cancer patients wait 10 extra years for the manufacturer to jump through FDA-imposed hoops, which unfortunately do little to make drugs safer.[56]

The marketplace already "regulates" electrical appliances privately. The UL certification mark is the seal of approval from Underwriters Laboratories, a private third-party certifying agency.

Our drugs would probably be safer with such third-party testing. Today, the FDA does no testing of its own, but only approves what the manufacturer submits.

Q *How do I convince my fellow health care professionals (who are often social democrats) and other citizens that government-mandated licensure will prove ineffective and costly?*

A Licensing enthrones today's practices and drives cost upward, while creating barriers for tomorrow's breakthroughs. When we or our loved ones need cutting-edge professional help, licensing regulations may force us to go underground, go overseas, or do without. Studies show that we can improve the quality of care while keeping costs down by turning to a system of certification instead of licensure.[57] Certification gives the patient the ultimate choice of a health care provider; licensure lets bureaucrats decide. Who do you want in charge of *your* health?

Q *What do Libertarians think about requiring licenses to practice medicine and requiring FDA approval for medicines used? Which party (Republican or Democrat) comes closest to sharing this belief?*

A Libertarians believe that the consumer, not the government, should choose which medicines and practitioners they patronize. After all, the patients live and die by these decisions, so the choice and the responsibility for those choices belong to them.

The Democrats and Republicans believe that bureaucrats should decide for the patients, without any liability for bad decisions. That's why we have Libertarians!

Q *In my political science class the other day, consumer protection was the topic and I mentioned private alternatives like UL. I told the class that even without the government imposing building and fire codes, our classroom would have to be fire-safe because if it weren't, the university's insurance premiums would skyrocket.*

I thought I had done a good job until the professor said, "Well, think of the 1700 people that died in the recent Turkish earthquake. The insurance companies didn't protect them."

How would you have responded?

A You were doing well. Your professor's comeback involved some illogical extrapolations. One possible approach might have been:

"In poor countries like Turkey, safety standards, whether imposed by the government or the marketplace, are lower than in wealthy countries. Safety standards for something that might happen are only affordable in countries where the necessities are already in abundance. That's why natural disasters always take a bigger toll in poor nations. To increase safety, a country should increase its wealth, a feat that only the free market can achieve. Studies show that countries which enjoy free markets have a more even distribution of wealth than regulated ones. Thus, the poor benefit most by the increased prosperity and safety."

With poor countries, like Turkey, you can bet that its economy is heavily regulated. If you had asked your teacher, "Does Turkey even have insurance companies?" he probably wouldn't have known. Asking such questions helps to establish whether the comment is well-grounded in fact.

If you're going to be sparring on the international front, you might want to get a copy of the Fraser Institute's Economic Freedom of the World Annual Report by James D. Gwartney (www.freetheworld.com). The report rates freedom in every country by a number of different criteria. Turkey is towards the bottom of both prosperity and freedom indicators. Government has impoverished its citizenry, making safety measures a low priority. Insurance companies probably can't function in such an environment.

If so, a good response might be, "You mean that government destroyed the economic freedom and prosperity needed to protect them!"

Health

The only way to make health care affordable is to do away with the excessive government interference that accounts for about 80% of the cost.[58]

Q *Drug companies don't investigate the relationship between diet and disease because there is not much profit in marketing broccoli and carrots to physicians! So, don't we need government agencies, like NIH, to fund this type of research?*

A Drug companies might not be interested in research on broccoli, but broccoli farmers are! The reason that growers' associations don't spend money on such research is that the FDA forbids them to advertise their findings. Producers of oat cereal were chastised by the FDA for making the "medical claim" that oats could help lower cholesterol. Without the FDA, you'd see a great deal of research on diet and disease sponsored by the agricultural sector.

As taxpayers, we first pay government to create the problem (e.g., FDA) and then pay once again for the government-mandated solution (e.g., NIH). Think of how many more lives would be saved if our resources weren't so carelessly wasted!

Q *I know you would rather not have government involvement in health care, but given that it is there, and it's probably not going away for a while, should the government try to improve the health of its citizens?*

A Two wrongs won't make things right. Trying to force better health habits on people ultimately costs more than the medical treatment would, because force is very, very expensive and inefficient. The War on Drugs, as an example of such a "self-improvement" program, has killed more people than drugs themselves. Do you really think that more government can correct the problems that too much government has already created?

Q *Wouldn't a "socialist" health-care plan work for the U.S.? It seems to work for other countries.*

A Actually, such systems only *seem* to work. Thousands of Canadians cross the U.S. border each year to pay for heart surgery, hip replacements, and other treatments. The "free" health care in their native land is available only after months, sometimes years of waiting, and many die before their number is called. In Britain if you're over 55, you'll probably be denied expensive treatments such as kidney dialysis. It's sad enough to watch loved ones die when a disease is incurable, but it's much worse to watch them die just because the line is too long.

The secret to lowering health care costs is to do away with the excessive regulation which drives up prices by 80% with no added benefit. Since the government can only get its money from us, high prices ultimately translate into health care rationing, regardless of who foots the bill.

Q *I saw an ad showing a hemophiliac child whose parents face $450,000 in medical bills annually. My wife, a social worker employed by the state to aid the mentally ill, said, "Now do you see why Medicaid is necessary?" I was and still am at a loss to answer that question.*

A If government did not make pharmaceutical manufacturers jump through so many regulatory hoops, it's likely that the cost of drug treatments would be about 80% of what they are now.[59] Such reductions would make medication affordable for more people.

Rare instances where an uninsured individual was not able to pay for care would still occur. However, health care providers would be more likely to take such charity cases if the cost of doing so was made more reasonable by getting government out of health care. An appeal to community charitable organizations might be sufficient to pay the lowered costs of marketplace health care as well.

Today, Medicaid does not pay the full cost of health care for individuals needing help. To remedy this situation, hospitals charge those with private insurance more for their services. This increases the cost of insurance, and fewer people can afford it. When these people get ill, they turn to Medicare/Medicaid and the cycle repeats itself.

A better solution would be to get the government out of health care at all levels so that costs and insurance plummet. Almost everyone could afford to be insured and have access to catastrophic medical treatment when they needed it.

Medicare/Medicaid is like putting a bandage on a hemorrhage. In the long run, it simply masks the true problem. Instead of treating the symptoms of high health care costs, let's cure the underlying disease – government intervention!

Q *What do libertarians think about requiring licenses to practice medicine and requiring FDA approval for medicines used?*

A Libertarians believe that the consumer, not the government, should choose which medicines and practitioners they patronize. After all, the patients live and die by these decisions, so the choice and the responsibility for those choices belong to them.

The Abigail Alliance (www.abigail-alliance.org) sued the FDA on the grounds that the Constitution protects the right of terminally ill patients to take the drug of their choice, even if it isn't FDA approved. Sadly, the courts ruled that no such constitutional right exists. Even if a new drug looks safe in early clinical trials, dying patients cannot take it until it gains FDA approval years later. How would you feel if you or your loved one wasn't permitted to buy a new, potentially life-saving medicine because a bureaucrat had not yet given permission?

Q *How would hospitals in a libertarian society treat indigent patients in need of medical care? How will the poor get necessary hospital treatment in a libertarian society if they can't pay? Isn't some government intervention needed here?*

A Without the excessive regulations that we have today, health care costs would drop dramatically. More people could afford preventative care, medical insurance, or even pay for their hospital stay directly.

Many people who could barely survive in today's society will be comfortable in a libertarian one, as businesses flourish and job opportunities abound.

Of course, even with improved health, lower medical costs, and better jobs, a few individuals would still need help. In a libertarian society, with its greater prosperity (an estimated 8-fold increase),[60] more help would be available for the fewer in need.

Charities might work directly with hospitals, so that no one was turned away for financial reasons. "Free" hospitals, staffed largely by volunteer heath care practitioners, might also come back into vogue.

Indeed, the real-life "Patch Adams," eloquently played by Robin Williams in the movie by that name, is planning to set up just such a facility in West Virginia (www.patchadams.org).

Q *I've been frustrated by some libertarians who think that compromising libertarian principles is the best way to get the libertarian message accepted by the public, on issues including mandatory health insurance.*

What about the idea of competing with insurance companies by fostering the creation of non-profit insurance and/or medical co-ops? In a co-op, any profits would stay in the co-op to offset the additional cost of helping those currently lacking basic care.

A   You've pretty much described the "mutual aid societies" that once protected Americans against medical disasters before government regulated them out of business for the benefit of the doctors and insurance companies.

David Beito's wonderful book *From Mutual Aid to the Welfare State* describes these associations in detail. Beito summarizes some of the government interventions that led to their decline at: www.heritage.org/Research/Lecture From-Mutual-Aid-to-Welfare-State.

For example, the American Medical Association (AMA) condemned doctors who worked for a flat fee for these societies. Since the AMA controlled the licensing boards, physicians didn't want to incur their wrath.

Even though the mutual aid societies served their members well during the Depression, insurance companies successfully lobbied for regulations requiring that mutual aid societies have large amounts of financial reserves on hand.

Thus, these effective co-op-like groups were essentially regulated out of business, putting us at the mercy of the often less efficient and less compassionate insurance companies.

The free market and human ingenuity creates amazing protection for us, including health care, but government intervention destroys it!

Trade & Tariffs

Free trade is the best national defense we could ever have. No country bombs their trading partners!

Q *Do you think it's appropriate for the U.S. government to use its power to open foreign markets to U.S. companies?*

A Individuals should be free to trade – or not trade – as they choose without government interference or tariffs.

If American consumers feel that they benefit from buying inexpensive Japanese goods, they should do so freely. If our government puts tariffs on Japanese cars because Japan won't buy American, for example, we hurt ourselves as a nation of consumers to protect a few auto workers.

These tariffs force us to pay more for cars, so we have less money to spend on other things. Production of these other things goes down, and the Americans producing them lose their jobs. In the end, protectionist measures put some Americans out of work so that others can make more.

Since we are all consumers as well as workers, even the protected workers lose in the end. Higher prices eat up the extra wages. It's a no-win scenario.

Instead of trying to keep the jobs of some Americans at the expense of others, we help everyone by stopping the taxation and regulation that limit job creation. Making well-paid jobs readily available keeps everyone happy!

Q *Isn't our government justified in establishing embargoes on nations that consistently violate human rights?*

A Embargoes themselves are a violation of human rights. Innocent traders are financially destroyed overnight when contracts are broken. Governments that torture their citizens will not change their ways because the innocent suffer. They will simply claim that the suffering is the fault of the nation that instituted the embargo. When we prevent ships carrying food and medicine to Third World nations, we violate their rights just as much as their tyrannical dictator.

Q *What do libertarians think of NAFTA and free trade?*

A Libertarians support free trade, but it doesn't take the five hundred plus pages of the NAFTA agreement to say "no more restrictions between us." NAFTA is obviously *not* a "free trade" agreement. Libertarians differ on whether or not NAFTA will give us more free trade or less.

Q *If you remove all tariffs and countries can sell their products to us for less, what about those who will lose their jobs here when American companies can't keep up?*

A When tariffs are eliminated, consumers pay less for foreign goods. They therefore have more money to spend on other things. Their spending creates more new jobs than those that are lost.

Inefficient domestic companies are put out of business by foreign goods, but competitive domestic sectors grow as consumers spend their extra cash. The net effect is job creation, because a dollar spent on efficiently produced goods buys more, increasing demand. The country, as a whole, becomes more competitive on the world market and better able to export to other countries.

Q   *In an economy without any trade barriers, where the market can be flooded by less expensive imported goods, at a price our domestic manufacturers cannot hope to compete with, what is going to stop domestic jobs from rapidly going overseas to cheap labor countries?*

A   Some jobs will go overseas, but here we'll experience a net gain in the number of jobs and the wages we're paid. Everyone wins. Here's how it works:

Let's assume that cheap labor countries can manufacture and ship clothes to us more economically than our domestic industry. Our clothing bill goes down, leaving us more money to buy something else, say, computers. More high-tech, high-paying jobs are created here to meet the increased demand. We'll experience a net gain in jobs, because our human capital is more efficiently allocated. Uneducated cheap labor is manufacturing, and skilled technical labor is innovating.

Of course, the domestic clothing workers will experience some trauma as they scramble to find new positions. Most will end up in jobs that are more interesting and demanding as our work force as a whole shifts to become more technical. Like the rest of the country, they will benefit from the lower clothing prices and the higher standard of living made possible by the more efficient division of labor.

Countries that "protect" inefficient industries with trade barriers, keep consumer prices high and prosperity lower than it otherwise would be. In the U.S., for example, we pay more for automobiles than we would if tariffs on imports were abolished. Every extra dollar we spend on automobiles is one less for the computer and other domestic industries that compete well in the international markets. Tariffs put our market leaders at risk to preserve inefficiency. Ultimately, all of us – even the automobile workers – lose by higher prices and the lower standard of living.

Q   *When the textile industry lost so many jobs to Mexico, Asia and elsewhere, the unemployed workers who were left behind were poorly trained and semi-literate. More, they are not very mobile. In short, they aren't very likely to be able to upgrade their skills to increase their productivity.*

So the short question then is: what do we do with these unemployable workers who are left? A short answer is needed. Thanks for your thoughts.

A While unskilled jobs are lost to machines, skilled jobs increase as more people are needed to build the machines. Workers need to upgrade their skills to stay competitive as technology advances.

In a libertarian society, people could gain new skills by working for an employer at a training wage. Today, minimum wage laws prohibit them from being paid to train. Instead, out-of-work employees must pay tuition to community colleges or other institutions to learn new skills. If they can't come up with the money, they're out of luck.

In a libertarian society, people could apprentice with plumbers, electricians, or carpenters to learn new skills in a short period of time. Today, out-of-work employees must spend a considerable amount of time and money meeting the requirements for licensure in these professions without a commensurate gain in skill level.

Today, unskilled workers are out of luck; in a libertarian society, they'd have a good chance of taking the next step up the proverbial ladder.

Q *As we have seen with our present examples of "free trade" (NAFTA), the free trade idea is not so rosy in practice. With no restrictions on imports, many industries, not just our textile industry, would leave! When companies can move every time they discover new and poorer workers to exploit (or when labor at home is unionized), then everyone loses. We lose jobs, and the new workers (slaves) lose for being exploited and having their local natural resources stolen from them. U.S. companies already have more rights than humans and more power than governments.*

A Thank you for voicing your concerns! Let me try to address them. No matter how many jobs go to other countries, we can easily create more if government regulations don't prevent it. Every nation's workforce has particular strengths and weaknesses. In the U.S and Japan, technological know-how is the strength. In less developed nations, low-cost unskilled labor is. Truly free trade (not NAFTA, as you correctly point out) allows each nation to do what it does best.

Jobs designing computers and other state-of-the-art electronic products cannot easily be moved to Third World nations. Technological know-how in several major disciplines is required. The level of education and experience needed just isn't available there.

Free trade means that our costs of living go down. Our clothing manufacturers can't compete with overseas products because imports are lower in price. If we pay less for the things that we buy, every dollar we earn goes farther.

People in Third World nations who are making the imported clothing receive very low wages. However, working in the clothing factory must be the best deal they can get, or they wouldn't stay. Face it – people in the poorer nations have fewer good choices than we do!

Certainly, big business today has enormous power. We gave them that power when we asked our government to regulate business. Government put regulations into place which only the large companies could meet. Government claimed that it would protect the environment for us, but turned it over to big business instead. The companies, in turn, reward the politicians with campaign contributions. Until we take away the power of government to regulate business, business will control government (and everything else)! That's why libertarians want to get rid of government regulations, which, as you correctly stated elsewhere in your letter, turn into the "freedom to oppress."

Q *How can libertarianism help underdeveloped countries?*

A We can help underdeveloped countries in three ways. First, we can lower trade barriers (tariffs, quotas, etc.), so that these nations can participate in the global marketplace. Bangladesh, one of the world's poorest nations, received billions in foreign aid to build garment factories. When it started exporting its products, developed nations erected trade barriers and the factories had to shut down.[61] If we are so willing to give a handout, why not give a hand "up" instead?

Second, we can make sure that our foreign aid doesn't keep aggressors in power. Most U.S. foreign aid goes for "security assistance" which enables tyrants to oppress their people, e.g., Marcos (Philippines), Seko (Zaire), the Shah (Iran), Hussein (Iraq), Taliban (Afghanistan). These governments create a labyrinth of regulations which business people must meet, so that it might take years and a number of bribes in order to get permission to provide a simple bus service. Consequently, about 80% of business in underdeveloped countries occurs in the black market.[62]

Third, we should set an example that can be easily imitated. A number of sincere governments in underdeveloped nations have tried to imitate the United States, but have been confused by our ever-increasing regulations. Giving underdeveloped nations a road map for success may be the best foreign aid of all.

Q *Why is it wrong to have some means to even out the playing field for at least some types of trade?*

A "Wrong" is raising our hand in violence against peaceful neighbors. Trade restrictions stop our neighbors from exchanging freely with foreigners – at gunpoint, if necessary – for the benefit of some Americans at the expense of others. If this is "right" action for us, it's right for others too. We'll take turns being victim and aggressor as our neighbors seek to retaliate in kind. This is a prescription for eternal economic warfare! Ultimately, aggression is a no-win scenario.

Q *How could we possibly be better off without import tariffs? Wouldn't that just make it more difficult for us to compete in the international marketplace?*

188 Short Answers to the Tough Questions

A Just the opposite! Import tariffs raise prices for the consumer, while protecting industries that can't compete in the international marketplace. Without these tariffs, consumers who buy inexpensive foreign goods have more money to spend on efficient domestic industries that do compete well internationally. Inefficient businesses go out of business – as they should!

Q *Wouldn't we be at a serious disadvantage if we dropped all subsidies on American products and tariffs on foreign products if other countries did not do the same? Couldn't foreign countries subsidize a particular commodity to drive U.S. competitors out of business?*

A The Japanese have tried (unsuccessfully) to do just that. However, when a business is subsidized, it doesn't have to be competitive to survive. Most subsidized businesses become inefficient, negating the advantage of the subsidy.

If other countries are foolish enough to subsidize their industries, their products simply become cheaper on the American market, benefiting U.S. consumers greatly. Americans making similar products can shift their expertise into areas where foreigners find it difficult to compete (e.g., computer technology). In the long run, our entire work force becomes more secure and the price of our consumer goods goes down.

Gun Control

Firearms are the great equalizer. Guns give the little guy (or gal) a fighting chance.

Q *How can libertarians be against gun control when the U.S. has so many murders?*

A We have many rapes in the United States as well. Should we castrate all of our men to prevent it? Just as a potent man can be a rapist or a lover, so too can guns save lives or take them.

Fifty percent of "murdered" spouses are wife beaters killed in self-defense.[63] Without easy access to a gun, the women may have been killed instead.

Q *Does anybody ever really use a gun in self-defense against criminals?*

A By the late 1970s, armed citizens were killing more criminals in self-defense than the police.[64] Many more would-be attackers and robbers are deterred from their crime when their intended victim simply brandishes a firearm.

Q *Those bumper stickers that read "when guns are outlawed, only outlaws will have guns" are really disgusting.*

A What's disgusting about the truth? Five-sixths of all criminals obtain their guns illegally.[65] Only law-abiding citizens make legal purchases.

Q *Isn't it true that a person is better off not resisting an aggressor? Wouldn't trying to defend oneself with a gun be risky?*

A A victim who submits is twice as likely to be injured as a victim who resists with a gun. Defending oneself *without* a gun does result in more injury than submission.[66]

Q *When are we going to realize that the violence in this country is linked to our liberal gun laws? Britain has a much lower murder rate because of their excellent gun control.*

A New Zealand, Switzerland, and Israel have more gun ownership than the U.S., yet in these countries, homicides are less frequent.[67] On the other hand, the District of Columbia has the toughest anti-gun laws in the nation, and has one of the highest murder rates in the U.S.[68] Clearly, gun ownership doesn't predict the homicide rate.

If anything, gun ownership decreases crime.[69] In Orlando, the police publicized a program to train women to use firearms. In the following year, rape dropped 85% and burglary fell 25%.[70] Similar results have been reported in other major U.S. cities.

Q *Wouldn't our neighborhoods take on a Wild West character if everyone carried a gun?*

A An armed society is a polite society, and the not-so-wild West was rather peaceful, in spite of Hollywood's violent portrayal.[71] As a legacy, in the rural West where every household still has firearms, crime is less than in eastern cities.

Q *Since 80% of handgun victims are relatives of the killers, doesn't this show that having a gun on hand is dangerous?*

A Between 67% and 80% of the killers in domestic shoot outs have prior arrest records, frequently for violent crimes.[72] Thus, the average domestic killer is not a model citizen corrupted by gun possession, but a person continuing a life of violence.

Q *I would never own or use a gun. Guns are disgusting and should be outlawed.*

A Outlawing guns would require your police to use guns to take guns away from your neighbors. Are you OK with using guns to implement your ideas?

Q *One of the major arguments of those against gun control is that crime drops with less gun control, because criminals don't know who is armed. How can you call our society "free" if people are controlled by fear? If people are so scared of their society that they want a firearm for protection, how can you call these people free people? People should feel free enough to give up their firearms willingly. If people can't do this, then they will never be free.*

A When libertarians talk about freedom, they generally mean freedom from aggression by government and individuals, not freedom from fear. Today, we have neither freedom from fear, nor freedom from aggression.

Ironically, many people lose their fear when they acquire a firearm. Their belief that they can adequately defend themselves frees them from fear. In other words, political freedom can lead to freedom from fear.

Hopefully, the day will come when we no longer need to fear our neighbors or our government. People can then lay down their weapons just as you describe. By moving our society away from aggression and towards political freedom, we hasten the dawning of that day!

Q *A friend asked me this question: "Why are there more guns than people?" I have a hunch that this isn't true. I wonder if such statistics are skewed to give support to an anti-gun position? What is your answer?*

A I'm not sure whether this is true or not, either. If it is, it may be because so many gun owners have more than one firearm.

Your questioner is really saying: "Something is wrong with our society because we have so many weapons." However, the best research suggests that even deranged shooters who fire into crowds are deterred by laws permitting law-abiding citizens to carry concealed weapons.[69] Rapists and burglars stay away from areas where women are publicly trained in firearms.

Once acquainted with such data, your friend may decide that more guns are the solution, not the problem.

Q *An acquaintance of mine often attacks my stance on individual liberties, especially those relating to firearms. He has said, "I would rather give up certain unnecessary rights if it would result in a safer environment in which to live."*

A If your acquaintance wants to give up his right to have firearms in order to live in a neighborhood free of them, he could do so in a libertarian society by moving into a private community (e.g., condo complex) that banned them.

Q *What can I say to someone who doesn't believe the data showing that there is less crime when people are allowed to have guns?*

A Invite your friend to post a sign in his or her yard that says "This home is a gun-free zone." You'll find that most people refuse to do so, knowing intuitively that such a post is an invitation to home invasion.

Education

I n 1990, the *Detroit News* endorsed me for the State Board of Education even though I ran as a Libertarian, because of my unwavering support for total educational choice.

Q *How would the poor be educated in a libertarian society, when all schools are private?*

A In a libertarian society, the poor would not have to pay school taxes through their rent. This money could be used to send their children to private schools, which cost half as much as public ones, and would be even more economical without today's government regulation.

Today, the poor are forced into ghetto schools because their parents seldom have enough money to pay both property taxes and tuition. Because attendance is compulsory, troublemakers disrupt classes and learning is difficult.

Traditionally, the poor have been the strongest champions of choice programs, which force educators to teach well or go out of business. In Harlem, school choice increased the number of children reading at their grade level from 15% to 64%.[73] Such dramatic results show that the poor can learn when given a choice.

Q *Private schools work great for the average student, but how about the difficult ones?*

A Private schools can specialize to help students at any level. One private institution specializes in students who are about

Short Answers to the Tough Questions

to drop out and boasts an 85% graduation rate.[74] Not bad, considering that none of these students were likely to graduate otherwise!

Q *Public schools aren't perfect, but private ones aren't that much better!*

A If private schools aren't that great, why are public school teachers twice as likely as other parents to send their children to one?[75]

Q *How could the poor afford schooling in a libertarian society?*

A A good education is a major factor in moving people from poverty to affluence. Today, however, our poor go to inner city schools where they are more likely to learn about drugs and violence than about computers and Shakespeare. Indeed, they are lucky to learn reading, writing, and arithmetic.

Not surprisingly, low income parents favor tax-funded vouchers which allow them to send their children to a school of their choice. Since private schools educate children for half the cost of public ones, sending every child to a private school with vouchers would slash educational taxes in half. In addition, children, especially the poor, would receive the superior education that private schools give. Many libertarians see vouchers as a good transitional step, although others fear it may result in total government control of private education, as well as public.

Today, even private school education is highly regulated, making it more costly than it otherwise would be.

We know that children learn rapidly from TV/video instruction, as evidenced by the success of the preschooler program, "Sesame Street." With freedom in education, TV producers would have a market for K-12 education, which could be brought directly into the home (or classroom) for the cost of cable. Advertiser-sponsored education would be virtually free. Rather than giving the same lessons over and over each year, teachers would be released from this drudgery to answer questions and tutor children having difficulties.

Implementing new teaching technology is difficult in a formal school setting today because of the regulations that apply to both public and private schools. Innovations are pioneered in after-hours teaching institutions (e.g., Sylvan Learning) and the home school network. Students enrolled in either generally outperform their peers.

In summary, when we start applying space-age technology to schooling, the cost of a quality education plummets. The poor benefit most, since inner city schools offer them little. Even quality home study with televised lessons would give them a better education, although even more options would be available to them in a libertarian society.

Part of the greater wealth of a libertarian society is the innovation that increases quality while decreasing cost. The greatest innovation would likely come in the most regulated sectors of our economy, including education.[76]

Q *If attendance weren't mandatory, very few children would go to school.*

A History suggests otherwise. In the early 1800s, a survey in Boston found that 90% of the school-age children were enrolled, even though attendance was not compulsory and public schooling was not widespread. At that time, the U.S. was considered the most literate nation in the world. We learned more when we weren't forced to do so!

Q *If education isn't compulsory, children whose parents don't care about education won't go to school. They'll grow up to be hoodlums, so society will end up paying in the long run.*

A The most significant factor in a student's success is the home atmosphere. If the parents aren't supportive, chances are that their children would only disrupt the classroom and learn next to nothing if they were forced to attend. Why penalize the students who want to learn by putting these troublemakers in their classes?

Q *As a public school teacher, I'm much better paid than I would be in a private school and I like it that way.*

A Instead of being limited to union-scale wages, teachers in a libertarian society will have unlimited potential. The teachers could own and operate the schools they work in, rather than being just employees. Because education in a libertarian society would use the latest technology for routine lectures, instructors could spend their time actually teaching. Teachers who excel could help design instructional videos and computer programs for their school, state, or nation and be paid handsomely in return. The only teachers who wouldn't benefit would be those whose teaching skills were marginal.

Q *I would like to know the libertarian stand on displaying the Ten Commandments on public property such as court house walls, etc. I also would like to know your position on school prayer.*

A Libertarians would replace government-run schools with privately run ones. Each school would make its own decision about school prayer, displaying the Ten Commandments, etc. Parents could send their children to the schools that best fit their values.

In a libertarian society, very little, if any, property would be public. Property owners would decide these issues based on their own beliefs.

Q *Numbers I have seen suggest that private schools are roughly ¼ the cost of their public counterparts per pupil. Public schools could be sold to private institutions with the proceeds going back to the public in the form of school vouchers or credits. Would this scenario be acceptable to libertarians in general?*

A Such a scenario might be a workable transition from state-run schools to totally private ones. I like the idea of giving the proceeds of the sale directly to the school children in some form instead of to the government in any form.

Q *Would libertarians be open to compulsory school taxes for all on a progressive scale with revenues being redistributed equally among the public for private schooling?*

A In general: no. Bad means invariably taint the good ends that we hope to achieve by using the aggression of taxation.

However, many libertarians believe that one way to transition into a totally private system is to refund established school taxes through a voucher program, preferably while phasing out the tax entirely.

Q *We do need a public education system. Literacy is so important to a democracy, that I'm not willing to let even a few children fall through the cracks, if parents or charity had to foot the bill.*

A Unfortunately, no system is perfect. There will always be some students who can't or won't learn. All we can do is to choose the system that minimizes the number who "fall through the cracks."

Did you know that we used to be the most literate nation in the world when the government wasn't involved in education? Since government has become involved, almost half of our children have become functionally illiterate.

What makes government involvement create such a poor outcome is its "one size fits all" approach to education. When instruction is individualized, as it is when education is private, fewer children "fall through the cracks." Since no system is perfect, shouldn't we choose the one which works the best?

Short Answers to the Tough Questions

Q *In a libertarian society, what would be the most noticeable change regarding the accessibility of a college education to qualified young people from lower-income families?*

A In a libertarian society, students might have the equivalent of today's college education before they turn eighteen, since course work would be more individualized and students would learn at their own pace.

Even children from lower-income families would have this opportunity. More people would be working and making good money, so fewer children would live in poor households. That portion of the rent that today goes to school taxes would be in the hands of the parents, not the near-worthless ghetto schools. Without labor restrictions, both parents and students could work at the schools to get credit toward tuition.

Most importantly, however, deregulating education would spur innovation and create inexpensive alternatives to sitting in a classroom (e.g., sophisticated educational TV channels, computer learning in game formats, group home-schooling, etc.). Of course, in a society where jobs were plentiful and the society was wealthier, those in desperate circumstances would have a better chance of getting scholarships as well.[76]

Q *Do you believe that all schools should be privatized, or just that there should more competition for the public schools? I believe the problem with private schools is that they concentrate too much on just academic results and exam scores. Students would leave school not having experienced such things as football and other sports and activities that help people learn to work in a team and to communicate with others. I would like to hear your opinion.*

A In a libertarian society, some schools might indeed emphasize academics. Others, however, would have strong sports orientation because many people, like yourself, value an education with a physically oriented team-building component.

Of course, some schools might choose to teach cooperation and communication by other means (e.g., helping students create and run their own businesses). Children, especially those from poor backgrounds, are enthralled by learning how to earn money. Indeed, one libertarian who teaches in an inner-city school has become a big hit with his students by showing them how to become entrepreneurs (www.nfte.com).

Some private schools might indeed charge high tuition. However, studies show that today most private school attendees come from the lower classes, not the upper ones. Public schools today are fine in well-to-do communities, but treacherous in the ghettos. Private schools often cater to the poor who want more for their children than an inner-city government school education. In a libertarian society, with lower educational costs and better paying jobs for parents, quality schooling for the poor would be more common, not less.

Q *What is the libertarian response to those who state that mandatory "community service" in elementary and high schools is an excellent idea?*

A "Mandatory" means forced – at gunpoint, if necessary. When we force people to do things, for their own good or the good of others, we violate their right of self-determination.

Libertarians respect the rights of others to choose their own path – that's what liberty is all about. If community service is such a good deal, we should have no trouble persuading people to do it voluntarily. If we can't convince others that our way is best, maybe we should humbly consider the possibility that it isn't!

Q *I live in England, where the private schools are derided by some, not because they are bad, but because they are thought of as unfairly benefiting the wealthy. I disagree. I believe that, because the offspring is an extension of the parent, he or she gains no unfair* *advantage; the school simply allows people to gain advantage from their own work. Do you agree?*

A I would agree. However, all schools, whether public or private, cost many times more in taxes or tuition than is necessary because of government regulations. Without these restrictions, ad-sponsored television programs like Sesame Street, special educational cable stations, Internet courses, and other advances we cannot yet envision could make high-quality education virtually free for everyone!

Q *I do not believe the libertarian state is minimal, for this reason: Kids who grow up without an education are more likely to turn to a life of crime, and I believe that public schools are cheaper than public prisons. So, I do not support a libertarian state because I believe it would waste my hard-earned tax money. Unless you can prove that your state truly is minimal, I do not see how you could justify forcing me to pay taxes for your government, as a libertarian state would do.*

A A libertarian state wouldn't have any taxes at all. Like you, we see taxation as forcing someone to give up their earnings for someone else's programs. We believe taxation to be immoral and impractical; the Libertarian Party's platform thoroughly denounces it. Without taxes, how could a government be anything but minimal?

You seem to think that we would have more ignorance without public education, but history tells a different story. Before the advent of public, tax-supported schools, private schooling was the norm. America was largely acknowledged to be the most literate nation on earth, in contrast to today, when supposedly no child is "left behind," but almost half leave school functionally illiterate.

Immigration

Immigrants built the U.S., yet their descendants often want to deny others the same opportunity their forbearers had.

Q *If you open the borders, won't the U.S. be filled with welfare types that destroy the economy, and workers who are willing to work for low wages, lowering our standard of living?*

A No! Studies show that immigrants tend to pay more taxes and use less welfare than the average American. The low-level jobs they do take are usually ones that Americans shun. By working for less, immigrants lower prices, giving the consumer a higher standard of living.

News reports in early 2012 described a reverse flow of immigrants, as people from Mexico returned home because of poorer work opportunities in the recession-hit U.S. economy. Clearly, most immigrants want to work – not stay here just to collect welfare.

Q *If low-skilled immigrants work for less, won't employers tend to hire these low-skilled immigrants over low-skilled natives? Even if there is no shortage in jobs, won't low-skilled immigrants eventually bring down the wages of the whole class of low-skilled Americans, simply by the rule of supply and demand?*

A Although that might happen in theory, in recent times immigrants appear to move into sectors that Americans don't populate. For example, migrant agricultural labor doesn't displace many Americans, who prefer flipping burgers to harvesting in the hot sun. Many Mexican laborers are used to hotter climates and thus tolerate farm work better.

Immigrants can move into hamburger flipping, but only when they have a reasonable grasp of English, so that they can understand instruction and interact with customers. Because of such advantages, Americans are preferred over immigrants even in many low-paying jobs.

Many immigrants seem to prefer running their own small businesses, rather than being an employee. Americans, on the other hand, often prefer employment, shorter hours, benefits (such as medical), and letting the employer take the entrepreneurial risks.

Some nationalities gravitate towards specific businesses. Asian Indian immigrants, for example, have jump-started the sleepy lodging industry in the past several decades, creating jobs for Americans rather than displacing them. Half of our Silicon Valley companies were started by immigrants, who have hired thousands of Americans in the process.[77]

Q *If we opened our borders, what would keep the mass of people around the world from descending on the United States like so many locusts?*

A In a libertarian society, all property would be private, including roads. Thus, immigrants could only enter the country by invitation of the property owner or by paying user fees for roads and other services. Without government welfare, immigrants could only stay if they earned their way or found someone to support them. These restrictions would keep the U.S. from being overrun, while allowing entry to those who could pay their own way through hard work or prior savings.

Q *I agree with you on all libertarian positions except the idea of opening our borders. Your arguments for open borders are very persuasive, but isn't it contingent on creating a free society first, then opening our borders to others? Therefore, opening borders should not be*

one of our first priorities, right? Let's open our borders when we have a
truly free society, but until then, it's best to keep foreigners out.

A Even without a free society, opening our borders is consistent with libertarian philosophy. For example, suppose that I wanted to invite a Mexican family into my home to live and work. The family goes back to Mexico when their employment ends, or they find other employment. Would you feel right about stopping them – at gunpoint, if necessary? Probably not.

As an interim step, we could simply require immigrants to have an invitation from a citizen willing to provide for them or help them find employment. If the hosts tire of this arrangement, the immigrants must find other sponsors or return to their native country.

Since all property would be private in a libertarian society, anyone entering the country could only do so if invited. Thus, the program described above better approximates a free society than current immigration restrictions. In addition, it could be implemented with relative ease today, even without any other libertarian reforms.

How to open borders while still burdened with excessive government is a hot discussion among libertarians. Please feel free to join in!

Q *Because of the accident of birth, I would like to keep America to myself and don't feel the need to share this land of plenty.*

A You may wish to keep America to yourself and could readily do so in a libertarian society, at least on the parcel that you own. As your neighbor, however, I may wish to host an immigrant, and would be free to open my home or even sell it to the guests of my choice.

Just out of curiosity, how would you feel if the "accident of birth" you mentioned were reversed and you were born, say, in Mexico?

Q *My sister and I are in a homeschooling debate club and this year the topic is immigration reform. We are taking the libertarian* *position that the borders should be opened, but I do have one problem. I can't seem to find anything anywhere that addresses what will assuredly be a hole in our argument that will be found by the other team: under an open border policy, criminals will be allowed in the country. Could you please help?*

A Most immigrant "criminals" are political refugees, rather than murderers and rapists. As documented in Joel Millman's book *The Other Americans*, most immigrants work long, hard hours to make their dreams materialize. On pp.52-53, he presents evidence that immigration does not result in an increase in crime. His supporting data is indirect, but enough for him to conclude: "What is certain is that crime didn't increase (in New York City) because of immigration. Throughout the peak years of immigration, arrests for rape, robbery, murder, and theft kept trending, stubbornly, down."

For the most part, thieves and violent criminals are looking for an easy way out. Immigration, which often involves a considerable amount of culture shock and even a new language, hardly falls into that category. Most immigrants come to the U.S. to work, not to plunder. For anyone, immigrant or not, who turns to a life of crime, the solution is to stop him or her, not punish thousands of innocents who simply want to work.

Q *I am in the difficult position of being both a libertarian and an immigration officer. I have arrested numerous immigrants, both illegal and legal, for crimes they have committed while they resided in the United States. Controlling for drug crimes, which would be eliminated in a libertarian society, we still estimate that the prison population in California is 15% immigrant. This is based on hard evidence compiled through interviews and record checks of inmates. Most of these are violent offenders who get turned over to me for deportation once their sentences are finished.*

I am for hard-working people being allowed to cross borders freely. But as libertarians we need to realize the fact that some enforcement posture against criminals and would-be terrorists needs to remain in place. Your "short answer" relies on only one source.

A Thank you for sharing from your personal experience. You do have a difficult position!

As you know, libertarians do have an enforcement posture against both criminals and terrorists, whether they are immigrants or not. Anyone who harms another should be stopped, preferably with as little force as possible. Depending upon the crime, restitution and/or imprisonment may be appropriate. Under our current system, deportation might be another option.

Q *Regardless of what the exact percentage of criminal immigrants might be in any one locale, shouldn't our focus be on apprehending the bad guys instead of trying to keep everyone out? One of the reasons that crime pays so well today is that our law enforcement agents are busy enforcing victimless crime laws.*

A When communities have elected private security instead of public police, crime plummets. Private security helps its clients prevent crime and diligently pursues the lawbreakers. If those employed by the Immigration and Naturalization Service (INS) were to switch to fighting crime this way, I suspect that we would have less of a problem than we have now, even if our borders were open.

I realize that the INS can't simply decide to pursue this course on its own. However, this exercise shows how we've misplaced our focus and resources by trying to control all border crossers because we fear what a few of them will do. Indeed, most regulation works just exactly this way: mismanaging everyone instead of pursuing the guilty few. The result, not surprisingly, is that the bad guys rarely get caught.

California may indeed have a higher incidence of criminal immigrants than elsewhere (the numbers I cited were from New York). However, the solution is the same: focus on those who harm others, not those who are harmless.

Q *Doesn't the fact that 9-11 terrorists were immigrants show the fallacy of open borders?*

A We don't have an open border with Mexico, yet thousands of illegal immigrants cross it each year. If common laborers can slip by our enforcers, well-trained terrorists will be able to do so too. Closing our borders won't keep out those determined to get in, but it will tie up a great deal of our enforcement personnel – to the great delight of the terrorists.

The alleged 9-11 lead hijacker, Mohamed Atta, entered the United States three times on an expired visa in 2001, even though officials were aware that he had violated it by taking flying lessons. Why wasn't he stopped at the border? If our immigration officers weren't so busy stopping peaceful Mexicans, maybe they would have had time to pursue the real threat.

Rather than proposing the abolition of all immigration screenings and border inspections, we should refine our policies to stop harassment of commerce and focus on defending the U.S. against crime, terrorism, and war. What do you think?

Terrorists capable of planning a successful attack most likely have the capability to get through a border check with false identification. Thus, putting more resources towards more immigration screening may not likely foil any serious deviants. If our goal is to stop terrorism, our resources could probably be better placed.

When we invest in border patrol, we have fewer resources to apprehend people who actually commit criminal acts. Freedom and practicality might be better served by open borders and stepped-up law enforcement. If criminals knew that they faced a high probability of apprehension and restitution, they wouldn't cross the border to rob or kill. Studies show that criminals do indeed respond to such factors, including the possibility of encountering an armed victim.

Perhaps the way to keep immigrants honest is to stop screening the multitudes who want to enter, and to deter criminality by making sure that the few who harm others are brought to justice.

Q *I have reservations about the consequences of a policy of open borders to the U.S. of "opening the floodgates" for immigrants to flow in freely. Obviously, the waiting lists for entry into America are very long in many countries. Since our society is currently far from a pure libertarian one in which all property is privately owned, I could easily envision a mass invasion by people from around the world seeking a better life, soon leading to an overpopulation crisis like we see in places such as India.*

Therefore, isn't there some reasonable justification to enforce some measures to ensure that all the valuable resources that make our country so attractive are not ransacked by the influx of literally hundreds of millions of human beings?

A Although the media does often refer to the "overpopulation" of India, that country has fewer residents per square mile than Hong Kong or Japan, which we don't consider "overpopulated." The difference is that India cannot provide for her people because government regulations stifle the production of wealth. Hong Kong and Japan are less encumbered and are able to produce enough. Even with a great influx of immigrants, therefore, we don't need to worry about "overpopulation" as long as we keep our economy free enough to provide for all.

Immigrants hardly have a history of "ransacking;" indeed, just the opposite is true. Without regulations to impede them, most try to start their own businesses or work at jobs that native-born Americans refuse (e.g., hand-harvesting crops). Indeed, half of the companies in Silicon Valley were started by immigrants who are now supplying jobs to thousands of Americans. When some of these immigrant CEOs were questioned by ABC's John Stossel, they claimed that regulations in their native lands prevented them from starting these businesses.

Immigrants leave their culture behind and come to a land where the customs and language are often very different. They have a great deal of courage and perseverance to undertake such a move. They are more likely to be "makers" instead of "takers." However, if our system rewards loafers rather than producers, our country will deteriorate as both native-born Americans and new immigrants choose welfare over work.

Q *On a recent Boston radio show, callers were asked to call in with their answers to the following question: "What should be done with illegal aliens?" The results: 2% chose "Amnesty"; 98% said "Arrest and Deport." How can the Libertarian Party and other libertarians continue to advocate an open border policy when such a high number of Americans are against it?*

A Libertarians base their positions on the non-aggression principle, not majority opinion. Libertarians don't say what they think people want to hear; they say what needs to be said.

Americans who disagree with an open border policy often do so because they don't understand the principles involved and have been misinformed about the true impact of immigration upon American prosperity. Our job is to counter misperceptions about immigration, and share information about the great benefits of immigration with the public in a positive, persuasive way.

Incidentally, the survey question you've cited is unlikely to be a referendum on open borders as much as one on law and order. "Illegal immigrants," by definition, are breaking the law; Americans generally don't forgive lawbreakers easily. Wouldn't you expect the numbers to be reversed if the radio audience had been asked, "What should be done with legal aliens?"

Unfortunately, our laws don't have a practical and legal way for many people, such as unskilled Mexican laborers, to get the green card required to work in the U.S. According to State Department data, it takes such an individual about 131 years, even if they have a sibling who is a U.S. citizen.[78] Obviously, such a person will never actually see a green card.

Q *Many libertarians advocate open borders. My question is: with open borders, does this not blur the distinct geographical borders* *of any country? Does this in any way diminish the sovereignty of a country?*

A A free flow of people doesn't diminish the sovereignty of a country any more than the free flow of goods does. However, the sharing of cultures that occurs during both activities historically has diminished the prospects of war. Since war is the greatest threat to sovereignty, immigration and free trade may actually strengthen it.

Q *Will open immigration homogenize nations? That is, will it make their cultures the same? Looking at the European Union we see a continent where an elite is trying to homogenize and unify it. Open borders are one of the tools being used.*

A Ultimately, societal attitudes contribute as much or more to homogenization than open borders. If each of us stayed in our own countries and never left, we wouldn't have intermarriage, which definitely contributes to homogenization. However, through TV, radio, and the Internet, we might all eventually adopt the same customs and lifestyle even if no borders were crossed.

On the other hand, some ethnic groups keep to themselves even when they enter a new nation. These communities are often large enough to make it possible for many immigrants never to even learn the language of their host country.

Some people think that homogenization means less strife. However, having similar physical characteristics, language, or customs is no guarantee of peace. Mutual respect, honoring our neighbor's choice, and righting any wrongs that we do (i.e., the libertarian philosophy), however, is a tried and true path to that end.

Switzerland, for example, is one of the most libertarian nations in the world. This wealthy and peaceful nation was founded to unite but not homogenize diverse groups of people. It has three national languages: French, Italian, and German.

Peaceful coexistence is about mutual respect and delighting in our differences, rather than feeling a need to force everyone into the same mold.

Q *The more I read The Liberator Online, the more I see situations from a libertarian perspective. I posted a comment to an online comments board regarding the issue of laws mandating "English Only" for businesses. Could my posting be considered a libertarian response to the question of "English Only" legislation? And how could I improve it?*

Here is what I wrote:

From a free-market, business standpoint, any legislation mandating either "English Only" or "Bilingual Necessary" is superfluous. In a free-market, laissez-faire atmosphere, I will conduct business with my customers in whichever language will assure that my business prospers. If it is necessary to speak Spanish to sell my product, I will speak Spanish. It's very simple: if I do not speak Spanish, I will not sell.

The opposite is also true. If it is necessary to speak English to sell my product, I will speak English. In this case also, it's very simple. If I do not speak English, I will not sell.

We see then that legislation is superfluous and impedes business.

*Will I demand that my monolingual Spanish speaking **buyer** learn English before I will **sell** him my product? How ludicrous! Of course I will not! I want my business to prosper. I will conduct my business in Spanish.*

*Conversely, if I am a **buyer** who speaks only English, and a **seller** who speaks Spanish demands that I learn Spanish before he will sell to me, I will show him the door and do business with a seller who speaks my language.*

By the way, the aforementioned is not theoretical. I have been a seller to both English and Spanish monolinguals. Let the free market operate, unfettered, and the question of "English Only" becomes moot.

 A That's an excellent answer! No improvement necessary!

Q *As with all peoples of the world, immigrants take with them the customs, religions, speech, language, holiday acknowledgements, etc. which they had in the country from which they are disembarking. This is human nature and is, in a free country, quite permissible as well as expected. Would libertarians support or embrace legislation designating a national language? If so, why?*

A No. Libertarians wouldn't force people to speak a particular language. Libertarians are against the initiation of force against anyone who is acting peacefully.

Local Issues

Local activism tells our neighbors what libertarians stand for and "who to call" when Big Brother comes knocking at their doors!

Q *What small, starting steps could libertarians in a city or county government take that would help move their community in a libertarian direction, but still be acceptable to the not-yet-libertarian voters (and which would hopefully show the success of libertarian ideas)?*

A Reducing taxes is very popular with voters, especially when services are improved as well. Suggest selling off business enterprises that your local government shouldn't be involved in (like golf courses or stadiums).

Contract out government services to the private sector via competitive bidding. The Reason Foundation in Los Angeles (www.reason.org) is a libertarian think tank specializing in local solutions and privatization (they coined the word "privatization"). Contact them for further ideas and details.

If the local government stops filling posts vacated by retirement or turnover, it can reduce the number of municipal employees painlessly as it privatizes.

Be sure and share your success stories with other libertarians so that they can follow your example!

Q *At the municipal level, city governments perform many functions: plowing and salting roads in the winter, coordinating senior citizens activities, evacuating residents in times of local* *emergencies, police protection, and so on. How would these services be provided in a libertarian municipality? What duties would a libertarian city rightfully have?*

A Most of the services could be supplied by private organizations on a local level. Some libertarians believe that the police and court systems would be the only government "services" provided in a municipality, but even these could be funded by user fees or community volunteers, not by taxes. Some libertarians believe that even these protective functions are best provided privately.

Q *What would a good libertarian sheriff say about DUI enforcement? Do I do blood tests to protect children and motorists from drunks? What do I tell the mother who lives next to the crack dealer?*

A If I were in your shoes, I'd explain to my constituents that I would focus my limited resources on stopping violent crime. Instead of giving tickets for a few miles over the speed limit or giving blood tests, my patrols would be instructed to get *all* reckless drivers off the street, whether they were drunk or distracted.

I'd be tougher on violent crime than any former sheriff, but soft on those behaving peaceably. The crack dealer would be told straight out that if the neighbors were happy, I'd be happy. If the neighbors felt that their kids were threatened by guns or physical abuse, I'd throw the book at them. Most sheriffs don't have the resources to make good such a threat because their officers are too busy locking up prostitutes, arresting people for smoking a joint on their back porch, and trying to control behavior that doesn't harm others.

I'd also try to show my constituents how to prevent crime, like the private police do. I'd encourage firearm ownership in the expectation that burglaries, rapes, and other violent crime would dramatically decrease. Punks brandish fewer weapons at the neighbors when the neighbors may be armed too.

Of course, my police force and constituents would need to buy into such programs. I think they might really enjoy trying liberty for a change!

Q *Like you, I too want to see prosperity within our cities. Yet how can cities and towns attract businesses and families if they are not allowed to give subsidies and special tax breaks? Would a libertarian town be able to advertise or in some other way promote that it is a good town for starting a business and/or raising a family? How would a libertarian town go about luring businesses to locate within its boundaries?*

A A libertarian town could lower property taxes dramatically by privatizing services like garbage collection. If nearby communities are still high-tax areas, people will come to you.

For almost 20 years, I lived in Kalamazoo, Michigan, where property taxes were some of the highest in the nation. The city government was concerned that the middle-class was moving out of Kalamazoo and into neighboring Portage. All the while, Kalamazoo kept raising property taxes, while Portage's remained relatively low.

When I campaigned for city commission, retired Kalamazoo home owners came to me in tears. They had paid off their mortgage, but property taxes had become higher than their mortgage payments used to be. As a result, they couldn't afford to retire in the homes that they had raised their children in.

Portage wisely kept its property taxes low. The middle class moved in. Businesses followed and Portage prospered. Any town can duplicate this model.

Q *I hope to run for state legislature. One of our major problems has been our roads. Many people have relocated to our area but our roads can't handle all the traffic. I need a libertarian solution to this problem.*

A If your local laws permit it, neighborhood associations or private companies could build, own and operate a private road network (such as is done in condo communities). Residents would contribute as a condition of using the roads. Only vehicles displaying their permit could drive there. People who didn't have a car and didn't want to use the new roads wouldn't have to pay. Unlike forcible taxation, involvement would be voluntary.

The bureaucrats, however, will likely make this approach difficult. Another, though less savory option, is to have the government build the road with taxes, but contract out the construction and maintenance to a private firm after competitive bidding. Other locales have saved 50-70% of the road cost using this approach.

Check with the Reason Foundation (www.reason.org) for back-up literature on this approach. Good luck!

Q *How would a libertarian government handle problems like a porn shop or other undesirable business moving into a residential neighborhood, without the use of zoning regulations? Would the solution be for homeowners to sue for a loss of property value?*

A If your neighbor does something to enhance your property values, would you feel obligated to share it with him or her? Probably not! Yet we often do feel cheated if our neighbor does something that decreases our property's value.

In a libertarian society, these ups and downs could be alleviated by building or moving into a community with restrictive covenants. Basically, the developer places restrictions into the deed of the property, to limit what subsequent owners can do or build.

For a real-life example, check out Houston, Texas. No zoning laws are in effect there, but some restrictive covenants are. On a smaller scale, condo communities often have used restrictions in their deeds.

The advantage of deed restrictions over zoning laws is that you know what you are getting when you buy. In today's system, your neighbor only has to get a variance from the zoning board or

city code enforcers in order to alter his or her property and change
the value of yours.

Q *You've talked a couple of times about "restrictive covenants" as
an alternative to zoning. I don't see much difference. Who would
establish a restrictive covenant? If someone placed a restrictive covenant
on my property, how would that affect me when I got ready to sell my
property? I might not be able to find anyone willing to put up with the
covenants that had been applied to my property. I find it hard to believe
that Houston never changes its covenants.*

A No one can put a restrictive covenant on your property except
yourself. When you buy property with covenants in place, you
voluntarily accept them as a condition of sale. In other words, no one
forces their covenants on you.

Zoning, however, is forcibly imposed by your local government and can change overnight, altering your property values radi-
cally. Libertarians believe that forcible imposition of taxes and regulations, such as zoning, should be outlawed.

Houston's residents do change their covenants, but they do so
by consent. In other words, if someone wants to put a commercial
building up in an area where covenants don't permit it, he or she
must have the explicit or implicit agreement of the neighbors. In this
way, changes are made by consent, not forcibly imposed.

Q *At times, there have been questions brought up about whether
people have the right to place and display anything they choose
on their own property. I do think that people should have this right;
however, this can lower the property value of surrounding properties.*

A In some communities (e.g., condominiums), owners can
contract to abide by standards that protect property value.
Such agreements could also be made among consenting neighbors.
Alternatively, many people will take down displays that concern
their neighbors if asked politely to do so.

Q *How should a libertarian city council handle the case of Elena Zagustin, the infamous "neighbor from hell" in Huntington Beach, California?*

She lived in a $500,000 house among other $500,000 houses, but allowed her property to go to pot. She never painted or maintained the building, threw trash and junk in her front and backyards, never cleaned the interior or threw out old newspapers. In short, she lived in a dump of her own making.

Her neighbors used every persuasive form they could think of to get her to shape up, but she kept resisting until they started attacking her with lawyers and zoning inspectors. It still took several years to bring the issue to a close. The city finally seized the property and sold it at auction to a developer who specializes in remodeling run-down properties.

*I admit I'm stumped. How could a libertarian city council protect Elena's property rights while still protecting the **neighbors'** property rights, too?*

A In a libertarian society, people would move into a community with deed restrictions, covenants, or condominium associations that required their preferred level of upkeep. Violating such an agreement would result in a breach of contract and well-defined remedies. Without such a contract, no one's rights are clearly defined.

Zoning ordinances usually require a certain level of upkeep, and were probably in place when Elena purchased her home. Thus, the neighbors felt justified in taking action against her, since technically she was breaking the law.

However, from a libertarian perspective, such a law infringes on Elena's right to do with her property as she wished. Elena didn't sign a contract with anyone to keep her property clean and neat, yet when she failed to do so, the city government forcibly took her home from her. Had Elena signed a contract, covenant, or condo regulation requiring upkeep when she purchased the property, she probably would have felt more obligated to comply.

So what do we do when rights are poorly defined? My preference is to err on the side of individual liberty. For example, Elena's neighbors could have held an occasional clean-up party for Elena and helped her restore her home. Perhaps such neighborly good will would have brought out the best in Elena, who in turn could have arranged to hire some help to keep her home up.

If Elena refused this generosity, the neighbors could have built an attractive fence around her property to hide the eyesore from view. Funds for this fence would come from neighbors who felt that Elena's property threatened the value of theirs.

Since the fence would actually stand on neighboring property or on the city's road easement in front of her house, Elena would have no grounds to object. She might even prefer to clean up rather than become enclosed.

The neighbors might also find a way to buy Elena out, fix up her property, and sell it at a profit.

All of these options protect Elena's right to do with her property as she sees fit. Instead of using the guns of government, the neighbors would need to invest some time and money, instead of imposing all of the cost on Elena as they actually did.

If we were Elena's neighbors, why would we choose the libertarian route over the convenience of having government enforce zoning restrictions? The answer is simple. By setting a precedent for liberty, we protect *ourselves* from potential problems later.

For example, what if most of the neighbors upgraded their property and voted that *we* must do the same? If we failed to comply, we'd risk losing our home, too, even though *our* level of upkeep hadn't changed at all.

We reap as we sow. If we want liberty's protection, we must first grant it to others.

Q *We live on a dirt road that wasn't paved because the developer went bankrupt, and the township won't maintain the road unless all who live on this road pay to have it paved. (I think a bank now has the deed.) As a result, we have major problems with kids riding dirt bikes and four-wheelers up and down the roads – very aggravating! The State Police say they can't do anything about this, because it's a private road. We have asked these kids to slow down and they are very rude and the parents are even more rude. We are at our wits' end. There are other neighborhoods around here with the same problem. What can we do?*

A If the bank has the deed, they might be willing to sell the road to you and your neighbors for virtually nothing. Indeed, if you and your neighbors formed a non-profit association to take possession of it, the bank might give it to you for a bit of free publicity.

As owners of the road, you could then ban dirt bikes or any other trespassers. Several neighborhoods in St. Louis, Missouri have bought their streets so that they too could regulate traffic and keep out undesirables. Ownership has its privileges!

Q *I'm not sure how to bring in libertarian principles at the zoning board, parks & recreation, library advisory, heritage commission, building standards, board of adjustment, etc. Any ideas?*

A In one community in which I was politically active, eminent domain was a big issue. Local governments across America are routinely condemning property, taking it over by eminent domain, and then selling it to big developers. Small business owners gratefully funded libertarians who successfully fought this battle for them.

If you sit through a few zoning board meetings, you'll see how they can devastate landlords and other small business people through a simple vote. In my area, one couple constructed a rooming house with all the applicable permits and approvals, only to have it condemned when the zoning board decided to change its designation. The board members had no sympathy for the financial devastation they caused.

That's just one issue. Privatization is another very popular solution to many local concerns; you can get a great deal of information about it at www.reason.org.

Read your local newspaper and you'll quickly get a good idea of how an active libertarian can help. Government aggression has become so pervasive that you'll easily find your local niche!

Miscellaneous Issues

S ome of the following are frequently asked questions that don't readily fall into the earlier categories. Many are just plain fascinating!

Q *Do you think that the post office should be run by the government or should it be a private enterprise?*

A Private, of course! New Zealand has had great success in turning their money-losing public postal monopoly into a profit-making private enterprise. Funding anything through the aggression of taxation taints the outcome. Honoring our neighbor's choice by refraining from aggression produces the win-win outcome we desire.

Q *I need somebody to protect me from my body being viewed as an object. I think pornography spreads negative stereotypes that people shouldn't be exposed to. As a woman, I want to be free not to be viewed as an object. If the government doesn't protect this freedom by outlawing hard porn, how can I be free?*

A No government can keep us free from the opinions of others, no matter how much we might wish it. Each of us must learn how to cope with criticism, rejection, and misjudgment. I like Mom's attitude best: "Sticks and stones may break your bones, but names will never hurt you."

Just a few short centuries ago, women were considered to be property of their men folk. Husbands could legally beat, rape, and even kill their wives. Today, society might have more pornography, but women are no longer considered property. History, not pornography, is responsible for the lingering few who still see women as sexual objects exclusively.

If we send our police after pornographers, we have fewer police to send after rapists. Where do you want your resources placed?

Q *If you remove all farm subsidies, what happens to the farmer when drought or flood hits and he loses his crop for a year?*

A Like other business people, farmers plan for bad years through savings, insurance, etc. If they fail to make such plans, they suffer the same fate as other businesses operating on the edge – they go under in tough times. They are bought out by someone who manages better. The displaced farmers find an occupation more suited to their particular talents.

Subsidies discourage good management and encourage inefficiency. As a result, consumers pay more for less.

Q *Without a national ID (for example, Social Security numbers or driver's licenses) how would banks and other institutions verify your identity for their services? How could they prove, for example, your claim to ownership of a piece of property or a car? How could they know you didn't just steal or forge a deed or title?*

A A government-issued ID can always be forged. Already today, a thriving underground black market exists in forged Social Security cards, passports, and driver's licenses.

Indeed, banks are losing so much money on forged ID and identity theft that many have started fingerprinting customers. With identification information, as in so many other areas, government does a very poor job.

As you have observed, identification proving that someone actually is who he says he is, or has the qualifications he claims, is a vital need in a market economy. Private institutions have an enormous stake in being able to quickly and accurately insure the identities of customers who, in today's global economy, may engage in transactions around the world.

In a libertarian society, banks and other financial institutions would establish the level of identity verification they needed to protect their interests, as has been the case in the past. Such institutions would have a strong interest in creating ways of identification that would not offend, burden or harm their customers.

Competition would quickly create new and innovative ways to meet this demand. We would expect to see the kind of constant innovation, low cost, ease-of-use, and concern for pleasing customers that we today see in other significantly unregulated areas of our economy, such as telecommunications, computers and the Internet.

People would be free to decide for themselves if they wanted to provide information in order to work with these institutions. Governments couldn't force individuals to carry IDs. The most innovative and customer-pleasing solutions would be the most successful.

There is a great need for identification services that aid consumers while protecting their privacy. Only the market – not government – can provide this.

Q *I have a question about Social Security numbers. This is something that has always bothered me. I have four children. Hospitals, schools, and other places demand Social Security numbers for my children and myself. Even when I protest, they insist it is mandatory. My children were told they would not get their grades or report cards. On one occasion my son said he couldn't go to school without it. I complied, but don't like it. What is the libertarian viewpoint on the issuance of Social Security numbers?*

A Most libertarians are as uncomfortable with Social Security numbers as you are. Many Christians wonder if they are not the "mark of the beast" referred to in the Bible, without which no one will be allowed to buy or sell. Clearly, such numbers are a means of governmental tracking, which most libertarians view as an invasion of privacy.

Some conscientious objectors have turned in their Social Security numbers in order to withdraw from the system. Of course, you have already seen that functioning without a Social Security number in today's society is problematic. Be aware that government officials do not always take kindly to those who no longer wish to follow their rules.

Building a strong movement for liberty and increasing awareness about these issues is the only way such abuses will be ended. You've taken a good start in that direction by learning more about libertarianism!

Q *Like you, I wish to live in a nonviolent and safe society. I do, however, support and attend rock concerts at clubs and arenas at which there is a large amount of slam-dancing and other reckless behavior. How would a libertarian government deal with this, if at all?*

A Clubs and arenas would all be privately owned in a libertarian society. Owners would police such events to maximize customer satisfaction and limit their own liability.

Q *Aren't the windfall profits landlords receive when society is progressing actually the property of society in general?*

A No! Landlords work hard for their money. I know; I once was one! My tenants felt sorry for me. One of them told me to stop trying to repair, paint, and improve. "Go on welfare, as I've done," she urged. "Then you can get some rest!"

Q *What about "biopiracy," the practice of patenting plants and cures for diseases? Would libertarians outlaw such patents in the name of freedom? If not, won't everyone become slaves to those who "own" what others require to survive? If libertarians would outlaw such patents, what about those for inventors or artists? Don't they need their*

*work protected in order to make a living from their talent or ingenuity?
In short, where do libertarians stand on intellectual property rights?*

A Most libertarians believe that intellectual property rights, such as copyrights, should be protected. Many libertarians believe that patent rights would likewise continue in a libertarian society, even though determining what constitutes a new invention can be arbitrary.

Some libertarians believe that intellectual property does not exist at all. Of course, software manufacturers could still license their product (as they do today) under the contractual condition that buyers wouldn't copy or sell it.

My personal belief is that medical patents such as you describe would cease to exist in a libertarian society. Patents are important in the pharmaceutical industry today primarily because the FDA makes drug development so unnecessarily expensive that costs can be recovered only with a few years of market monopoly. In a libertarian society without the FDA, patents wouldn't drive the industry as they do today. They'd be less necessary, much less valuable, and eventually more trouble than they were worth.

Q *They want to foreclose our house for not paying property tax. Is this really legal? Can they really come in and put all of our belongings on the front lawn?*

A Yes, they can legally take your property – but they couldn't do so in a libertarian society. Libertarians recognize that taxation of any kind is theft. If you don't pay, your property is taken – at gunpoint, if necessary. Help libertarians legalize freedom instead of theft!

Q *I'm a very frequent flyer (20 flights per month), which is what brought this hypothetical question to mind.*
In a perfect libertarian world, how would a conflict of interest over property rights be resolved in an emergency or investigation that is handled by the NTSB or FAA? In other words, if a plane crashes on

Mr. Smith's farm, what obligation is Mr. Smith under to allow any governing body or rescue operation on his property? Would it be the state government who would compel Mr. Smith to cooperate? I realize that 99.99% people would not need to be coerced in this type of situation, I'm just curious about those that do.

A In a libertarian society, if you felt that someone "needed to be coerced," you would do so at your own risk. For example, your Mr. Smith might sue for restitution if you trespassed on his property. Even if the jury awarded Mr. Smith compensation, you (or those whose lives you saved) might feel it was a small price to pay. Most likely, however, Mr. Smith would not want to risk neighborhood scorn and ostracism by making a public claim against rescuers, especially if he operated a local business which could be boycotted by disgusted neighbors.

Q *I hear a lot of talk about a proposed anti-flag burning amendment. On one hand it seems that this amendment would be a violation of the First Amendment, on the other it seems that the measure is only decent. After all, why should we allow our own citizens to show disrespect for our great country and every man, woman or child that has ever died for it? What would a libertarian think about such an amendment?*

A If a person burns a flag which they have purchased, they are not aggressing against another human being. Specifically, they aren't assaulting, defaming, cheating, or stealing from anybody. They are making a peaceful protest. The right to criticize our country or government is paramount to our freedom, the ideal represented by that flag.

If we throw flag burners in jail, take their money in fines, or otherwise cause them harm, we become the aggressors. This is not the libertarian way. Libertarians do not harm others except in defense of themselves or their property.

You believe that flag burning shows disrespect towards those who have fought to preserve our freedoms. Punishing protestors shows an even more profound disrespect for the ideals that these people died for. An intact flag is worthless if it no longer stands for freedom. A flag burned to ashes challenges us to remember just exactly what freedom is.

Q *I am wondering about the future of property rights in outer space when we finally do explore and colonize extensively. Since most of the "land" in space on the Moon, on Mars, and other planets isn't currently owned by anyone, what would be a good way to distribute the property? In light of the fact that there are private-sector space-faring associations and corporations that are trying to set up the private sector to make voyages into space, it seems that this will soon be an important question to answer.*

A The moon and other planets, in the absence of government interference, would be "homesteaded" and claimed by individuals or groups. For example, a group might establish a moon base and expand to cover a sizable area. The second group would have to choose to establish their camp from land not "homesteaded" by the first.

In all likelihood, some boundary disputes would arise. The difficulty and expense in making space voyages, however, will provide great incentives to settle these peacefully.

Unfortunately, if the governments of the world become claimants, the probability of armed conflict will increase dramatically. Since politicians don't personally pay for the wars that they start – or die on the battlefields – they have less incentive to negotiate.

Q *I understand that Congress shall make no law abridging our freedom of speech, but I also understand that we are not to harm another person or their property. So, I wondered how a libertarian society would deal with libel and slander. Would speech that truly harms another person deserve some punishment?*

A Libertarians are divided on this issue. Some believe that lying about a person, and thereby causing them to lose business, etc., should be cause for restitution. Other libertarians believe that lying is not fraud in the same sense that breaking a contract would be. The line between stating our opinion about someone and actually telling a falsehood can be fairly thin at times. "Bill Clinton (or George W. Bush) is a bad person" could be a lie or the truth, depending upon how one sees it!

Q *What would happen in a libertarian society to people who plagiarize Dr. Mary Ruwart's answers to tough questions? Not that I am admitting to anything!*

A In today's society, copyright law allows you to publish excerpts from another person's writing as long as you cite the source. This falls under the generally recognized concept of "fair use."

Written material is considered intellectual property, that is rented (not sold) to the reader. Most computer software is marketed this way as well.

Many libertarians believe that copyrights would function similarly in a free society. The copyright notice would act as contract between the author and the reader.

In regards to my *Short Answers*, please feel free to "plagiarize" them in your discussions and campaigns; that's what they're for! In your writings, just give credit where credit is due.

Q *The first question I got from a friend with whom I was discussing libertarian philosophy (I had said just before that the basic tenet was that a person could do what he wanted as long as it didn't hurt anyone else or commit force or fraud against anyone) was: "How about a guy standing on the street corner exposing himself? That isn't hurting anyone but I sure wouldn't want my 5 year-old child seeing that!"*

I replied that in a libertarian society, the street corner might be private property so that would be trespassing, but she just pooh-poohed that answer. What is the short answer to this problem of public nudity?

A The streets in a libertarian society are likely to be owned by individuals or groups who prohibit activity that they or their customers find offensive. In most family-oriented neighborhoods, nudity is likely to fall into that category. In those areas, flashers would be deterred by the possibility of prosecution much as they are today.

You did well with the essence of your reply. Sometimes you just have to spell it out, step by step.

Q *How can you balance the budget, pay off the debt, and slash spending without doing away with entitlements, like Social Security and Medicare, that people have paid into for decades?*

A We can only balance the budget by privatizing entitlements like Social Security and Medicare and ending foreign wars. The *only* way we can keep the promises made to our seniors without massive inflation is to increase our rate of wealth creation. One way to do that is by deregulating business. Each regulator destroys about 150 private sector jobs each year, so each one fired is true "economic stimulus."

Another way to increase wealth creation is to cut the tax rate and end tariffs and other barriers to importation. This drives domestic capital into efficient businesses, stimulating the economy further. Even at lower tax rates, a robust economy means more tax dollars collected to offset the entitlement programs, which should be privatized ASAP so that young people aren't forced into these Ponzi schemes.

Q *I find these references to the "Founding Fathers" of the United States disturbing. You are recalling a time that has similarities to the Unilateral Declaration of Independence days of Ian Smith's Rhodesia. Surely those references are invalid for libertarians, since they legitimize the theft of lands and destruction of lives and livelihoods that forms the basis for your present occupation of other people's property and continuing denial of their rightful place in society?*

A The Founding Fathers referred to by Americans are those who helped gain independence from Britain. Many of the Founding Fathers were admirers of the Native Americans and lived peacefully with them, just as many of them strongly opposed the institution of slavery that then existed. Others had an expansionist approach because they felt that the indigenous population, women and blacks did not have the same rights that as white males did. Clearly, libertarians do not agree with those who held the latter viewpoint.

Q *Who pays for long term R&D? Certain basic technologies we rely upon, such as the Internet, artificial satellites, etc., required a huge investment in R&D for a long period of time before they became profitable. If governments won't have the resources to do it, even if they do it in a wasteful manner, who will?*

A "Government resources" are really funds pirated from the private sector. Since government uses them inefficiently, less money is available for other projects. More government therefore means less useful research, long term or short term. Business has no trouble raising money for profitable projects, even long-term ones. Pharmaceutical companies, for example, face a 15-year development time after they discover a new drug that they want to take to market.

Q *I am greatly in agreement with libertarian principles, but as a college student preparing for a career in the hard sciences, I can't help but question one issue: scientific research. How would a libertarian society address such issues as scientific research of a purely academic nature at a scale that cannot necessarily be carried out at a university level? I am thinking of such government-operated laboratories as Brookhaven National Laboratory and the Relativistic Heavy-Ion Collider, a project which no business or university could ever conceivably carry out. Without government-funded laboratories, how do we fuel new research of such a nature that would be inherently unprofitable to any private enterprise?*

A In his 1996 book, *The Economic Laws of Scientific Research*, Terence Kealey presents evidence that only 10% of new technology comes from academic (government-funded) research. He also finds that increasing funds for government research tends to depress privately funded efforts, resulting in a net loss of new scientific progress. In other words, government funding of research, like most forms of aggression, backfires. My own experience in 25-plus years of both industrial and academic research supports these findings.

If a libertarian society didn't have a Brookhaven National Laboratory or a Relativistic Heavy-Ion Collider, it would most likely have something that was more highly valued by society at that point in time. Who knows, you might even like it better!

Of course, in a libertarian society, research could be funded privately. For example, the Life Extension Foundation (www.lef.org) currently supports anti-aging research so successfully that its discoveries have been patented.

Q *It seems Americans have a veil over their eyes because corporations fund the media and therefore control it. In a libertarian society, how would the people get true quality information about the world?*

A In a libertarian society, big businesses wouldn't be so big, since they couldn't destroy their competitors through government regulation. Without government control of the airways, more radio and television stations would be available and could not be shut down on political whim. Thus, the average person would have much better quality and quantity of information.

Today, the unregulated Internet provides the most diversity of views and cannot be easily controlled by politicians or corporations. Some people have even dubbed the "blogosphere" (to also include the huge number of independent news and opinion-oriented websites) the "alternate media," which many have come to trust more than they do the "old" or "mainstream" media. Freedom catalyzes the spread of innovative ideas and information.

Q *If we remove the FCC entirely, there will be nobody allocating frequencies to radio stations, and preventing interference between broadcast stations. How could we deal with this problem without something like the FCC?*

A One way to eliminate the FCC would be to auction off all of the frequencies and allow them to be bought and sold like other property. Trespass by other stations would be handled just like trespass on land. Bandwidths useful for new applications could be "homesteaded" just as land once was.

Q *What would happen to scientific missions such as Mars Pathfinder if NASA were privatized?*

A Any group (non-profit or for profit) could sponsor space missions and reap the benefits (e.g., pictures, technology, information), much as NASA does today. Individuals, such as yourself, would have more influence on the direction of such missions as contributors or stock holders instead of taxpayers.

In a libertarian society, we're likely to have more and varied space exploration because of the 1) greater wealth overall; 2) profit potential of space exploration, 3) two-fold greater efficiency of the private sector.

Q *I am a graduate student and have a small family. As are current teachers, future teachers are very poorly treated, and graduate students often live well below the poverty line.*

My question is: what would you recommend to a libertarian (as I am) who finds himself forced to use government programs such as food stamps and HUD subsidies in order to provide for his family and follow his dream?

Every time I go to pick up food stamps, I feel like a traitor. When I am able to give food to my kids, I feel better, but I think there has to be a better way. I have visited private non-profit food banks, but they often give food that we do not like, or cannot eat (allergies). So their help, while appreciated, is not very useful.

This is a predicament and I was wondering what you would recommend?

A We can always arrange our life differently in order to meet our goals. Some people in your situation might choose to work for a few years to build up enough savings to attend school without deprivation. Others might take on an additional job. Still others might arrange for a loan from family, friends, or commercial sources.

My personal choice during my undergraduate years was to live very inexpensively. Instead of a car, I rode my bicycle to class, even in the snowy winters of Michigan. I lived in a dilapidated dwelling where the floors had a noticeable slant and the carpet had odors that no cleaning would remove. My clothing consisted of hand-me-downs from relatives and friends, which I altered to fit. Sometimes my only affordable source of protein was a plate of chicken necks. My usual stock was tuna fish and chicken potpies which I could buy on sale for ten cents each. In the summer between my undergraduate and graduate years, I literally lived in the laboratory and cooked over a Bunsen burner because I didn't have enough money for apartment rent. (The university newspaper even ran a cartoon based on my unusual housing situation!)

I could have borrowed money for my education, but I didn't like the idea of graduating with a debt. Because I was doing what I wanted to do – going to school without borrowing – I didn't feel at all deprived. The only legacy from those days is a refusal to ever eat chicken potpie again!

I share this story only to suggest that if we feel strongly about our goals and our means to them, there's a path for us to follow. First, though, we must determine what our goals really are. If you truly want to get an education and feed your children without taking welfare, you'll find a way.

On the other hand, many libertarians believe that taking such services when needed constitutes a recovery of our stolen tax dollars.

This is a perfectly moral argument, but it does have a glaring flaw. If each of us tries to recover exactly what we've put it in, we will find that only a fraction is available, because our money has been wasted, not invested. Liquidation of all government assets, including almost half of the U.S. landmass, is probably the only way that all of us could even come close to recovering what government has taken from us.

When making such difficult decisions, let your conscience be your guide. No one can advise you better.

How to Get There
from Here

T he marketplace works in mysterious ways. Who can say how
and when the win-win libertarian philosophy will manifest?

Q *How many Libertarian Party members are there in the U.S.
House and Senate?*

A To the best of my knowledge, the only member of Congress
who has claimed formal affiliation with the Libertarian Party
is Representative Ron Paul from Texas, who was the 1988 Libertarian
Party (LP) presidential candidate and a lifetime member of the LP.
Dr. Paul has had 12 terms in Congress as a Republican, in spite of
intense opposition from GOP regulars.

When Congressman Paul is asked why he left the Libertarian
Party, he responds: "I never did." Congressman Paul believed that
he could only continue to win his seat if he was on the Republican
ticket. As of this writing in 2012, he is waging a campaign for the
Republican presidential nomination, while planning to retire from
Congress at the end of his current term.

Q *Do libertarians have an example of a working model that
subscribes to your ideals? Is there a success story anywhere in
the world?*

A Almost every aspect of the libertarian ideal has a real-
life success story, but not necessarily in one time or place!

Contrasting libertarian-like and statist societies where they co-exist is especially enlightening.

Today, fishing rights in Britain's rivers are privately owned, so rivers are protected from pollution, unlike in the U.S. In Kenya, elephant hunting is banned and the herds are rapidly decreasing. In neighboring Zimbabwe, where elephants can be owned, sold, and hunted, their numbers are increasing dramatically.

Modern-day Costa Rica has no standing army, yet it is one of the most peaceful places in Central America. Switzerland has a part-time national government, yet the Swiss enjoy one of the highest standards of living in the world. Until recently, their currency was still backed by gold, so their inflation rate was low.

Scottish banks in the 1800s had free banking which protected its depositors while neighboring English banks went under. Canadian banks, which were not as highly regulated as U.S. ones, experienced fewer failures during the Great Depression.

Hong Kong prospered as a free trade zone with low taxes and few regulations. It went from one of the poorest countries in the world to one with a per capita income comparable to that of the U.S. in just 50 years.

Q *Is there scientific evidence that supports libertarian ideas?*

A There is indeed! My book, *Healing Our World*, is probably the most comprehensive listing of these studies, but it probably covers only half of the available literature. You can download the 1992 version for free at my website, www.ruwart.com or purchase the expanded 2003 edition there or from the Advocates.

When I first wrote *Healing*, I wanted a few illustrations of how liberty works in the real world. To my amazement, I found that almost every aspect of liberty has been tried at some time in history with remarkable success. In many cases, we are unaware of this history, perhaps because of the pro-government history taught in government-run schools.

We all suffer when liberty is lost. We lose the wealth that would have been created, the health that would have come from innovations, and the wisdom that comes from the discovery and implementation of truth. Thankfully, in the long run, we all gain when liberty is restored. One day, when we realize this, government aggression will be seen as undesirable and we will no longer harm ourselves by encouraging or accepting it.

Q *Why is libertarianism so strong in the United States, as contrasted with Europe, where there seems to be much less interest?*

A Most of the people living in the U.S. are descendants of people who immigrated specifically to enjoy the blessings of freedom. In the 1800s, the U.S. was probably the freest nation in the modern world. That heritage clearly remains.

Q *You are completely unrealistic. Governments exist because people love power.*

A When people realize, as most will one day, that they hurt themselves, as well as others, when they try to coerce and manipulate through politics, the world will change dramatically.

At one time in the world's history, we believed that the earth was flat, that slavery was necessary to maintain civilization, and that if man were meant to fly, he'd have wings. Changing our minds about these things has changed our world.

People go after power because they think it will make them happy. Ultimately, bending others to their will is found to thwart that goal. Since people greedily go after what brings them happiness, one day they will also reject the desire for power over others as a means to their ends.

Q *How we can get the passive American population to stop complaining and get off their butts and work for change?*

A My perception is that people haven't realized that liberty will give them everything that politicians promise but can never deliver. Consequently, my time and energy is spent pointing out this simple fact.

However, most change in society is made by a small percentage of dedicated individuals. If you want to be part of that dedicated group, ask yourself what YOU think needs to be done. What do *you* feel called to do?

If the answers seem elusive, you might get inspiration from the last chapter of my book, *Healing Our World*, entitled "How to Get There From Here." You can download the 1993 version free from my website at www.ruwart.com.

Q *What do you think about the Free State Project? Its goal is to get enough liberty activists to move to a single state (New Hampshire) so that, working within the political framework there, they can influence its politics towards more freedom.*

A We probably need a wide range of activism and activist organizations to move our nation and the world in a libertarian direction by creating "the perfect storm" of libertarian activities and resources. The Free State Project, in my opinion, is making a significant contribution to the cause of freedom.

Some of my other favorite activist organizations include the International Society for Individual Liberty (www.isil.org), something you, as a European, might be especially interested in, as they work with liberty activists around the world.

The Advocates for Self-Government (www.theadvocates.org) has brought the World's Smallest Political Quiz to both the Internet and our nation's schools and is helping libertarians become successful communicators of the ideas of liberty.

The U.S.-based Institute for Justice (www.ij.org) is successfully overturning government interference with small business and changing the way state and local governments use eminent domain.

The Libertarian Party (www.lp.org) has placed hundreds of candidates in local office.

For students, libertarian activist organizations include Young Americans for Liberty (www.yaliberty.org) and Students for Liberty (www.studentsforliberty.org). Check them out!

If we chop off enough tentacles from the octopus of aggressive government, we can render it harmless. Multiple approaches may ultimately be more effective than a single "silver bullet."

Q *I've had many email discussions with a dear friend of mine (a liberal, as I formerly was) regarding the benefits of libertarianism. However, my inexperience led me to botch my efforts. Maybe the sensible thing to do would be to just move on to others, but I can't bring myself to give up.*

A Sometimes it is more sensible to move on. When we spend our time with those resistant to liberty, we aren't spending it with those who would be more receptive. Our time, unfortunately, is limited. Sometimes it's best to agree to disagree.

However, because we love those close to us, we especially want them to share the sense of uplift, enlightenment, and hope that libertarianism engenders. We especially hate to see our friends and family voting for things that actually do the opposite of what they intend.

Many liberals are deeply committed to helping the disadvantaged. In low-key emails, you could send your friend links to stories about libertarians who are making a big difference to the disadvantaged. Don't push your friends for a reaction. Let them come to you. Just send them a tidbit now and then.

Some examples: The Institute for Justice (www.ij.org), a pro-bono libertarian legal non-profit, has led a number of fights to keep big government from regulating minority entrepreneurs out of business. They took eminent domain to the Supreme Court to protect a lower middle class neighborhood from developers. You may want to browse their site and find some cases that would illustrate how liberty is the only champion of the disadvantaged.

Another example: libertarian Steve Marrioti began teaching low-income at-risk adolescents how to start their own businesses after he was mugged for $10. His National Foundation for Teaching Entrepreneurship (www.nfte.com) has gained numerous awards and is funded almost exclusively from private donations.

You might also find what issues most concern your friend. If he is anti-war, pro-civil liberties, against corporate welfare, etc., he will find no stauncher allies than libertarians. You can build common ground on such issues and find much to agree on. That may open his mind on other issues.

Finally, don't be so hard on yourself! Effective communication doesn't come without some practice. We're all still learning. Take a break. Back off for a while and prepare yourself for the time when your friend wants to know more.

Q *How do we get from here to our libertarian ideal? Even if libertarians held every office in the country tomorrow, how could they convert our current system of social democracy into a libertarian system?*

A Exactly how the transformation will come about is difficult to predict. Who would have thought that the Berlin Wall would come down so easily or that the Soviet Union would fall without the clash of armies? Who would have predicted the Industrial Revolution or even the success of the American colonies breaking with England? Who would have envisioned instant communication anywhere in the world via the Internet?

Truth is generally not only stranger than fiction, but stranger than we can imagine. However, the marketplace is already moving us in a libertarian direction. The average economic freedom score for the world rose from 5.53 (out of 10) in 1980 to 6.74 in 2007, according to the Economic Freedom of the World Report (www.freetheworld.com).

More restitution, e-gold as a substitute currency, home and Internet schooling, private security, private roads, and other government-service substitutions are on the rise. These alternatives will eventually replace their governmental counterparts simply because they are more efficient.

Q *If you don't like it here in the U.S., why don't you leave?*

A I love the principles of freedom and individual rights that this country was founded upon. I want to help the U.S. return to the ideals that made her great.

Q *As a libertarian who is considering a run for public office, why should I not accept public funding? I am opposed to the government owning roads, yet I still use them to go to work every day. I am opposed to the government subsidizing education, yet I go to a state college. Using public funds would make things a lot easier for a young person like me to run for office. Public funds would give me a chance to win, just as public roads give me a chance to get to work each day.*

A Libertarians differ in how they view accepting matching funds or any other tax-supported programs. Some libertarians believe that we shouldn't accept this "stolen" money in any form. Others believe that we should recover our tax dollars as much as possible from the bureaucratic "thieves."

Most libertarians turn down matching funds regardless of which view they hold. Voters often challenge us: "How do we know that you'll lower our taxes? Other politicians promise that too, but never come through!" When we point out that we've already turned down campaign subsidies, we gain voter respect.

The official Libertarian Party position on matching funds is that candidates must decide this issue for themselves. This issue was revisited in a recent strategy session and reaffirmed.

Q *Dr. Ruwart, I have tried to use some of the answers you suggest to questioners, but these are often only assertions, without evidence. Perhaps references to credible sources would help.*

I'll grant that the questioners usually cannot provide any more evidence for their assumptions. But since it is their belief that we are out to modify, isn't the burden of proof on us? What do you think?

A Many of my short answers are designed to surprise the listener so that they come back with a question or challenge that encourages dialog. Of course, when making such statements, which are contrary to popular belief, it is indeed helpful to be able to point to supporting evidence.

Consequently, my short answers often include a phrase like this: "For details, see Chapter XX in my book, *Healing Our World*, available as a free download at my website, www.ruwart.com" to indicate where such references may be found. If, in an answer, I use information that can't be found in *Healing Our World*, I usually include its source.

Needless to say, making the case that liberty works requires more information than simply pointing out that it is right. Big government proponents gained the upper hand by convincing people that liberty doesn't work in the real world. When we can show people that liberty works, and does so predictably because it is right, big government will be quickly cut down to size!

Q *The libertarian prospect is bleak because the human prospect is bleak. People are, for the most part, lazy or stupid. Furthermore, history demonstrates that, so far, the universal condition of mankind has been tyranny.*

A When we look only at the short term, prospects for liberty do seem bleak. Although people seek their own self-interest, they frequently don't recognize it. Our job, of course, is to help them do so!

When we look over the long term, however, we can see a great deal of progress. Within the last couple hundred years, most societies have rejected slavery, recognized that women and people of color are fully human, condemned torture, and abandoned rule by monarchs.

The long-term view shows progress away from tyranny. We will probably continue to take two steps forward and one step back, but the overall direction is towards liberty. For example, the average economic freedom score for the world rose from 5.53 (out of 10) in 1980 to 6.74 in 2007, according to the Economic Freedom of the World Report (www.freetheworld.com).

In the U.S. after 9-11, we've experienced that step back. Our mission, should we chose to accept it, is to point out the folly of fighting tyranny with tyranny. I expect a reversal on the War on Terrorism much like we saw with the war in Vietnam. It's just a matter of time…

Q *Why should we sit back and watch the government strip us of our liberties? I appreciate your column, but I disagree with your idea that we as a people must be strong and patient and eventually government will change.*

A The solution is not to be strong and patient and wait for the government to change. Obviously, we've had a miscommunication here!

Our government will not change unless we change first. Until we honor the peaceful choices of our neighbors and insist that our government do the same, things will not get better.

What is the mechanism by which we educate our neighbors and enlist them in pulling out the fangs of government? How exactly do we stop the Frankenstein monster that we've created? Each of us will have different ideas and each of us should try to implement them. Together, the sum of our efforts will change the world for the better just as surely as our early actions changed it for the worse!

Q *I've been frustrated by some libertarians who think that compromising libertarian principles is the best way to get the libertarian message accepted by the public. When I disagree with them, I am derided as a purist. How do I answer them?*

A Those who want to soft-sell the libertarian message are really saying that they wish to deceive the public to gain votes, a clear violation of the non-aggression principle. If we don't believe in our principles enough to live them, how will we persuade others of their practicality?

Oftentimes, those who suggest that the libertarian message is too extreme for the mainstream voter generally don't know how to present libertarian ideas in a compelling way. Consequently, they fear ridicule when they come across in an unconvincing manner.

Sometimes, they themselves aren't fully convinced that liberty works in a particular area. This is not at all unusual. When we fail to see a way that liberty works in the real world, we tend to believe it doesn't. When someone provides us with real-life examples of how liberty works for just about everyone, we quickly become good advocates for self-government.

You can get hundreds of examples showing how liberty works from my book, *Healing Our World*, available either from the Advocates (updated 2003 edition) or as a free download from www.ruwart.com (the older 1993 edition). The Advocates for Self-Government web site provides a number of resources to help present the libertarian message in a compelling manner.

Finally, libertarians often believe that they can't be effective unless they are elected to public office. History tells us otherwise. Even though only a few Socialist Party members were elected in the past century, most of the major economic planks of their 1928 Socialist Party platform were quickly adopted by the Democrats and Republicans and became, to a major degree, U.S. law.

"In our opinion, the Socialist Party was the most influential political party in the United States in the first decades of the 20th Century," wrote renowned libertarian economists Milton and Rose Friedman in their 1980 book, *Free to Choose*. Maybe we should be less focused on election outcomes and more focused on winning hearts and minds, something that we can't do by compromising our message.

Q *Considering the shared grievances and policy views of many Libertarians and Greens, why aren't these parties mutually supporting candidates in joint efforts to further their viewpoints?*

A Green Party members are natural allies of Libertarian Party members, except for one important stumbling block. Most (but not all) Greens believe that big government is the sole solution to their concerns, especially environmental ones.

Libertarians understand that government is the fox in the hen house. The U.S. military dumps more toxic waste than the top 3-5 chemical companies. It may very well get the prize for being the world's greatest single polluter because of the large number of contaminated U.S. military bases throughout the world. Naturally, the government can invoke sovereign immunity so that it doesn't have to clean up its mess.

In addition, most, but not all, Greens believe that public ownership results in better environmental stewardship than private ownership, in spite of the wealth of data showing otherwise.

These are two of the major factors that keep the Greens and Libertarians from joining forces, although members of the two parties often do help each other get on the ballot by passing dual sets of petitions for voters to sign.

Once Greens realize that the environment can best be protected through private ownership and restitution, rather than big government, the two parties may very well become one!

Q *If you could repeal 10 federal laws, reverse 10 Supreme Court rulings or dismantle 10 federal agencies, which laws, rulings or agencies would you do away with? I guess what I'm looking for is the libertarian "hit list."*

A Each libertarian might answer this differently, so I can only give you my personal favorites. If I could magically change our government ten ways, I would end all taxation (1), confiscation (2), and eminent domain (3), effectively cutting off the government's revenue. The borrowing powers of the government would be rescinded to prevent it from deficit spending in retaliation (4). Any outstanding obligations would be retired (5), as much as possible, from sales of government property (including about 42% of our country's land mass).

Without the means to compel payment for government services, all government agencies would have to operate like any business by voluntary exchange with its customers. Agencies that failed to provide satisfactory service would have to shut their doors. Since some people would undoubtedly be willing to support a government that regulated in their favor, any initiation of force, by government or individuals, would be outlawed (6).

Sovereign immunity would be eliminated (7), making government officials subject to direct prosecution by their victims. For example, bureaucrats in the FDA, if they managed to survive the above reforms, could be held liable for deaths that they caused by denying the American consumer access to drugs of their choice or information about them.

Gold and silver would likely become legal tender, by simply ending the Federal Reserve's monopoly on currency issue (8). I'd make a declaration of war by Congress necessary for sending troops overseas (9), taking away the president's power to wage war by naming it something else. Finally, I'd save my last wish for something critical that I may have missed!

Q *People love to hear about cutting taxes, but they don't like hearing about cutting social programs, especially when faced with the hysterical "all our children will become starving drug addicts" response from conservatives and liberals alike. Given that some of the libertarian positions are hardly mainstream, how can we overcome the horrified reactions of most people to our ideas?*

A Education is the primary means of overcoming ignorance. Our mission, therefore, is to explain how liberty works and government doesn't. Social studies provide ample evidence that only liberty can take the drugs out of our schools, protect the environment, and help the poor.

The 1996 and 2000 Libertarian Party presidential candidate, Harry Browne, often asked people if they would give up their favorite social programs if they never had to pay income tax again. The response was overwhelmingly in the affirmative; progress is indeed being made.

Q *When are we as Americans going to start fighting the fascist government that we are letting be created around us without the majority of the population even knowing it? What is your advice to our people?*

A Your question contains the answer: we are creating "the fascist government" because we know not what we do. The solution, therefore, is to educate those around us who don't understand that in trying to control others (through government), we find ourselves controlled.

The truth will literally set us free. When we discover that our actions and attitudes empower aggressive government, we'll simply change our behavior, thereby disempowering the aggressors.

Many people look up to government as sort of a super-parent and resist the truth, just as abused children have difficulty admitting that their parents are harmful to their health. Such children are healed by caring adults who gently lead them to the truth. For best results, our attitude should similarly be supportive, not judgmental or abrasive.

Sometimes our task seems overwhelming. When it does, remember the words of American anthropologist Margaret Mead: "Never doubt that a small group of committed, thoughtful citizens can change the world. Indeed, it's the only thing that ever has."

Q *I fear that we may do a disservice to freedom by implicitly conceding logical points in an attempt to appeal to illogical people. For example, feminists push for equality of results as if that, in itself, is* *a moral imperative. If we respond by assuring them that libertarianism will provide a greater "equality," don't we concede the premise in an effort to win the support? Doesn't the cure become worse than the disease?*

Shouldn't our first goal be to persuade people that logic is the tool to discover truth, rather than cultivating unthinking support?

A Truth presents itself differently to people, depending upon how they see the world. Some people accept an idea when it appears logical; others only go along with what is practical; still others are moved only by love. Logic is a wonderful way to truth, but not the only way, or the only "right" way.

Like most truth, liberty can be discovered by logic, pragmatism, spirituality, or love. A feminist might embrace liberty because it will indeed promote equality and then discover why liberty creates such beneficial outcomes through the logical derivation of human rights.

I'm fond of saying that "Liberty works because it is right; the proof that liberty is right is that it works." Morality and practicality are two sides of the same coin – inseparable. Does it matter what side of the freedom coin that a person looks at first? Once the coin is in hand, both sides become apparent.

Historically, libertarians have clustered around the logical thinking of intellectuals, and some find any other derivation of liberty questionable. I wrote *Healing Our World* in part to illustrate that the non-aggression principle clearly derives from the heart as well as the head, from the practical as well as the moral. Truth can be seen from whatever direction an individual comes from.

Now that you've explored the logical side of liberty, why not explore its other facets?

Q *There is one main reason I believe the libertarian philosophy will never see the light of day now or in the future. America as a country is now predominantly female in numbers, and women continue to rise in circles of power.*

Women by nature are collectivists and not prone to risk-taking. These female tendencies were developed over millions of years. What I believe we continue to see in America is the feminization of our society.

I will continue to vote Libertarian because I am voting with those who believe in my principles. But I believe the die is cast and nothing will stop the inevitable result. What can I do to change my thinking or am I hopeless?

A No one is hopeless, not even the female of the species! My belief (and I'm a woman!) is that collectivism attracts caretakers because it masquerades as a loving philosophy. My book, *Healing Our World*, was written to show that only liberty protects the environment, helps the poor, etc. When nurturing women recognize that only liberty is consistently caring, they become the staunchest libertarians of all.

Q *In Harry Browne's essay "A Libertarian's New Year's Resolutions" (recently printed in the Liberator Online), he stated "My purpose is to inspire people to want liberty, not to prove that they're wrong." How do you inspire people to want liberty? Some people just don't seem to have any sense of self-determination. How do you tell someone in words what liberty should feel like?*

A People want what is in their own self-interest. Liberty surely is, but politicians have persuaded the public otherwise. Our mission is to show that liberty, not big government, gives us what politicians promise but never deliver. Even people without a sense of self-determination gravitate towards more wealth, better health, less crime and all the other blessings of liberty. Just show people how liberty will make their lives better; they know exactly what that feels like!

Q *What can I do, personally, to advance the libertarian ideal? I'm not quite old enough yet to run for president, but it's never too early to start thinking about it.*

A Your help is limited only by your imagination! If you want to run for office, start with a local one and learn the ropes. Contribute money and/or time to the Libertarian Party or to its campaigns. Talk to your friends about libertarianism. Keep learning and growing yourself so that you can speak to the concerns that people have instead of preaching to them. Finally, practice the non-aggression that you teach!

Q *Your maxim is that aggression is always a lose-lose scenario, but please consider the following thought experiment (which I do not endorse).*

Assume the libertarian movement gains control of the public schools, and teaches everything from a libertarian perspective, and refuses to allow opposing perspectives. Further assume that this situation continues for five to ten years. Given the predictable outcomes of education, most students so exposed would be libertarians, or at least libertarian-leaning. The few dissidents would not be able to cause many problems, and we would in turn become a more libertarian country.

Given the above hypothetical situation, it would seem that aggression (mandating what would be taught and how) would result in a win-win situation (a country that practices non-aggression, with all the inherent benefits).

Is my logic flawed?

A Actions speak louder than words. If teachers extol the virtues of liberty to students forced to attend class, the students will see the hypocrisy. By failing to practice what we preach, we teach others that we don't believe our own words so they won't either. Instead, the students would conclude that liberty is a nice theory, but just isn't practical. In later life, when the students had to make political policy decisions, they would likely choose aggression as a means to their ends, too.

Liberty is not just a formula that can be learned through memorization – or forced indoctrination. Liberty is a spiritual choice, a way of life. When our understanding of liberty is superficial, we can easily be lead astray.

The American public was tricked into believing that liberty was old-fashioned and impractical, so aggression was necessary. Because liberty wasn't fully understood and appreciated, we went down the wrong path. I believe that your thought experiment would end this way as well.

Of course, even to try such an experiment today would require libertarians to force their way in. Once we become aggressors ourselves, it's not easy to suddenly become tolerant in all areas except education. Power (in the context of government aggression) corrupts; using it destroys the very thing we are seeking.

Q *It seems like most people want to live in a Nanny State today! How can libertarians combat this apathy or laziness that permeates our society?*

A Many people are abdicating responsibility to the Nanny State and giving it power over their lives. However, others are actively reclaiming their personal responsibility (e.g., New Agers, members of the human potential movement, those interested in spirituality [as opposed to religion], pacifists, etc.). These individuals are very receptive to the libertarian message because they are firm believers in non-aggression and personal responsibility. When they understand that taxation and regulation bring the guns of government to bear on peaceful people, they become staunch libertarians.

As an example, my record sales for my book, *Healing Our World*, happened, not at a libertarian gathering, but a New Age/spiritual one. I did not even speak at the conference, but simply put my book out on one of the tables. Fifty percent of the gathering bought a copy.

Thankfully, most change comes about because of a passionate, dedicated minority. The majority that you've described just go along. For more on this subject, see Malcolm Gladwell's *The Tipping Point*.

Q *In The Liberator Online, you said: "Liberty is a win-win scenario, even for those opportunists and their hordes of followers who erroneously believe that they profit by making war and controlling others. Once the aggressors understand that they get more of what they want (e.g., wealth, health, happiness) in a free society, they will selfishly become libertarians."*

I have to strongly disagree with this. What opportunists in government want is power. They want to control the lives of other people for their own gratification. Wealth is desired only because it helps to increase power. Power is the desired end, not the means!

A Power and control are sought as a means to an end as well; that end is happiness. I once had the opportunity to chat with a man who helped to deceive the American people so that they would acquiesce to government aggression. First, I asked what his goals were; he replied, "Power and money." Since he had both, I asked him what he thought would make him happy, since he didn't seem as if he had accomplished this universal goal. He replied that he felt separated from the rest of humankind and that to be happy, he felt he needed to feel connected instead.

When we deceive or otherwise aggress against others, we first separate ourselves from them. Only then can we harm them, because now they are different from us: stupid, naive, evil, etc. This gentleman deceived the entire country as part of his job, so he had to first separate himself from just about everyone.

At some level, he recognized that this disconnection stood in the way of his happiness. He did not understand why he felt disconnected.

Aggression backfires on us because it requires us to forfeit the connectedness that is a prerequisite for human happiness. Thus, in going after power, money, or control of others through aggression, we sabotage the happiness that we want these things to give us.

When the psychological as well as the political impact of aggression is widely understood, few people will choose to sabotage their happiness by engaging in it.

252 Short Answers to the Tough Questions

Q *When I look at the welfare state I live in, it seems unlikely that it could ever be transformed into a libertarian state. So many people depend on the government for everything I don't see or understand how they could make the transition from dependence to independence. People often ask me this question when I am discussing libertarianism, and I have yet to come up with a suitable response.*

A Countries can move from a welfare mentality to self-responsibility rather rapidly. New Zealand, for example, was bankrupted in the mid-1980s by its high taxes, trade protectionism, and subsidies. In desperation, a government was elected that understood how markets work.

By lowering taxes, doing away with subsidies, and getting rid of trade barriers, New Zealand went from a Fraser Institute Economic Freedom Rating of 60 out of 107 nations to 3 in just a few short years (www.freetheworld.com)!

These changes took New Zealand from consuming more than they produced (a negative annual Gross National Product(a measure of wealth creation)) to one that produced more than they consumed. Britain (1983-1989) and Ireland (1987-1996) experienced the same growth spurt when they made similar changes.

As the bumper sticker says, "Shift happens."

If you're interested in this topic, the Fraser Institute (www.fraserinstitute.org), as well as other freedom-oriented organizations, annually rank countries according to the amount of economic liberty they allow.

Q *How can libertarians ever get a foothold into politics without the ability to easily generate funds like their major competitors? Other politicians and parties use their powers to blackmail industry (where the real money is) with the threat of passing unfavorable laws. Both industry and other wealthy PACs will buy votes for things that benefit them. Libertarians will never have either of these groups throwing much money at them because you only promise freedom! No money, no power?*

Or are valid ideas enough? It takes money to disseminate valid ideas like libertarianism. Where is it going to come from?

A Today, money is used to promote the idea that we can benefit by forcing our neighbors to our will through government. Once we realize that coercion backfires every time, this propaganda will fall on deaf ears.

Our mission, should we choose to accept it, is to educate our friends and neighbors about the benefits of liberty. The truth costs little to share, but pays big dividends.

Q *What do you say to people who think if they vote Libertarian it is a wasted vote?*

A Many people want to vote for the lesser of two evils in order to slow down the spread of evil. I felt this way myself once, until I realized that what a politician does after the election is very different than what he or she promises to do. I realized that I couldn't tell which candidate would actually turn out to be more evil; indeed, any difference was likely to be so small as to be immeasurable. Under these circumstances, my vote had the most impact as a protest vote, signaling the career politicians that they'd better change their tune or lose popular support.

If everyone who wanted libertarians to win actually voted that way, we'd have many Libertarians in the Senate and Congress. What could be more wasteful than casting your vote for someone you don't want?

Q *I consider myself a libertarian, but I'm struggling with how to use my vote in the November elections. My theory is that if a libertarian were to be elected president without a substantial number of libertarians in Congress, the inevitable political gridlock would virtually guarantee a disastrous four years of stalemated initiatives to reduce the size and influence of government.*

Such a situation would surely damage the libertarian and conservative parties, possibly opening a door of opportunity for liberal big-government advocates. As a result, I'm inclined to vote for a Republican presidential candidate, while voting for Libertarians for the Senate and House. My hope would be to build up Libertarian representation and influence, thereby making the election of a Libertarian president practical.

What are your thoughts on this?

A Most likely, a libertarian president without Congressional support would not pass many legislative reforms. However, the president is very powerful and can do a great deal on his or her own, without Congressional approval.

For example, a libertarian could rescind the Executive Orders that allow our President to seize control of American communications, power, food, transportation, etc. A libertarian president could pardon non-violent "criminals," such as marijuana users, languishing in federal prisons (approximately 50% of the inmates). He or she could address the nation through TV, radio, and the press, gaining support for libertarian ideas.

As Commander-in-Chief, a libertarian president could call our troops home and keep them here. A libertarian president could fire employees (if not abolish the departments) of the DEA, IRS, FDA, etc. He or she could sell off federal lands and return the proceeds to the people in some manner. For example, Harry Browne, Libertarian Party presidential candidate in 1996 and 2000, suggested turning Social Security into private annuities.

My all-time favorite: a libertarian president could refuse to sign the budget. Government employees, including Congress, might have to go without a paycheck until expenditures were trimmed back to their constitutional limits.

If this were all a libertarian president could accomplish, his or her four year term would restore a great deal of freedom to the American people. Are you sure you'd rather waste your vote on politics as usual?

Q *Should you vote for the person who holds the ideals that are close to your own, or should you vote for the person who is most likely to win, and might at least sway policy towards (instead of away from) your ideals?*

A In this matter of conscience, I can only share my personal views with you. After I became a libertarian, I sometimes voted for the lesser of two evils. I abandoned that practice when I observed that campaign rhetoric and reality seldom matched, so I was really voting blind. I now vote Libertarian to support those I believe in, register a protest vote, withdraw my support from the Demopublicans, and send a message to officeholders that I want them to act more libertarian.

Even though our vote total is small, the Republicrats are beginning to woo the libertarian vote by using some of our rhetoric. They do pay attention to small numbers of lost votes, even if only with lip service.

I'd be delighted if the underfunded Libertarian Party was as successful in this century as the Socialist Party was in the last one. While Socialists won few elections, their platform has been incorporated into both of the so-called major parties.

Remember, too, the Republican Party was also once a minor party, so there's no reason that the LP can't become mainstream.

Q *How do libertarians propose to bring their vision for a libertarian society into being? How do libertarian theorists propose to wean the majority of society from the teat of government liberality? Do you really believe that Americans, after generations of being accustomed to trusting government for nearly every public amenity and service, will give up those carrots for the stick of self-reliance and personal responsibility? Aren't libertarians trusting awfully heavily on the assumption of personal initiative and good faith on the part of parties to any agreement or treaty?*

A Libertarians rely on good, old-fashioned self-interest, not personal initiative or good faith, to create a free society.

Libertarians understand that only liberty can give people all those things that politicians promise but never deliver: more wealth, better health, less crime, a cleaner environment. Even those who think they benefit by big government do better in a free society.

The libertarian strategy, therefore, is to help people see that liberty works better for them than government coercion. We offer the carrot of liberty instead of the stick of coercion.

Not all libertarians agree exactly how best to proceed. Some are trying to elect libertarians to office. Others are trying to educate the public directly. Some focus on their friends and family. Libertarian novelists deliver the message of freedom through entertaining media. Most likely, all these approaches are needed, since people don't all respond in the same manner. Libertarians are, in essence, producing a marketplace of ideas, where each customer buys in from a different angle.

In the days of brawn, people fought for freedom with the sword. In today's society of intellectual prowess, people persuade with the pen. You know which one is mightier!

Q Someone said that "a vote for the Libertarian party or the Green Party or any other independent party may as well be a vote for the Democrats, as we all know none of those independents will ever win so why waste your vote?" How do I answer this, both to myself and to others?

A People who believe that conservatives are likely to slow the growth of big government more than liberals need look no farther than the George W. Bush administration. If the 9-11 terrorists wanted to destroy our freedoms, they did a great job by provoking a conservative president to enact measures that effectively voided most of our remaining constitutional rights. President Bush even spent more on non-military programs than Bill Clinton did.

Conservatives and liberals are both big government advocates, just with different emphasis. As the saying goes, conservatives want to control you in the bedroom; liberals want to control you in the board room. Libertarians don't want to control you at all.

Does this mean that all conservatives and liberals are equally undesirable in office? Of course not! You might choose to support a conservative or a liberal who seems to be "on their way" to becoming libertarian. Ultimately, you'll need to decide this on a case-by-case basis.

Q *Having wealth can mean getting the legislation you want, getting it interpreted in the courts the way you want, and having your side of the case argued more competently.*

A You're right! In today's society, money can buy regulations that hurt the competition, resulting in cartels and monopolies. In a libertarian society, the government is forbidden to make such regulations, so money is less influential.

Q *Almost all candidates for public office are professional office seekers. They spend the majority of their time before and after winning an election soliciting campaign funds. How does the average voter tell the difference between bribing a public official and "supporting" that official?*

A I suspect that you are asking me to confirm what you already know. People contribute to campaigns to get legislation passed in their favor. In other words, contributors want the guns of government pointed at others for their benefit. People who bribe public officials do so for the same reasons. The only difference is that contributions are legal and bribes are not. Similarly, taxation (government theft) is legal, but private theft is not. This schizophrenic logic is responsible for much of the chaos in society today.

Q *My short question is: Do you believe there will be a "Mary Ruwart brand" or type of libertarianism? I have read your book* Healing Our World, *and find I agree with you on just about*

*everything. Is your view of libertarianism the consensus among the
majority of libertarians? You seem to be one of the most Christian political philosophers I've ever seen.*

A Libertarians all use non-aggression as their guiding principle,
but have traveled different paths to arrive at the same place.
Some are atheists who derive non-aggression through logic; others
are pragmatists who recognize that only liberty works; some understand that love means never bending another to your will. Of course,
Christians who embrace the Ten Commandments and Christ's
teaching come to libertarianism through these revelations.

One of the reasons that I wrote *Healing Our World* was to
show people that liberty was a multi-faceted diamond reflected in
any paradigm that withstood the test of time (logic, pragmatism,
love, revelation). Before that, it was fashionable for logical libertarians, who were in the majority, to ridicule those who took the other
paths. Since a house divided against itself cannot stand, I attempted
to provide an integrated view that would heal this rift. I like to think
that such healing would be an evolution in the libertarian philosophy, rather than a separate "brand" of libertarianism.

Q *I find it very hard to find flaws in the liberty ideal. Still, I am
asking a lot of questions about libertarianism, and probing the
libertarian philosophy deeply, because I want to make sure it is truly
the ultimate answer to the world's problems. What are your thoughts
on this?*

A We always need to question our values and keep open minds.
Otherwise, where is freedom of thought?

You say you are asking questions to determine whether liberty
is the "ultimate answer" to the world's problems, whether liberty will
ever fail us. I would say, as trite as it sounds, that love is the ultimate
answer and that liberty, or political freedom, is one aspect of that
love. Without love, liberty will be fleeting. If you are looking for the
ultimate answer, you need to look one step beyond liberty.

If we are loving towards each other, we won't assault, steal from, or defraud one person to give to another. If someone is in need, we give of ourselves. If another person doesn't want to help, we honor their choice out of that same love. When we love, we are not tempted to aggress.

Perhaps the price of liberty is not so much eternal vigilance, as universal love.

Notes

What Is a Libertarian?

1. For more detail, see the chapter entitled "Helping the Poor" in this book and Chapters 3-12 in my book, *Healing Our World*.

What Would a Libertarian Government Look Like?

2. For more detail, see the chapter entitled "Restitution" in this book and Chapter 13 in *Healing Our World*.

3. JR Edwards, "The Costs of Public Income Redistribution and Private Charity," *Journal of Libertarian Studies* 21: 3-20, 2007.

Restitution

4. RE Barnett, "Restitution: A New Paradigm of Criminal Justice," *Ethics* 87:293, 1977.

5. JW Johnston, ed., "The Missouri State Penitentiary," *Illustrated Sketchbook of Jefferson City and Cole County* (Jefferson City, MO: Missouri Illustrated Sketchbook, 1900), pp. 250-251.

6. J Shedd, "Making Goods Behind Bars," *Reason*, March 1982, pp. 23-32.

7. JK Stewart, letter to *Wall Street Journal*, July 26, 1989.

8. JO Haley, "Confession, Repentance, and Absolution," in *Mediation and Criminal Justice: Victims, Offenders, and Community*, M. Wright and B. Gallaway, eds. (London: Sage, 1989), pp. 195-211.

9. TL Anderson and PJ Hill, "An American Experiment in Anarcho-Capitalism: The Not-So-Wild, Wild West," *Journal of Libertarian Studies* 3:9-29, 1979.

Roads

10. For a review of some of these studies, see Edmund Contoski, *Makers and Takers* (Minneapolis: American Liberty Publishers, 1997), pp. 97-99.

The Environment

11. JS Shaw and RL Stroup, "Gone Fishin'," *Reason,* August/September 1988, pp. 34-37.

12. RT Simmons and UP Kreuter, "Herd Mentality: Banning Ivory Sales Is No Way to Save the Elephant," *Policy Review,* Fall 1989, p. 46.

13. For example, see DR Leal, "Homesteading the Oceans: The Case for Property Rights" in *US Fisheries* (Bozeman, MT: Political Economy Research Center, 2000), pp. 7-22; B Runolfsson, "Fencing the Oceans: A Rights-Based Approach to Privatizing Fisheries," *Regulation* 20: 57-62, 1997; RJ Agnello and LP Donnelley, "Prices and Property Rights in the Fisheries," *Southern Economic Journal* 42: 253-262, 1979.

14. US Bureau of the Census, *Poverty in the United States, 1999*, Current Population Reports Series P-60, No. 210 (Washington, DC: Government Printing Office, 2000), p. 15.

15. For details, see H DeSoto's groundbreaking book, *The Mystery of Capital: Why Capitalism Triumphs in the West and Fails Everywhere Else* (New York, NY: Basic Books, 2000).

16. TL Anderson and DR Leal, *Rekindling the Privatization Fires: Political Lands Revisited*, Federal Privatization Project, Issue Paper No. 108 (Santa Monica, CA: Reason Foundation, 1989), p.12.

National Defense

17. R Flick, "How We Appeased a Tyrant," *Reader's Digest*, January, 1991, pp. 39-44.

18. "Town to Celebrate Mandatory Arms," *New York Times*, April 11, 1987, p. 6.

19. G Kleck, "Policy Lessons from Recent Gun Control Research," *Journal of Law and Contemporary Problems* 49: 35-47, 1986; A Krug, "The Relationship Between Firearms Ownership and Crime: A Statistical Analysis," reprinted in *Congressional Record*, 99th Congress, 2nd Session, January 30, 1968, p. 1496, n7.

20. JR Lott, Jr. and WM Landes, *Multiple Victim Public Shootings*, John M. Olin Law & Economics Working Paper #73 (Chicago: University of Chicago Law School, 2000), p. 9.

21. "Court Rules U.S. Not Liable in Deaths from Atom Tests," *San Francisco Examiner*, January 11, 1988, p. A-1.

22. For details, see Chapter 15 of *Healing Our World*.

23. For example see D Gieringer's "The Safety and Efficacy of New Drug Approval," *Cato Journal*, 5: 177-201, 1985.

24. For detail, see J Gwartney et. al., "Economic Freedom and the Environment for Economic Growth," *Journal of Institutional and Theoretical Economics,* 155: 643-663, 1999.

25. For a sample of one of the many interviews in which bin Laden makes these statements, see www.time.com/time/magazine/article/0,9171,1101011015-178412,00.html.

26. J Lott, Jr. *More Guns, Less Crime* (Chicago: University of Chicago Press, 1998).

27. For some examples, see Chapter 20 of *Healing Our World*.

28. "Persian Gulf Policy" in *Cato Handbook for Congress*. 105th Congress (Washington, DC: Cato Institute, 1999). www.cato.org/pubs/handbook/hb105-46.html.

29. R Marcinko, *Rogue Warrior* (New York, NY: Pocket Books, 1993).

30. For further details, see www.mikenew.com.

31. www.gpo.gov/fdsys/pkg/CREC-2003-03-07/html/CREC-2003-03-07-pt1-PgE397-2.htm.

Jobs and Wealth Creation
32. For details, see Chapter 12 of *Healing Our World*.

33. J Fermino, "705G for Cab Medallions," *New York Post*, Aug. 8, 2011; also, "New York Cab Medallions Worth More Than Gold," Bloomberg.com, Aug. 31, 2011.

34. MB Kibbe, "The Minimum Wage: Washington's Perennial Myth," *Cato Policy Analysis #106*, p. 5; S. Warne Robinson, "Minority Report," in *Report of the Minimum Wage Study Commission*, Vol. I. (Washington, D.C.: U.S. Government Printing Office, 1981), p. 187.

35. W Williams, *The State Against Blacks* (New York, NY: McGraw-Hill, 1984).

36. T Sowell, *The Economics and Politics of Race* (New York, NY: William Morrow, 1983), pp. 174-175.

37. See the Fraser Institute's *Economic Freedom of the World Annual Report* at www.freetheworld.com.

38. See Chapter 7 of *Healing Our World*.

Discrimination
39. C Vann Woodward, *The Strange Career of Jim Crow* (New York: Oxford Press, 1955).

40. For more detail, see W Williams' *The State Against Blacks* (New York, NY: McGraw-Hill, 1982), pp.89-98.

41. For details, see Chapters 3 & 4 in *Healing Our World*.

Helping the Poor
42. "Welfare and Poverty," *NCPA Policy Report #107* (Dallas, TX.: National Center for Policy Analysis, 1983), p. 1; Robert L. Woodson, "Breaking the Poverty Cycle: Private Sector Alternatives to the Welfare State," (Harrisburg, PA.: The Commonwealth Foundation for Public Policy Alternatives, 1988), p. 63; JR Edwards, "The Costs of Public Income Redistribution and Private Charity," *Journal of Libertarian Studies* 21: 3-20, 2007.

43. J Fermino, "705G for Cab Medallions," New York Post, Aug. 8, 2011; also, "New York Cab Medallions Worth More Than Gold," Bloomberg.com, Aug. 31, 2011.

44. T DeLeire, "The Unintended Consequences of the Americans with Disabilities Act," *Regulation* 23: 21-24, 2000.

45. TR Dye and H Ziegler, "Socialism and Equality in Cross-National Prespective," *Political Science and Politics* 21: 45-58, 1988.

46. For details, see Chapter 11 of *Healing Our World*.

47. H de Soto, *The Mystery of Capital: Why Capitalism Triumphs in the West and Fails Everywhere Else* (New York, NY: Basic Books, 2003), p. 251.

48. W Tucker, *The Excluded Americans: Homelessness and Housing Policies* (Washington, DC: Regnery Gateway, 1990); W Tucker,"How Rent Control Drives Out Affordable Housing," *Policy Analysis* No. 274 (Washington, DC: Cato Institute, 1997).

49. E Bierhanzl and J Gwartney, "Regulations, Unions, and Labor Markets," *Regulation* 21: 40-53, 1998.

Family Values and Children's Rights
50. In recent years, this practice has changed due to the libertarian pro-bono legal organization, the Institute for Justice (www.ij.org/othercases/1386).

The War on Drugs

51. J Ostrowski, "Thinking About Drug Legalization," *Cato Institute Policy Analysis #121* (Washington, D.C.: Cato Institute, May 25, 1989), p. 1.

52. For details, see Chapter 15 of *Healing Our World*.

53. R Lewis, "Dutch View Addicts as Patients, Not Criminals," *Kalamazoo Gazette*, September 24, 1989, p. A-6; Ostrowski, p. 3.

Consumer Protection

54. SL Carroll and RJ Gaston, "Occupational Restrictions and the Quality of Service Received: Some Evidence," *Southern Economic Journal* 47: 959-976, 1981.

55. For details, see Chapter 7 of *Healing Our World*.

56. For a review, see Chapter 6 of *Healing Our World*.

57. For more detail, see Chapter 5 of *Healing Our World*.

Health

58. S Pipes, *The Top Ten Myths of American Healthcare* (San Francisco, CA: Pacific Research Institute, 2008). www.pacificresearch.org/docLib/20081020_Top_Ten_Myths.pdf.

59. For details, see "Deadly Secrets behind Soaring Pharmaceutical Prices" at www.youtube.com/watch?v=0Yvt8CsujzY and Chapters 5-6 of *Healing Our World*.

60. See Chapter 12 of *Healing Our World*.

Trade and Tariffs

61. J Bovard, *The Fair Trade Fraud* (New York: St. Martin's Press, 1991), pp. 46-47.

62. H De Soto, *The Other Path: The Invisible Revolution in the Third World*. (New York: Harper and Row, 1989).

Gun Control

63. DB Kates, Jr., *Guns, Murder, and the Constitution: A Realistic Assessment of Gun Control*, (San Francisco: Pacific Research Institute for Public Policy, 1990), p. 25.

64. M Lorenz Dietz, *Killing for Profit: The Social Orientation of Felony Homicide* (Chicago: Nelson-Hall, 1983), Table A.1, pp. 202-203.

65. J Wright and P Rossi, *Armed and Considered Dangerous: A Survey of Felons and Their Firearms* (New York: Aldine, 1986), p. 185.

66. PJ Cook, "The Relationship Between Victim Resistance and Injury in Noncommercial Robbery, *Journal of Legal Studies* 15: 405-406, 1986.

67. Kates, Jr., *op.cit*, pp. 37-38, 40-43.

68. "Fifty-One & Counting," *Spotlight,* Feb. 13, 1989, p. 2.

69. J Lott, Jr. *More Guns, Less Crime* (Chicago, IL: University of Chicago Press, 2000), pp. 100-103, 196-197,

70. G Kleck, "Policy Lessons from Recent Gun Control Research," *Journal of Law and Contemporary Problems* 49: 35-47, 1986; Alan Krug, "The Relationship Between Firearms Ownership and Crime: A Statistical Analysis," reprinted in *Congressional Record,* 99th Cong., 2nd Sess., January 30, 1968, p. 1496, n.7.

71. TJ Anderson and PJ Hill, "The Not So Wild, Wild West," *Journal of Libertarian Studies* 3:9-29, 1979.

72. DB Kopel, "Trust the People: The Case Against Gun Control," *Policy Analysis #109*, (Washington, D.C.: Cato Institute, 1988), p. 6.

Education

73. JM Hood, "Miracle on 109th Street," *Reason,* May 1989, pp. 20-25.

74. C Lochhead, "A Lesson from Private Practitioners," *Insight,* December 24, 1990, pp. 34-36.

75. DT Kearns and DP Doyle, *Winning the Brain Race: A Bold Plan to Make Our Schools Competitive* (San Francisco: Institute for Contemporary Studies, 1988), p. 17.

76 For a detailed description of such a system, see Chapter 10 in *Healing Our World.*

Immigration

77. For more details on how immigrants enrich our nation, check out Joel Millman's *The Other Americans: How Immigrants Renew Our Country, Our Economy, and Our Values* (New York, NY: Penguin, 1997).

78. "Let Them In," by Philippe Legrain, *Forbes Magazine,* June 28, 2010. www.forbes.com/forbes/2010/0628/special-report-immigration-opening-borders-mexico-let-them-in_2.html.

SUCCESSFUL
LIBERTARIAN OUTREACH

More outstanding products from the Advocates for Self-Government

Tools

World's Smallest Political Quiz cards: The world's most popular libertarian outreach tool! An instant eye-opener and mind-changer. Fast and fun.

Operation Politically Homeless (OPH): The acclaimed "libertarian event in a kit" has everything you need to start finding new libertarian recruits by the dozens in your community. Fun for newcomers and veterans alike.

Books and Free Newsletter

Secrets of Libertarian Persuasion and *Unlocking More Secrets of Libertarian Persuasion* by Michael Cloud. Learn to quickly and simply win people's hearts and minds to liberty.

Liberty A to Z: 872 Libertarian Soundbites by Harry Browne. Nearly 1,000 short, powerful, thought-provoking, and highly quotable remarks on virtually every topic.

Libertarianism in One Lesson by David Bergland. The excellent short primer that is perfect to give to anyone who's curious about the ideas of liberty.

The Liberator Online is the free email newsletter of the Advocates. Articles on effective libertarian outreach and much more.

Speakers and Workshops

Mary Ruwart, Michael Cloud and Advocates President Sharon Harris are available to speak or conduct workshops on successful libertarian communication. Learn exciting, proven ways to greatly enhance your libertarian outreach!

Acknowledgements

The author and publisher would like to express gratitude to the following people:

Steve Smith of Chapel Hill, North Carolina, for his excellent editing; Justin Arman, Donna Dodson, Evan Hanson, and Evelyn Hanson for proofreading; Susan Monahan for the index.

James W. Harris for originating and working with the "Ask Dr. Ruwart" column in the *Liberator Online;* Catherine Hanson and Zachary Varnell for their work on designing and posting short answers to LibertarianAnswers.com.

And the readers of the *Liberator Online* for their questions and thoughtful comments.

Want more from Dr. Ruwart ?

Visit her website:
www.Ruwart.com

Get a copy of her wonderful book
Healing Our World in an Age of Aggression
http://store.TheAdvocates.org/product_p/opp.htm

Subscribe to the Advocates' popular newsletter
the *Liberator Online* to read her
"Ask Dr. Ruwart" column:
www.TheAdvocates.org

**Find all her short answers online
in searchable form:**
www.LibertarianAnswers.com

**Arrange for her to speak at your next event:
Call the Advocates at 800-932-1776**

About the Author

D r. Mary J. Ruwart is a research scientist, ethicist, author, and libertarian activist.

She holds a B.S. in biochemistry and a Ph.D. in biophysics from Michigan State University, and has held faculty appointments at St. Louis University's Department of Surgery and at the University of North Carolina in Charlotte.

As a senior research scientist at the Upjohn Company in the 70s and 80s, she was involved in developing new therapies for a variety of diseases, including liver cirrhosis and AIDS.

Dr. Ruwart worked extensively with the poor through her decade-long efforts to rehabilitate low-income housing in the Kalamazoo, Michigan area. She was also an active member of the Kalamazoo Rainforest Action Committee and has been profiled in *American Men and Women of Science, Who's Who in Science and Technology, World Who's Who of Women, International Leaders of Achievement, Who's Who of American Women, Community Leaders of North America,* and several other prestigious biographical works.

Since 1982, Dr. Ruwart has been involved in societal ethics with a focus on the political theory and practice of libertarianism. Her award-winning international best-selling book, *Healing Our World*, demonstrates how the ethical application of libertarian principles has historically created harmony and abundance.

She has run for public office as a Libertarian Party candidate numerous times, using those opportunities to educate voters on the impact of ethical choices on their personal and financial well-being. She has also served on the Libertarian National Committee.

Dr. Ruwart currently serves as Chair of the Board of the International Society for Individual Liberty (ISIL) and Secretary of the Board of the Foundation for a Free Society.

For over 15 years, she has been the author of the very popular "Ask Dr. Ruwart" column in the Advocates for Self-Government's *Liberator Online* newsletter.

Readers are invited to contact Dr. Ruwart through Facebook, her website at www.Ruwart.com, or via email at Ruwart@ TheAdvocates.org.

Index

St. Louis, Missouri, 219
Stalin, Joseph, 80
Standard Oil, 171
State Against Blacks, The (Williams), 119, 121
State sovereignty, 99-100
Steinbeck, John, 116
Stossel, John, 168, 207
Students for Liberty, 238
Sudan, 91
Suicide, assisted, 164-166
Sweat shops, 110, 114
Switzerland, 9, 17, 74-75, 77, 190, 209, 235
Sylvan Learning, 195
Syria, 91

T

Taliban, 83, 86, 187
Tariffs, 182, 183, 187-188, 228
Taxes, 244
    Christian principles and, 12
    consumption (national sales), 18-19
    criminal justice system without, 21
    for education, 197, 200
    excise, 19
    Fair, 18-19
    feasibility of abolishing, 16-17
    income, 17-19
    national defense without, 73
    percentage of income paid in, 94
    property, 214, 224
    range of libertarian perspectives on, 14-15
    reason for libertarian opposition to, 2, 17-18
    reducing at the local level, 212
    sales, 18-19
    single people discriminated against via, 153
    United Nations funded by, 98-99
    wages and reduction of, 112-113

Taxicab industry, 109, 116, 117, 127
Teenage pregnancy, 126, 136-137
Telephone/telecommunications industry, 116-117, 171-172
Terrorism, 82-92. *See also* September 11 terrorist attacks
    airline prevention of, 168
    gun control and, 76-77
    immigration and, 90, 205, 206
    intervention in foreign affairs and, 90-92
    relinquishing of liberties to fight, 82-83
    suggested responses to, 85-90, 93-94
    War on, 85, 242
THC (oral form of), 159. *See also* Marijuana
Theft, 1, 37
    restitution for, 20-21
    taxation as, 12, 15, 18
Third World, 65, 114, 186
Tipping Point, The (Gladwell), 250
TIT-for-TAT, 7
Titus, Herbert W., 100
Tocqueville, Alexis de, 9
Toll roads, 40, 46
Trade, 182-188, 235
    embargoes on human rights violators, 183
    freedom of choice in, 182
    job loss and, 182, 183
    job outsourcing and, 185-186
    "leveling the playing field" and, 187
    NAFTA and, 183, 185, 186
    peace encouraged by, 85
    subsidies and, 188
    tariffs and, 182, 183, 187-188, 228
    underdeveloped countries and, 186-187
    unskilled workers left behind by, 185
Tragedy of the commons, 66, 67-68
Transportation Safety Administration (TSA), 168